Refashioning Secularisms in France and Turkey

Over the past few years, secularism has become an intrinsic component of discussions on religious freedom and religious governance. The question of whether states should restrict the wearing of headscarves and other religious symbols has been particularly critical in guiding this thought process.

Refashioning Secularisms in France and Turkey documents how, in both countries, devout women have contested bans on headscarves, pointing to how these are inconsistent with the 'real' spirit of secularism. These activists argue that it is possible to be simultaneously secular and religious; to believe in the values conveyed by secularism, while still remaining devoted to their faith. Through this examination, the book highlights how activists locate their claims within the frame of secularism, while at the same time revisiting it to craft a space for their religiosity.

Addressing the lacuna in literature on the discourse of devout Muslims affected by these restrictions, this book offers a topical analysis on an under-studied dimension of secularism and is a valuable resource for students and researchers with an interest in Religion, Gender Studies, Human Rights and Political Science.

Amélie Barras is a post-doctoral fellow at the University of Montreal with the Chair Religion, Culture and Society and the Canadian Religion and Diversity Project. Her research interest is in religion and politics, with a special focus in gender, law and Islam. She has published articles on these topics in *Democratization, Journal of Human Rights* and in *Mediterranean Politics.*

Routledge Islamic Studies Series

This broad ranging series includes books on Islamic issues from all parts of the globe and is not simply confined to the Middle East.

Historians, State and Politics in Twentieth-Century Egypt
Contesting the Nation
Anthony Gorman

The New Politics of Islam
Pan-Islamic Foreign Policy in a World of States
Naveed Shahzad Sheikh

The Alevis in Turkey
The Emergence of a Secular Islamic Tradition
David Shankland

Medieval Islamic Economic Thought
Filling the Great Gap in European Economics
S.M. Ghazanfar

The West and Islam
Western Liberal Democracy versus the System of Shura
Mishal Fahm al-Sulami

The Regency of Tunis and the Ottoman Porte, 1777–1814
Army and Government of a North-African Eyâlet at the End of the Eighteenth Century
Asma Moalla

Islamic Insurance
A Modern Approach to Islamic Banking
Aly Khorshid

The Small Players of the Great Game
The Settlement of Iran's Eastern Borderlands and the Creation of Afghanistan
Pirouz Mojtahed-Zadeh

Interest in Islamic Economics
Understanding Riba
Abdulkader Thomas

Muslim Diaspora
Gender, Culture and Identity
Edited by Haideh Moghissi

Human Conscience and Muslim–Christian Relations
Modern Egyptian Thinkers on al-damīr
Oddbjørn Leirvik

Islam in Nordic and Baltic Countries
Göran Larsson

Islam and Disability
Perspectives in Theology and Jurisprudence
Mohammed Ghaly

Producing Islamic Knowledge
Transmission and Dissemination in Western Europe
Edited by Martin van Bruinessen and Stefano Allievi

Refashioning Secularisms in France and Turkey

The Case of the Headscarf Ban

Amélie Barras

Routledge
Taylor & Francis Group
LONDON AND NEW YORK

First published 2014
by Routledge
2 Park Square, Milton Park, Abingdon, Oxfordshire OX14 4RN

and by Routledge
711 Third Avenue, New York, NY 10017

First issued in paperback 2016

Routledge is an imprint of the Taylor & Francis Group, an informa business

British Library Cataloguing in Publication Data
A catalogue record for this book is available from the British Library

Library of Congress Cataloging in Publication Data
Barras, Amelie, author.
Refashioning secularisms in France and Turkey : the case of the headscarf ban / Amelie Barras.
pages cm
Includes bibliographical references and index.
1. Hijab (Islamic clothing)--Law and legislation--France. 2. Hijab (Islamic clothing)--Law and legislation--Turkey. 3. Muslim women--Legal status, laws, etc.--France. 4. Muslim women--Legal status, laws, etc.--Turkey.
5. Freedom of religion--France. 6. Freedom of religion--Turkey.
7. Laicism--France. 8. Laicism--Turkey. I. Title.
KJC5156.B37 2014
342.4408'52975674--dc23
2013045853

ISBN 13: 978-0-415-79086-4 (pbk)
ISBN 13: 978-0-415-82178-0 (hbk)

Typeset in Times New Roman
by Taylor & Francis Books

Contents

Acknowledgements vii
Abbreviations xi

1 **Introduction: the hegemony of secularism, gender and space** **1**
Locating refashioning secularisms 3
On methods and ethics 10
Summing up the argument and outlining the structure of the book 16
Notes 18

2 **A tradition of regulations: shedding light on the paradoxes of the languages of secularism** **21**
Paradoxes of the languages of laïcité *and* laiklik *22*
Conclusion 36
Notes 38

3 **The slow exclusion of pious women from French and Turkish societies: (re)producing spaces** **43**
The exclusion of pious Muslim women and the making of spaces 44
'Making room' for public spaces 45
Conclusion 62
Notes 63

4 **French Muslim activists: promoting a *laïcité* ante** **69**
A short overview 70
The March 2004 Law and the extensions of exclusions: sketching an argument 76
Conclusion 88
Notes 90

5 Turkish devout activists: reconfiguring *laiklik* with human rights **94**
Setting the context: a discursive shift 95
Religious rights activists: a window into understanding how laiklik *can be refashioned 98*
Conclusion 112
Notes 114

6 A rights-based discourse: a door to multiple sites of challenges **118**
Litigation at the national level: the work of French activists 119
Access to international sites 122
Conclusion 135
Notes 136

Conclusion: an invitation to transcend the secular/religious divide **140**
Unwinding the argument 141
Evaluating the success of this (re)articulation 146
Notes 151

Bibliography 152
Index 165

Acknowledgements

I remember reading through the acknowledgements I had rushed to write before sending my PhD thesis to my committee a few years ago and realising, to my great dismay, that I had forgotten to thank many people. Since this book is a revised version of my PhD, it is almost as if I now have a second chance 'not to forget anyone'. But this seems to be, in itself, a herculean task as writing this book has been a process, a journey, influenced of course by friends, colleagues and family who I have known all my life or met along the way, but also by improbable encounters and fragments of conversations on boats, in cafes, planes, libraries, conferences, classes, and other improbable places. This is to say that I am unfortunately unable to remember the names of all the people that have contributed in a myriad of ways to my on-going reflection, but I will always be sincerely grateful for their generosity and time.

I am deeply indebted to all my interviewees for their patience and generosity of time, for sharing insights on their life experience and struggles, and for their enthusiasm about my project. Without them this book would simply not be. Particular thanks go to Belkıs Kılıçkaya for sharing her address book with me and for our endless conversations on Turkish politics; to Murat Ardag and Ece Özçelik for their kind help during field work in Turkey; as well as to Emmanuelle Andréani-Facchin and Ugras Oguz for ensuring that I felt at home in Paris, Ankara and Istanbul.

Research for this project was made possible by generous PhD grants from the Social Sciences and Humanities Research Council of Canada, the London School of Economics, and the University London Central Research Fund. My post-doctoral fellowship, funded by the Swiss National Science Foundation, with the Chair Religion, Culture and Society at the University of Montreal and with the Canadian Religion and Diversity Project, has provided me with the needed time and space to transform my PhD manuscript into this book.

John Chalcraft, my supervisor at the LSE, provided on-going support for this project. He believed in it from its infancy, encouraged me to persevere even in times of great doubt and diligently read and criticized various drafts. I am deeply grateful for our thought-provoking conversations, and for his introduction to post-colonial and critical studies. I thank as well Katerina Dalacoura for having read, and commented thoughtfully upon, several chapters of this work. Her sense of detail and her good knowledge of the Turkish case were greatly appreciated. Jeffrey Haynes also expressed enthusiasm for this project from its early stages. I am deeply thankful for his constant support and his careful reading of my work, as well as for introducing me to a vibrant network of scholars working on religion and politics. I thank Nadje Al-Ali, who pushed me outside my comfort zone and introduced me to a body of literature that has deeply expanded my intellectual horizon, and continues to do so. Finally, I am grateful for the precious comments I received from two anonymous reviewers who helped me bring this book to completion.

I had the opportunity to present parts of this research in different forums, including the European University Institute Mediterranean meetings, the International Studies Association annual meetings, the Middle Eastern Society Association annual meetings, and workshops at LSE, Princeton, Cambridge and the University of Geneva. I am grateful for the feedback I received at each of these occasions, and for having been able to meet colleagues who generously contributed to my reflection. When I was doing fieldwork in Paris I was invited to participate in the Doctoral Gratianus Programme, where I met doctoral students from across Europe and expanded my knowledge of the relationship between state, law and religion in Europe. I would like to extend a special thanks to Professor Basdevant-Gaudemet for welcoming me to the programme, as well as to Professor Margiotta-Broglio and Rossella Bottoni for putting me in contact with Turkish experts.

I have written parts of this book in different institutions, all of which provided me with a vibrant and supportive intellectual community. My gratitude goes to friends and colleagues whom I met at the London School of Economics, the University of Geneva, the Open Society summer school, during field work, as well as those working with the Religion and Diversity project. A special thanks goes to Anna Fukuda, Natalie Fukuda, Jasmine Gani, Francesca Biancani, Dia Dabby, Sarah Nicolet, Sebnem Gümüşçü, Michael Bloch, Jasmine Lorenzini, Sara Pupi, Laure Betris, and Günhan Akarçay for their generosity of mind and heart, and their friendship. I am grateful to all my students at the University of Geneva, the Graduate Institute, the Open Society summer school and now at the University of Montreal, who have, at different occasions, encouraged me to ask different and new questions. I feel deeply fortunate to have been surrounded by wonderful mentors. I thank Matteo Gianni for his excellent comments on parts of this work and Xavier Guillaume for our endless conversations, for encouraging me to engage further with theory, and for his friendship (which has kept me sane more than once). The work of Beth Hurd sparked, in many ways, my intellectual curiosity that led me to embark on this journey, and has been an inspiration throughout. I am grateful for her support and for her invitation to a thought-provoking workshop at Princeton in April 2011 on Law and Religious freedom. Solange Lefebvre has provided me over the past two years with a stimulating and supportive environment at the University of Montreal, and has introduced me to the realm of religious studies. I am deeply thankful to Lori Beaman for encouraging me to finish this book, for our refreshing conversations and projects, and for her inspiring scholarship. Finally, Sandra Harding's reflection has provided me with the impetus and courage to finish and send off this manuscript:

> You have to put your ideas out in public. Realize you're never going to be 100 percent right, and trust that for now you are the least wrong you could manage to be.
>
> (Sandra Harding, 2013)

I am indebted to my family, including my siblings, for *always* grounding me in reality. Those that know me, know that my family is big and noisy. Family dinners have been occasions to share, test and defend ideas. These conversations have, as far as I can remember, always been sources of inspiration. I am deeply grateful to my parents for having raised me in a home where curiosity, free thought, travelling and love for learning was part and parcel of our everyday. A special acknowledgement goes to my mother for having read more than her share of drafts of this book, always providing thoughtful comments, and for asking provocative questions. Our conversations have and will continue to inform, in many ways, my thinking. I would like to thank Karim for his constant companionship and love over the years, for making me laugh, and most importantly for crafting with me a home for our marvellous daughter: Nour. Finally, I dedicate this book to my paternal grandparents for their insatiable energy, love and support.

Parts of Chapters 2 and 3 appeared in 'Contemporary *laïcité:* setting the terms of a new social contract? The slow exclusion of devout Muslim women' *Politics, Religion & Ideology* 11.2 (2010): 229–47. Permission to reprint this material has been granted by Routledge Journals. Portions of Chapter 3 appeared in 'Sacred secularism and the politics of religious resurgence in France: consequences for the right to religious freedom' *Mediterranean Politics* 18. 2 (2013): 276–93. Parts of Chapters 4 and 5 appeared in 'A rights based discourse to contest the boundaries of state secularism? The case of the headscarf ban in France and Turkey' *Democratizatio*n 16.6 (December 2009): 1237 – 1260. Permission to reprint this material has been granted by Routledge Journals. An earlier version of Chapter 6 appeared as: 'Transnational understandings of secularisms and the right to religious freedom – exploring UN and ECHR cases' *Journal of Human Rights* 11.2 (2012): 263–79. Taylor & Francis has granted me the right to reproduce it. Portions of Chapter 5 appeared as: 'Devout Turkish Women Struggle for Full Citizenship' MERIP 262 (Spring 2012): 32–35. I thank MERIP for giving me the right to reproduce the material. A paragraph in Chapter 6 appeared in 'Considering the gender dimension of European debates on the Muslim "other"', in S. Behloul, A. Tunger-Zanetti and S. Leuenberger (eds) *Debating Islam*, Transcript

Publishing House (2013). I thank Lori Beaman, the Canadian Criminal Law Review and Carswell for giving me the permission to reproduce a stand-alone quote at the beginning of my conclusion. Finally, I am grateful to the collective *Maman Toutes Egales* (Mothers All Equal Collective, http://www.mamans-toutes-egales.com) for allowing me to reproduce two of their prints located at the beginnings of Chapter 3 and Chapter 4.

Abbreviations

AKDER	Women Rights Organization Against Discrimination
AK Party	Justice and Development Party
CCIF	Collective Against Islamophobia in France
CEDAW	United Nations Convention on the Elimination of All Forms of Discrimination against Women
CFCM	French Council of the Muslim Cult
CFPE	Collective Feminists For Equality
CEPT	Collective a School For All
CHP	Republican People's Party
CMF	Muslims' Collective of France
ECHR	European Convention on Human Rights
ECtHR	European Court of Human Rights
EMF	Muslim Students of France
HALDE	High Authority for the Fight Against Discriminations and for Equality
HCI	High Council of Integration
ICCPR	International Covenant on Civil and Political Rights
IPU	Inter-Parliamentary Union
JMF	Young Muslims of France
MAZLUMDER	Organization of Human Rights and Solidarity of the Oppressed People
MTE	Mothers All Equal Collective
NPA	New Anti-capitalist Party
ÖZGÜR-DER	Free Thought and Education Rights Association
PSM	Muslim Spirituality and Participation
TESEV	Turkish Economics and Social Studies Foundation
UMP	Union for a Popular Movement
UOIF	Union of the Islamic Organizations of France
UN	United Nations
YÖK	Higher Education Council

1 Introduction

The hegemony of secularism, gender and space

Responding to harsh criticisms attacking her decision to participate in the 2010 regional elections while wearing a headscarf, Ilhem Moussaid, a 22-year-old member of the new French anti-capitalist Party (NPA) explained: 'I am a secularist, feminist and anti-capitalist' (Ilhem, cited in Alemagna, 2010). Ilhem and her small white headscarf created the headlines in newspapers in early February 2010, and became the prime subject of discussions among intellectuals, politicians and even members of her own party. Martine Aubry, leader at the time of the French Socialist Party, argued that a candidate wearing a headscarf would not have been accepted on the list of her party. For her, religion had to be separated from politics – it had to remain in the private domain and not disturb what she understood as the neutral realm of the secular Republic. Members of the French Right presented another type of argument, stressing that the young girl had been instrumentalised and manipulated by her own political party, as she lacked the rationality and the autonomy to be an independent agent of her actions (Zappi, 2010). In the midst of such a cacophony, Ilhem's voice and political opinions were barely audible, and when they were they were quickly disregarded as a non-sense or an aberration. Her headscarf was sufficient, from the outset, to define her identity. After a few days, Ilhem finally reacted in an email to the turmoil she had created:

> I am very sad to see 8 years of my life reduced to my headscarf. I am very sad to hear that my personal belief is a danger for others, when I am promoting friendship, respect, tolerance and equality between all human beings […] I am a citizen like all others.
>
> (Ilhem, cited in Gurrey 2010)[1]

Ilhem's discourse and responses to her detractors are a good illustration of the conundrums that pushed me to embark on this project. I began research for *Refashioning Secularisms* in 2006, not long after France passed a law banning visible religious symbols in public schools (15 March 2004). Although the wording of the law seemed to affect all religions, it was quite clear from the start that its first aim was to ban girls from wearing headscarves in public schools. Women and girls wearing a headscarf were facing similar restrictions in Turkey where, after the 'soft' coup of 28 February 1997,[2] a ban on the headscarf was enforced not only in schools, but also in universities, public buildings, courts, and so on. In both countries, these bans have been justified as protecting and fostering secularism – or rather *laiklik* in Turkey and *laïcité* in France.[3] More precisely, policy makers, as in the case of Ilhem, have articulated their narratives around different aspects attributed to *laiklik* and *laïcité*, such as the separation between religion and state, the neutrality of 'public' spaces, and/or respect for gender equality in these spaces. In so doing, they have 'pushed' these 'overtly' religious women back into the 'private' realm, participating in the (re)production of powerful binaries, where (in)visible religion coupled with gender delineates the frontiers between private and public.

Amidst these efforts to regulate the bodies of women wearing headscarves, what caught my attention was how these women reacted to this process of exclusion. In France, on the eve of the law, some of them protested in the street by wearing headscarves with the colours of the French flag and carrying banners, on which they proclaimed their belief in *laïcité*, and denounced this law as being a betrayal of the spirit of this principle. In Turkey, several activists positioned themselves against bans by making similar references to the 'real' essence of *laiklik*, arguing that bans were a direct infringement on their right to freedom of choice, self-emancipation, and gender equality. In other words, like Ilhem these activists were arguing that it was possible to be at the same time both secular and religious, to believe in the values conveyed by secularism while still remaining pious: '*Laïcité* yes, my headscarf also. My headscarf yes and *laïcité* also' (slogan in protests, in Bouzar and Kada, 2003: 134).

Being myself deeply influenced by the binaries around which dominant secular tropes have been organised,[4] I was, at first, quite puzzled by these reactions: How could pious women argue that they were at the same time religious and secular? This felt like an almost visceral inconsistency. Their discourse, I thought, seemed to be blurring the sacrosanct dichotomy between the religious (and, in particular, Islam) and the secular present in many of the works that had marked my training as a social scientist. In effect, their argument was not located outside secularism, but rather within this discourse. I felt compelled to analyse more thoroughly how this could be the case. Thus, I embarked on a journey that was going to unsettle my own intellectual boundaries and in which I would seek to tackle several questions, including: How could these women challenge headscarf bans by making reference to the same aspects of secularism used by states to enforce them? What was their reading of the term and were they able to find space within it to accommodate their religiosity? What effect did this have on their understanding of religion and the right to religious freedom?

This book, therefore, does not offer a discussion of how Islamic modernities can be conceived in opposition to secular ones. Rather it embarks on an exploration of how challenges can be located within secularism. It invites the reader on a journey into the hegemonic power of secularism in Turkey and France. In so doing, it highlights the shifting character of secularism – a character that facilitates its (re)appropriation. By embracing a micro-approach in order to document the power of secular tropes on the lives on individuals, *Refashioning Secularisms* also offers a discussion of the importance of women and gender relations in the discourses of secularism. In fact, while I did not intend to focus on pious women at first, I realised that not only were they key to the articulation of secular tropes, but that they were also actively involved in the production of alternative discourses on secularism.

Locating refashioning secularisms

Excavating the power of secularism

> I believe we must try to unpack the various assumptions on which secularism – *a modern doctrine of the world in the world* – is based. For it is precisely the process by which these conceptual binaries are established or subverted that tells us how people live in the secular – how they vindicate the essential freedom and responsibility of the sovereign self in opposition to the constraints of that self by religious discourses.
>
> (Asad, 2003: 15–16 (author's emphasis))

Throughout this project, I have remained amazed by the power secular tropes have been able to exercise on contemporary imaginaries. Not only was I surprised when I realised the role these tropes played in shaping policies both at the national and international levels, but I was also quite puzzled when I discovered that respondents were working within the frame of secularism. Yet, this is revealing of the 'paradigmatic' (Casanova, 1994: 17), or rather hegemonic, status of secularism. Scholars have not been immune to that spell. On the contrary, it has had direct consequences on how different disciplines in the social sciences have thought of and approached the relationship between religion and politics (on this see Wilson, 2012; Shakman Hurd, 2008).

In effect, many scholars, deeply influenced by the secularization thesis, have believed that with modernity religion would automatically retreat to the private realm, and that secularism would not only be the sole framework available to modern societies but would also be a prerequisite for democracy. Secularism in this story was imagined as corresponding to the separation of 'church' and state,[5] yet the modalities of this 'separation' were left unexplored. This standpoint explains the lack of interest, particularly on the part of political and international relations scientists, in the study of religion as they understood it as an object located outside of politics; that is, outside their area of interest (e.g. Haynes, 2005: 399, 400). Secularism, in other words, was approached as a universal and static paradigm, and little effort was put into investigating how the concept was situated in history, how not all understandings of the term were compatible with democratic principles, and, finally, how rather than being opposed or superior to the religious it could articulate itself in relation to the religious.

It is only recently that scholars have started to problematize this 'paradigmatic' status, and have sought to understand how and why secularism has been able to acquire such power over our contemporary imaginaries (e.g. Shakman Hurd, 2012, 2008; Jakobsen and Pellegrini, 2008; Scott, 2007; Cady and Shakman Hurd, 2010; Asad, 2003; Wilson, 2012; Knott, 2005; Calhoun *et al.* 2011). In so doing, secularism has been approached as a powerful discourse that 'works across [...] institutional sites' (Jakobsen and Pellegrini, 2008: 7), and one that is intimately related to understandings of religion and religious freedom. The reflections in this book are deeply indebted to this critical approach, and seek to contribute to this discussion. This standpoint is particularly interesting, inasmuch as it opens the door to exploring how the boundaries of what is understood as belonging to the categories 'religion' and 'religious freedom' shift in terms of secular narratives. It is based on the premise that there is not one model of secularism, but rather multiple modes of religious governance that differently shape assumptions about religion. In a sense, therefore, this viewpoint is less interested in evaluating to what extent religion is separated from politics in a particular country, and more with investigating *how* something comes to be constructed as religious and/or as political, and *who* is vested with the authority of (re)producing, and policing, those boundaries (Shakman Hurd, 2008: 16; Knott, 2005: 217). Rather than being about the retreat of religion, secularism is thus approached as a powerful mode of governance that shapes the boundaries of what is religiously acceptable. Elizabeth Shakman Hurd sums up this understanding nicely:

> Rather than take secularism to be a neutral or natural space for politics that emerges once religion has been privatized, displaced, or diminished, it takes shape here as a contingent series of legal and political claims and projects that are deeply implicated in the definition and management of religion, religious freedom, toleration, diversity and so on. Secularism is not the absence of religion, but enacts a particular kind of presence. It appropriates religion: defining, shaping and even transforming it.
>
> (Shakman Hurd, 2012: 955)

Many of these critical works have remained theoretical (e.g. Warner *et al.* 2010) or have chosen to adopt a macro and state-centred approach (e.g. Shakman Hurd, 2008; Kuru, 2009; Cady and Shakman Hurd, 2010; Calhoun *et al.* 2011; Bowen, 2007a, 2007b; Scott, 2007; Wilson, 2012). *Refashioning Secularisms* proposes shifting the lens. It invites the reader to adopt a more micro perspective, looking not only at the consequences and authority of secular tropes on the lives of pious women in France and Turkey, but also at how these tropes shape the reactions of devout activists.

Going beyond Europe: comparing secularisms and secular policies

Until the last decade, few scholars had compared French and Turkish secularisms. In fact, those who had discussed the two cases had highlighted their great differences, and had almost ruled out comparison on that basis (Berkes, 1998 [1964]; Mardin, 1995). This lack of comparative studies was not surprising, as it was partly a consequence of the 'paradigmatic status' of secularism discussed above, in which it was approached as a unique, universal and static model. On top of that, the idea that the French and Turkish cases were incomparable due to their great differences has to be understood in the light of a strong, culturally essentialist narrative. In this account, 'separation' between 'church' and state was only ever possible in countries with a Christian heritage, as Christianity contained an open recommendation 'to render unto Caesar, the things which are Caesar's' (Lewis, 1993:179). On the other hand, because no such advice was present in Islam, states in countries with an Islamic heritage saw themselves forced to 'control' religion to ensure that it would not disturb or take over state affairs (Lewis, ibid.; Gellner, 1983). This 'control versus separation' thesis has come under serious criticism in recent scholarship for overlooking the diversity of models of religious governance that exist across countries with similar religious traditions (Keddie, 1997; Lapidus, 1996), as well as for working with a static and essentialist reading of 'religion' (e.g. Kuru, 2009). Yet, as it will be discussed later in the book, it remains a powerful narrative, including at the policy level.

Over the last decade, a comparative tradition of secularism has started to gain ground. Scholars here are not only proposing a study of 'secularisms' (e.g. Shakman Hurd and Cady, 2010; Calhoun *et al*, 2011), but are also embarking on projects, in which they debunk essentialist narratives (e.g Kuru, 2007, 2009; Stephan and Kuru, 2012; Elver, 2012). For instance, Kuru (2007, 2009, 2012) and Shakman Hurd (2008), in their attempts to classify different models of secularism, have made the case that, despite their different religious heritage, the French and Turkish models belong to the same category – that is, 'assertive secularism' (Kuru, 2007) or 'laicism' (Shakman Hurd, 2008) in which the state actively intervenes in religion to push it out of the public realm. Thus, they are among the first works to develop an argument for putting French and Turkish secularisms in the same comparable category. While this book focuses on exploring *how* the French and Turkish models of secularism are similar, rather than explaining *why* they are similar (e.g. Kuru, 2007, 2009; Stephan and Kuru, 2012), embarking on a project that highlights the similarities of both models speaks to my positionality as a scholar. In effect, this endeavour aims to be a contribution to post-colonial scholarship that seeks to question the inherent differences between the 'East' and the 'West', and unravel how 'western' discourses on the Muslim world and Islam are intimately related to constructing and projecting a particular and different image of the 'Christian' 'West' (e.g. Saïd, 1979).

Amidst this rather recent exploration of the power of secularism, the question of headscarf bans, as an example of a secular policy, has been extensively discussed (e.g. Laborde, 2005; Bowen, 2007a; Scott, 2007; Salton, 2007; Najmabadi, 2006; Kavakçı, 2010; Elver, 2012). While the majority of these works have focused on the French law banning headscarves in public schools in 2004, some have compared policies banning headscarves in different states (e.g. Salton, 2007; McGoldrick, 2006), including in Turkey and France (e.g. Elver, 2012; Gökariksel and Mitchell, 2005 and Göle, 2005). As the reader will come to realize, these discussions have been invaluable in helping me understand the debates around headscarf restrictions, and in documenting contemporary shifts in the dominant understandings of secularism. Moreover, a few of these studies were particularly insightful, inasmuch as they have discussed how these policies participate in the construction of 'modern' gendered identities (e.g. Scott, 2007; Najmabadi, 2006; Kavakçı, 2012; Göle, 2005). Yet, the majority of these works focus on discussing state secularism, rather than on exploring the responses of individuals affected by these policies. Joan Scott explains this elegantly when she outlines the aim of her book: '*this is not a book about French Muslims; it is about the dominant French view of them*', and notes that there are: 'not many Muslim voices in this book' (2007: 10 (original emphasis)). Again, while this project is indebted in many ways to these top-down approaches, it stresses the importance of complementing them with bottom-up perspectives, which opens the door to capturing facets of the hegemony of secularism otherwise easily left unexplored.

Women at the centre of the comparison: unravelling gendered and spatial narratives

When I first started this research I had not intended focusing mainly on headscarf bans, but I quickly realised the importance of these bans in unravelling how and where the languages of secularism are used, as well as the content they are given and how this can change and/or get (re)articulated. In fact, because contemporary France and Turkey have allowed very little space for non-regulated religious expressions in the public realm, headscarves have become one of the key symbols of the struggle taking place over the meaning given to secularism. Focusing principally on these policies has not only facilitated the comparison between my two cases, but allowed me to track debates in both societies, locate groups and individuals affected by and challenging bans, as well as the sites and key points in time that marked these controversies. In effect, this focus helped me to delimit the time frame for the larger part of this study, which starts in the late 1990s and runs until approximately 2011, with a particular interest in the periods after the 1997 coup in Turkey and the March 2004 law in France. During these periods, the governments in both countries have been openly tightening their control over the visibility of Islam – enforcing headscarf bans in various public spaces – and justifying these actions by making references to the languages of secularism and pushing Muslim activists to clearly articulate their concerns with respect to this climate.[6] This focus means that women occupy an important place in the comparison.

I found the literature on gender and nationalism to be helpful in providing elements of answers to explain *why* such a central place has been given to women. This literature makes reference both to the centrality, but also to the ambivalent and vulnerable position, of women in the (re)production of the boundaries of modern projects (e.g. Yuval-Davis, 1997a; Kandiyoti 1991a, 1991b; Moors and Salih, 2009). In their work, Anthias and Yuval-Davis (1989) have argued that women are imagined as symbolically reproducing the boundaries of ethnic and national groups (ibid.). Here, women are perceived as 'border-guards', where they are markers of the rules and regulations of who is allowed to belong to the community and who is not, and in what fashion. This is why they are often constructed as the carriers of the community's 'honour' and culture throughout the generations (Yuval-Davis, 2009: 11). In a sense, therefore, as Kandiyoti notes, 'demands of the "nation"' can be as restraining for women as demands enforced by 'individual patriarchs' (1991a: 429).

This special place given to women explains why they are also given a pivotal role in national discourses in times of social change and transformation (e.g. Kandiyoti 1997; Moghadam, 2003; Abu-Lughod, 1998). Women, for instance, have found themselves at the centre of 'modernising' projects, where they have been asked to emancipate themselves from their community and become active in collective life, while at the same time still being responsible for protecting the boundaries of what is culturally understood as feminine (Kandiyoti, 1991a: 432–33). These projects have therefore often been less about increasing the autonomy of women, and more about ensuring that they protect and foster new national goals and regulations (ibid.). Likewise, the modern state's ability to penetrate and modify gender relations (through, for instance, the control of personal status laws) should be understood as ensuring the supremacy of one moral project over another (e.g. Kandiyoti, 1998: 272; Najmabadi, 2006; Abu-Lughod, 1998):

> The national projects of most 'modernising' states may seem to introduce a tug-of-war between private and public patriarchy. Indeed, one finds battles over women's souls (exemplified in debates over educating women) and their bodies (seen in debates over fertility control) and between the bureaucrat or the district commissar versus the male household head, the tribal chief or the local mullah.
>
> (Kandiyoti, 1991a: 430)

This battle over the place and role of women has, in fact, been important to the encounter between the West and Muslim societies during colonisation and after (Salih, 2003: 103). The veil was identified in the colonialist discourse as a sign of cultural backwardness, as well as of 'gender homosociality' favouring same sex practices. Unveiling symbolised the eradication of 'women's backwardness', as well as the boundaries of 'normative sexuality' (Najmabadi, 2006: 246). What is interesting here is less whether perceptions of the veil and sexuality were grounded or based on misconceptions, but rather that these were part and parcel of an attempt to articulate a new morality that had to define itself against an uncivilised 'other'. 'Like all regulatory discourses, the ideal of modern bourgeoisie domesticity needed its civilizational "others", and the normalization of certain forms of sexuality and gender was predicated upon a critic and stigmatization of others' (Kandiyoti, 1997: 117).

Because women issues have been central to colonial and modernising endeavours, it has also become the focus of attention of anti-colonial projects – symbolising culture change (Yuval-Davis, 2009). For instance, the insistence of colonial powers on 'de-veiling' women has rendered it a key symbol of anti-colonial resistance (Ahmed, 1992: 164). Today, with migration and globalisation, debates over women's bodies and the veil as a marker of backwardness or cultural 'authenticity' are far from being settled (Salih, 2003: 103; Najmabadi, 2006). Immigrant women often find themselves in a confusing situation where they are understood to be the bearers of the tradition of their communities, and are, at the same time, the first target of assimilationist policies that encourage them to reproduce the 'values' of the dominant culture:

> Family migration is generally associated with female migrants (…) who are primarily seen as introducing traditional practices, such as arranged marriages, authoritarian gender and generational relations and religious practices into secular, modern and liberal societies.
>
> (Yuval-Davis *et al.* 2005: 519)

In a sense, therefore, acknowledging the central place of women in the articulation of modern projects sheds some light on why they have been, and continue to be, one of the first targets of social transformations, which renders their status as fully-fledged citizens particularly vulnerable (Kandiyoti, 1991a: 435).[7] By making reference to women as 'border-guards', this discussion also makes the connection between women and the codes they (re)produce, and the (re)production of space and boundaries. This connection is key to understanding the gendered spatial workings of secularism. In effect, as Gökariksel (2007), Knott (2005, 2010) and others have highlighted, and as will be discussed extensively in the next chapters, the (re)production of space plays a crucial role in the articulation of secular tropes that delimit particular spaces as 'secular' or 'public' and others as 'religious' or 'private':[8]

> Just like any other political ideology, secularism operates through the construction, organization and encoding of spaces that represent, embody

> and sometimes enforce 'secular' values, norms and practices [...] Women's bodies, dress, and practices are key to the construction of each space as secular, modern, or religious.
>
> (Gökariksel, 2007: 62)

However, far from being secured or fixed, these boundaries have to be repeatedly (re)produced, policed and enacted. 'A sphere marked out as "private" at one stage of nation-building may reappear with the full trappings of the 'public' at another, their boundaries being fluid and subject to redefinition' (Kandiyoti, 1991a: 430).[9] As the reader will come to realise, since women are assigned a key role in the (re)production of these boundaries, they are here again often among the first to be affected by these shifts.[10]

Bridging the two discussions

By focusing, in part, on how the discourse of secularism is being altered by devout women, I see this project as being located, in some ways, at the crossroads of two literatures: a literature on secularism as a model of religious governance that has generally situated its analysis at the level of states and institutions, and a literature on gender and modernity that has embraced a more micro-approach, interrogating categories of the modern in specific contexts. Critical scholars contributing to the first discussion have highlighted the interdependence of religion and secularism, and the power of the discourse of secularism that ends up shaping the boundaries of what is religiously acceptable in a nation-state. Yet, as noted, while most of these studies stress that secularism is a social construction, they have yet to investigate systematically whether and how subjects affected by these policies alter, challenge and reframe this discourse. Few works, in fact, have explored *why* women's bodies and gender equality have become important in contemporary secular narratives, and how this relates to the geography of secularism. This is precisely why I consider that investigating these questions is important, as women's bodies and performances play an important role in grasping the delimitations and (re)production of boundaries between the 'religious' and the 'secular'. The literature on gender and modernity, on the other hand, provides elements of the answer to *why* women have come to occupy a key place in modern projects. Doing so has allowed these scholars to warn us about the ambiguous and vulnerable status of women as fully-fledged citizens. They have, however, only recently started to point out the importance of looking at the power and the impact of contemporary dominant secular tropes on the exclusion of devout women (e.g. Moors and Salih, 2009; Gökariksel, 2007; Gökariksel and Mitchell, 2005; Göle, 2010), or to record women's understandings of secularisms (Al-Ali, 2000). In this book, one of my contentions is that analysing and comparing how these exclusions unfold in specific contexts is relevant, inasmuch as it highlights how religion, coupled with gender differences, can mediate access to full citizenship, and facilitate the (re)production of spaces. Such an exploration is an invitation, also, to focus on the discourses and practices of the women at the centre of these tensions.

On methods and ethics

Conceptualising secularism

As already discussed, *Refashioning Secularisms* adopts a similar reading of secularism to the one developed by critical scholars. That is, it approaches it as an authoritative discourse that defines the boundaries of the religiously acceptable. Yet, since one of the aims of the book is to capture how secularism shifts, gets (re)articulated and transformed with time and contexts, I suggest complementing this approach with a Gramscian idea of hegemony. Hegemony is not understood here in the traditional sense of the term, as a form of static political dominance, but more as an open-ended process that can be transformed and altered:[11]

> A lived hegemony is always a process […] It is a realized complex of experiences, relationships, and activities, with specific and changing pressures and limits […] Moreover (and this is crucial, reminding us of the necessary thrust of the concept), it does not just passively exist as a form of dominance. It has continually to be renewed, recreated, defended, and modified. It is also continually resisted, limited, altered.
>
> (Williams, 1977: 112)

Approaching secularism as a hegemonic process is interesting in several respects. This reading does not only convey a sense of power, but also a sense of change and dynamism. In effect, a hegemonic process has to be alert to possible threats and adapt itself to 'contain, transform or even incorporate them' (ibid. 1977: 114) – leading to a possible (re)articulation of its terms.

Concretely, using this definition allows me to do two things. First, it facilitates the exploration of the authority of dominant understandings of secularism, as well as how these evolve with time, affecting the boundaries of what is considered to be religiously acceptable in a modern nation-state. Exploring this shifting character also sheds light on some of the tensions, inconsistencies and contradictions that are present within this hegemonic discourse. Second, it facilitates the exploration of how religious activists have been challenging the dominant understandings of secularism and, more particularly, bans on headscarves in France and Turkey. Challenges are understood, here, as the claims of religious activists positioning themselves publically against the bans. As such, this project resonates with recent studies that stress the importance of exploring the practices and strategies of devout Muslim women who find themselves at the heart of secular tensions (e.g. Moors and Salih, 2009; Gökariskel, 2007). However, it does not focus on the practices and day-to-day tactics of these women, but rather on the study of their public discourses, i.e. on their contributions to public debates on secularism and headscarf bans. This specific investigation serves as an entry point to evaluate whether activists refer to tensions and shifts in dominant secular narratives to base their claims, their success in (re)articulating the terms of this discourse, as well as identify possible limits to their endeavour. Indeed, the fact that they are locating their claims within this hegemonic discourse does not preclude the possibility that they can develop innovative ways of accommodating their religiosity with secularism.

> It would be wrong to overlook the importance of works and ideas which, while clearly affected by the hegemonic limits and pressures, are at least in part significant breaks beyond them, which may again in part be neutralized, reduced, or incorporated, *but which in their most active elements nevertheless come through as independent and original.*
>
> (Williams, 1977: 114 (author's emphasis))

To embark on this investigation, it is important to identify the key terms of this hegemonic discourse, the terms that have been referred to in the dominant interpretations of secularism and that have also been (re)produced and (re)appropriated by religious activists. In other words, I see secularism as containing several languages, whose contents shift over time and are subject to (re)articulations. Four languages of secularism, which are deeply interrelated, run through the different chapters of this book. The first one conveys the idea of separation between state and religion. Yet, the terms of this separation and how it is enforced are not fixed and they differ according to who is referring to them and the political circumstances. The second one conveys the idea of neutrality. Here, as well, who is affected by this neutrality principle and what this neutrality precisely implies remains changeable. For instance, in some cases it is used to convey the neutrality of the state and then, in other instances, the neutrality of public spaces or individuals. Linked to this notion of neutrality is the third language: the notion of individual autonomy. For some, this state can only be reached when individuals are 'neutral' when navigating public spaces; for others autonomy requires the state to be neutral and to refrain from interfering in the subjectivities of individuals. Finally, the fourth language is gender equality. The meaning given to this language is, as one will come to see, deeply intertwined with notions of neutrality and autonomy. Here again, how this equality is attained varies in accordance with the different understandings of the role of the state and individuals in a secular polity. One becomes aware, therefore, that although these languages are used as justifications in determining the terms of the relationship between politics and religion, the precise content they are given influences drastically what this relationship is and, consequently, the form, role and place of religion in a nation-state.

Researching secularisms

In order to map out the historical, political and sociological stories of secularisms both at national levels (Chapters 2 and 3) and at the transnational level (Chapter 6), this book is indebted to existing works in political science, law, history, gender studies, anthropology, religious studies and sociology. Discussions in the aforementioned chapters also draw on governmental and non-governmental reports, speeches, newspapers articles, government policy statements, laws and law proposals as well as court rulings. Moreover, Chapters 4, 5 and, to a lesser extent, Chapter 6 are organised largely around an analysis of the material produced by devout activists in France and Turkey,[12] as well as on a series of loosely structured interviews with some of these activists.

Here again, concerns over headscarf bans were useful in guiding me through selecting the individuals to interview, as well as the material to analyse. Since I was particularly interested in analysing the public discourse of Muslim activists with respect to headscarf restrictions, I focused on individuals in both countries who were involved in this activism. It is important to note that my aim in this project has not been to unravel individual subjective understandings of secularism and the differences that could exist between them.[13] My focus has rather been on analysing the discourse and arguments of devout activists in public debates, i.e. the discourse they produce when they are publically positioning themselves vis-à-vis state policies, public opinion, and/or the international community. This focus, I have found, is of particular relevance, inasmuch as it allows for an evaluation of whether their discourse is built on the inconsistencies found in the dominant discourses on secularism, how it is both constrained and enriched by contextual specificities, and whether activists are able to find the space to be heard and gain credibility. This explains why, in the second part of this book, I put a particular emphasis on analysing the written discourses produced by activists in which they articulate their concerns with respect to headscarf bans and secularism (e.g. reports, pamphlets, press releases, testimony books, open letters, and so on). While these documents have, to my knowledge, not yet been the focus of systematic scholarly attention, I believe that they are a direct contribution to controversies on headscarf bans, as well as to our conceptualisation of secularism and its power. In France, these documents were mostly all written in French, and I generally had no problem reading, analysing and translating part of these documents since I am a fluent French speaker. In Turkey, many of them have been translated into English by the activists themselves, an indication that their communications and claims were targeting not only national audiences, but international ones as well. For documents not available in English, I was helped to fully grasp their content by a research assistant, as I was learning Turkish.

Interviews and conversations have been helpful to capture some of the complexities of secular politics. These interactions have helped me establish a network of relevant activists, understand the context (e.g. who are the activists publically challenging headscarf bans; why, how and since when have they been involved in this type of activism), and access documents unavailable on the web. They have equally been useful in grasping the argumentative approach of activists better, as well as the nuances and paradoxes that mark their struggle. Finally, I was able, through these conversations, to get a sense of the practices of my interviewees (e.g. who were they allying themselves with; since when and why; what means of pressure did they use (national courts, international lobbying and/or protests), and so on).

To embark on this journey, I conducted fieldwork in France from October 2007 to March 2008 in the cities of Paris and Lyon (and did a few interviews in Strasbourg), and did follow-up interviews in April 2012. My first fieldwork visit to Turkey took place from April 2008 to August 2008 in the cities of Ankara and Istanbul. I did follow-up visits in April 2009, August 2010 and August 2011. The first couple of weeks in both countries were dedicated to conducting informal interviews with a series of public figures (e.g. journalists, scholars, politicians) to get a sense of the broad context and to try and identify the activists who were playing a significant role in fighting headscarf bans. At the early stage of this project, I was also introduced to a Turkish journalist who grew to become a key informant, and a friend. This reporter, who had worked in both Turkey and Paris, greatly facilitated my fieldwork experience in Turkey, as she kept me updated on the situation and debates and put me in contact with politicians, columnists and activists, who were in turn able to direct me to activists involved in headscarf debates.

In both countries, I used a snowball method to contact interviewees.[14] After identifying several key players through this mapping out phase, I asked these individuals if they could put me in touch with other activists involved in a similar struggle or with whom they had been collaborating. While I tried to interview a large sample of activists, my selection was still limited. In both cases, I was constrained by time, space, financial factors and, in the Turkish case, by language. Although I decided to conduct research in each country in two large cities known for their vibrant civil society (Ankara and Istanbul and Paris and Lyon),[15] my interview sample remained constrained within the borders of these urban centres. Moreover, while in France interviews were conducted in French, in Turkey most of them were conducted in English, and when my interviewees only spoke Turkish I was helped by a research assistant. Despite this assistance, I still felt it was easier to build rapport with interviewees who spoke English. As a result, the conversations conducted in English were often more detailed and most of the interviews that were conducted more than once were with these respondents.

In Turkey most of the activists interviewed were women in their mid-20s to early 40s, who had been affected by restrictions on headscarves, members of the new Turkish devout bourgeoisie, urban, well-travelled, and educated (often fluent in English).[16] Many of my interviewees were members of, or collaborated closely with, rights-based non-governmental organizations located in Ankara and/or Istanbul that had been fighting headscarf restrictions. While activists produced written material on headscarf bans as part of their collaboration with these organizations, some also published documents outside these frameworks (e.g. petitions and pamphlets). In France, my respondents had been active in challenging the March 2004 ban, and in recording and denouncing its extension beyond students in public schools. Even while I still interviewed more women than men, my interview sample was relatively more mixed than in Turkey. Most of my interviewees were in their mid-20s to late 30s, second or even third generation Muslims, whose parents had emigrated from the Maghreb. Many of them grew up, and still live, in French suburbs (e.g. Lyon, Paris, Lille, Strasbourg or Marseille), and were well educated with at least one university degree. In fact, most considered themselves to be French citizens of Muslim faith, an appellation often used to indicate a will to be active in French society while remaining pious. They also participated in the activities of the organizations and collectives where fighting the bans had become a priority.[17]

Finally, it is important to note that this is not a study of French or Turkish 'Islamic communities'. Needless to say, these 'communities' are extremely diverse, marked by generational, political, doctrinal and class divergences. Rather my goal is to analyse the public discourse produced by some of these activists. In so doing, it has a natural bias since it excludes individuals who cannot or who do not want to take a public stand.

Thinking about the interview process and ethical concerns

I conducted loosely structured interviews organised around a series of themes and open-ended questions that I wanted to cover with my respondents. The length of the interviews varied in light of the rapport that I was able to build with my respondents, but was approximately between one hour and one and a half hours. Most of the time, I met with my interviewees in their offices and in coffee shops, but sometimes on university campuses or in their homes. As previously mentioned, I interviewed some respondents a couple of times. This was especially useful once I had read documents that they had given me during previous meetings and when I had further questions, or if I wanted to build on an issue that had come out in another interview. For instance, towards the end of my fieldwork in Istanbul I discovered that some activists were participating in protests and alliances with LGBT associations and felt compelled to explore this new issue further with respondents I had already interviewed.

As with any type of research involving fieldwork, my positionality – as a woman researcher studying in the UK, of Canadian and Swiss origins, but who had lived in multiple places and was fluent in French – played an important role in explaining how, and to what extent, I was able to build a rapport with respondents. While I am not convinced that being a woman eased my access to women respondents, since activists met regularly with male journalists, activists and scholars, it might however have facilitated my ability to build rapport with a few respondents, who invited me to visit them in their homes. I was also quite surprised by the fact that it was somewhat easier to build rapport with my respondents in Turkey than in France. One of the reasons for this might lie in the way I speak French with a 'French' accent, rather than with a 'French Canadian' one. Although my mother comes from Montreal, because we did not live in Canada during my childhood I did not pick up French Canadian. This explains why, when I first started contacting my respondents in France, they thought from the sound of my voice that I was French, and expressed suspicion with regard to my motives in conducting a research on Islam and secularism. This reaction can partly be understood by the fact that over the last decades Muslims in France have been the focus of many journalistic, and even scholarly, accounts portraying them in quite a negative light. It is only when I told them that I was studying in the UK working on a comparison of French and Turkish secularisms, and that I had previously worked and lived in Montreal, that they became more comfortable and were willing to engage in conversation. Several of them even started our meeting by mentioning that they had family or friends leaving in Quebec, and that Canada was generally more open to religious diversity. They also reminded me on several occasions that the situation in France was very different from the one in Canada, the UK or Turkey, and that French *laïcité* was unique in its genre.

I suspected at first that conducting research in Turkey would be harder, especially because I did not know Istanbul or Ankara very well and had a limited knowledge of Turkish. However, meeting respondents and gaining access to material was easier than planned. This is probably due in part to my research inquiry – which invited respondents to share their struggles with me – as well as to my position as a western foreigner (some of the implications of this position are discussed below). On the other hand, during the mapping out session, when I tried to meet with members of known Kemalist and nationalist associations, I was more than once confronted with negative answers or no answers at all.[18] This, I believe, is again partly because of the character of my research inquiry, the socio-political climate of when I conducted fieldwork, and also, perhaps, because I was not fluent in Turkish.

These latter tensions, which were partly linked to my positionality and my choice of research inquiry, bring me to some of the ethical dilemmas I faced during fieldwork. Since the topic of secularism, and more particularly its relationship with Islam, is not only an intellectual concern but also the source of deep emotional and ideological struggles in both countries, my project found itself more than once in the midst of heated discussions. This happened during casual conversations when I presented it to friends or acquaintances in France and Turkey, who defined themselves as 'secularists' – positioning themselves in favour of an assertive type of secularism. Several tried to convince me that the (re)appropriation of secularism by devout Muslims was simply a facade to hide a 'fundamentalist' agenda, and even urged me to find evidence that would contribute to the validation of this thesis. I responded to these comments by stressing that the aim of my research was not to validate or invalidate a thesis, but rather to shed light on the discourse of devout Muslims who had been affected by secular polices. My unsatisfying answer was often brushed away by comments that pointed to my naïvety and my position as an outsider and foreigner – a position that had gone from someone that could unravel the 'truth' to being ill-placed to understand the situation. These conversations, even with friends, made me feel quite uncomfortable and anxious, as they pointed to the fact that these struggles were deeply ingrained in personal lives. Likewise, several of my respondents also articulated high expectations with respect to my project. In Turkey, devout activists expressed hopes that my research would participate in their own efforts to inform the 'West' of their predicaments, while in France one of my respondents saw my project as a means to tell an untold aspect of history.[19] In both contexts, the fact that I was a non-Muslim, western, foreign researcher interested in their struggles was perceived as positive, as it had the potential to give certain credibility to their endeavours beyond their circles. While my response to these expectations was to again restate the limited scope of my research, clarifying my position to my respondents also led me to deepen my reflection on my position as a scholar in politically delicate situations. Although I had read accounts in which researchers were faced with impossible expectations and reflected on their role and emotions in the research process, it was only when I was faced with this reality that I fully understood the complexity of this process. In fact, when I began fieldwork I found a certain level of comfort in my 'foreignness'. I thought it would allow me to stay 'outside' ideological struggles. However, I soon realised that, in the eyes of my respondents and my other acquaintances, my research project and my positionality were political. Moreover, while I was naïve enough to think that the boundaries between being a researcher and an advocate were clear, I quickly realised that these were thinner than expected, and that I had limited control on the position I was assigned by others.[20] These difficult predicaments that have unsettled my own boundaries, and that will continue to mark my personal and scholarly journey, direct our attention, as noted by others (e.g. Coutin and Hirsh, 1998), to the need to be more attentive to how we negotiate our own positions in and beyond fieldwork. While this is a process that I have only begun, I hope that I have at least succeeded, through pointing out some of my dilemmas, in shedding light on the political conditions in which this research is situated.

Summing up the argument and outlining the structure of the book

The central aim of *Refashioning Secularisms* is to explore the shifting character of secularism and how this affects what is considered to be religiously and politically acceptable in a polity. In other words, I will investigate how the languages of secularism in Turkey and France evolved with time, context, and as a consequence of who is articulating them, as well as the impact this has on understandings of religion. The structure of the book lends itself to this exploration. The first part of the discussion (Chapters 2 and 3) focuses on exploring the authority of dominant understandings of secularism, as well as how these understandings shift. Doing this sets the stage for the second part of the book (Chapters 4, 5 and 6), which analyses more specifically how devout Muslim activists have been challenging these dominant understandings. By focusing on headscarf bans, this exploration highlights the importance of gender in the discourses of secularism. In fact, this comes out not only through documenting the ambivalent position of women in dominant understandings of secularism, but also through the study of the discourse of devout Muslims, a discourse that is often articulated by women themselves and that is structured around the inclusion of devout women in the public realm.

Chapter 2 highlights the importance of taking into consideration the historical legacies of secular discourses. It starts by situating and shedding light on the different layers of meaning embedded in secular languages in Turkey and France. In so doing, it investigates how, as early as the nineteenth century, secular languages have been used to justify state interference in selected subjectivities, an interference that has been central to the construction of both Republics. For instance, I posit that the language of separation has been used to locate, regulate, and control religions and religious subjectivities. In this story, regulation has been considered necessary in order to 'prepare' these religions for 'full' separation. Moreover, by looking into the specific examples of how religious minorities and women have been subject to this process of regulation over time, this chapter starts to unravel how secular tropes are deeply intertwined with discourses on modernity, in which the regulation of family and sexuality occupy a key role. Chapter 3 continues to explore the multi-vocal and shifting character of secular languages. It does so by offering a detailed comparative analysis of the evolution of headscarf bans in both countries. By exploring how exclusions unfold in multiple sites, it invites the reader to become aware of the intimate relationship that exists between secular tropes, the production of space, and gender. This discussion captures how the boundaries of what is considered public space extend or retract in response to different times and political climates. I argue that this is not without consequences for the lives of devout women. In effect, by documenting these movements, one is able to clearly realise their vulnerable position as they find themselves at the margin of spaces; their ability to enjoy their citizenship rights varies therefore in respect to these shifts.

Chapters 4 and 5 suggest that the evolving character of the content attributed to the languages of secularism have facilitated their (re)appropriation by Muslim activists challenging headscarf bans. Chapter 4 explores how this unfolds in the contemporary French context and highlights that religious activists have generally been relying on national jurisprudence to publically challenge the March 2004 law and its extensions. This has been less the case in Turkey, where, as discussed in Chapter 5, Turkish courts have had a tradition of producing rulings confirming the exclusion of headscarf wearers from public spaces, leading activists to rely on international human rights conventions, as well as on a national process of political liberalization, to develop their arguments. Despite these differences, these chapters highlight how in both cases activists have been (re)appropriating the languages of secularism to redefine the terms of state intervention in religion, and to justify full citizenship rights for devout women. While they still end up defining the boundaries of the religiously acceptable in a nation-state, they attempt to widen them so that expressions of personal piety are not considered to be incompatible with collective life. Finally Chapter 6, by exploring the concrete means used by religious activists to challenge bans (e.g. national and international mechanisms), gives a transnational dimension to our exploration. I examine how restrictive national legal contexts have been pushing activists to send complaints to, and to lobby in, international human rights forums (i.e. UN human rights bodies and the Strasbourg European Court of Human Rights (ECtHR)). In so doing, one realizes that secularism and the meanings given to its languages have become a source of debate in transnational spaces as well as national ones.

Notes

1 Please note that I translated the French quotations throughout the book into English, and that I am responsible for any shortcomings.
2 The 28 February 1997 coup is qualified as 'soft' because the army did not directly take control of the country. It did, however, demand that the Welfare Party (a political formation with an Islamic leaning) ruling the country at the time in coalition with the centre-right True Faith Party restore secularism. To do so they asked the coalition in power to take measures to restrict the number of Imam Hatip schools (religious schools), increase mandatory secular education from five to eight years and control religious orders. This created an impasse within the ranks of the Welfare Party, as it was too divided on these issues. This 'soft' coup was backed up by the Constitutional Court, which later expelled the Welfare leader from parliament, banned him from political participation for five years and took all the party's assets (Esposito, 2000: 6). The consequences of this coup are discussed in greater detail in Chapters 3 and 5.
3 The terms *laïcité* and *laiklik* are used throughout this book to refer to French and Turkish secularism respectively. Although they can be translated as secularism, these terms remain very context specific. Several authors, in fact, have expressed concerns with this translation, as they believe secularism only partially reflects their meanings (Troper, 2000; Bowen, 2007a; Davison, 2003). Nevertheless, for concision purposes, the term secularism is used when I am referring to both the French and the Turkish cases.
4 The expressions 'dominant understandings of secularism' and 'dominant secular tropes' are used to refer to understandings of secularism referred to by state elites (e.g. bureaucrats, policy makers, and so on), courts and parts of society, and leading to a spread of restrictions on the wearing of headscarves in the public realm.

As the reader will come to realise, there are inconsistencies and tensions within these understandings.

5 Note that secularism was mostly understood in terms of its relation to Christianity, which explains the persistent use of the expression, 'separation of *church* and state'.

6 The expressions 'visibility of Islam' and 'visible Islam' are used in the text in reference to the growing presence of headscarves in the public realm.

7 Access to citizenship is therefore gendered. When one speaks of the gendered character of citizenship, it is equally important to bear in mind the heterogeneity of the category 'women'. In effect, access to citizenship varies not only in function of the ideology of a state but also of the ethnicity, race, religion, class, and age of an individual (Yuval-Davis, 2001: 122 and Lentin, 1999: 130). Women can, thus, be subject to double discrimination not only because of their individual positionality, but also because of the positioning of other communities they might belong to, such as local, cross, and trans-national communities (Yuval-Davis, 1997a, 1997b, 2001 and Yuval-Davis and Werbner, 1999; Lentin, 1999). This is of particular relevance for devout Muslim women in Europe who, because of their visible bodily attire, are often narrated as belonging to 'threatening' alternative communities (sub- and trans-national communities) and this in turn influences their full inclusion in the polity (Moors, 2009; Moors and Salih, 2009; Najmabadi, 2006).

8 Words, such as religious, neutrality, public, private and secular are used with single quotation marks to indicate that the boundaries and meanings given to these notions are not stable or essential, but are rather constructed and change over time and in different political climates. While quotation marks are only used the first time these terms are mentioned, they continue to be approached as unstable and constructed categories throughout the book.

9 Joseph and Slyomovics (2000: 35), Yuval-Davis (2001) and Knott (2010) develop a similar argument.

10 It is important to stress that although boundaries shift with time, this does not mean that they are porous. As the reader will come to realize, individuals that are prohibited from participating in different activities of the polis do experience these prohibitions as direct hardships in their lives and have to go through a series of hurdles to contest them.

11 For a detail discussion of this understanding of hegemony see Williams, 1977: 108–14 and Chalcraft and Noorani, 2007: 1–16.

12 It is important to note that I feel a certain level of uneasiness in using the terms secular, religious, faith-based or devout to refer to different groups and/or individuals, as this tends to essentialize identities and overlook the diversity of positions. For instance, women members of a secular group can consider themselves non-religious while still making theological judgements on which behaviours are religious obligations and which are not. Yet, during my interviews, this dichotomy was inevitably used to make a distinction between groups and individuals motivated by a religious ethic and those who were not. This is why, while keeping in mind these nuances, these categorizations are mobilised.

13 Al-Ali (2000), for instance, embarks on a project that has this particular focus. She investigates the understandings of secularism of Egyptian women involved in secular-oriented activism, pointing to the heterogeneity of their interpretation of the term.

14 With this mapping out phase, I conducted approximately 65 interviews.

15 I chose Ankara and Istanbul in Turkey because they are considered to be two urban centres with a vibrant civil society. In France, the choice of Paris and Lyon was motivated by the fact that they are the two largest centres, with Marseille, of Muslim population (Laurence and Vaisse, 2006: 21). Because of time and financial constraints I was not able to explore the civil society landscape in Marseille.

16 Several of these activists have been unable to go to university in Turkey because of headscarf bans, and have studied abroad in English, including in Sweden, UK and

Malaysia. For a further description of these activists and the organizations they have been working with see Chapter 5.

17 For a detail description of these activists, as well as of the organizations they have been working with see Chapter 4.

18 Turam (2006: 75) in her study of the *Gülen* movement in Turkey faced similar challenged when she tried to meet with Kemalists. This was linked, she argues, to the character of her research inquiry.

19 Deeb (2006: 40) in her study of public piety in Shi'i Lebanon, discusses how she faced similar expectations from her respondents.

20 For an insightful discussion of how ethnographic analyses are implicated in political contexts, and the complex position of researchers in these contexts, see Coutin and Hirsh (1998).

2 A tradition of regulations

Shedding light on the paradoxes of the languages of secularism

Secularism is often understood in terms of a separation between religion (or rather church) and state. Yet the precise terms of this separation, as well as the role the state should play in enforcing it, remains to this day an area of great debate at academic and policy levels. Some, for instance, consider secularism and the role of the state to be quite different whether it is applied in a Muslim or a Christian context (e.g. Lewis, 1993; Huntington, 1993). In the first, the Muslim context, they argue that due to the 'nature' of Islam, the state has to control religious affairs in order to ensure that state institutions and the public realm remain free from religious interference. In the latter, due to the 'intrinsic characteristics' of Christianity, which it is argued contains from its inception a recommendation 'to render unto Caesar, the things which are Caesar's' (Lewis, 1993: 179), the separation of power is easier and the state does not need to exercise a high level of interference. This thesis has been used by some to outline the core differences between French and Turkish secularisms (e.g. Berkes, 1998 [1964]). Yet, as discussed in the last chapter, this approach has been considered to be problematic in more ways than one. It attributes essential and ahistorical characteristics to religions, and thus fails to acknowledge that religions change and adapt in response to the context in which they are exercised. Likewise, it does not take into consideration that national models of religious governance can take different forms and mean different things depending of the historical and political contexts in which they unfold, regardless of the religious beliefs they seek to 'govern' (e.g. Lapidus, 1996; Keddie, 1997; Bowen, 2007b; Fetzer and Soper, 2007; Silvestri, 2007; Kuru, 2009).

This thesis is, nonetheless, interesting in so far as it feeds the narratives that have been mobilized to justify the governance of particular religions and religious subjectivities, and this regardless of whether a state legally keeps to the principle of separation. Scholars, in fact, have suggested that rather than take the idea of separation or control (when it comes to 'particular' areas of the world or religions) for granted, it is more relevant to look at the power produced by these statements (e.g. Shakman Hurd, 2008; Bowen, 2010; Knott, 2010). That is, how and by whom the boundaries between politics and religion are being established, how these are (re)produced and sustained throughout time, and the impact this has on the organization of the religious. The importance of engaging with the politics behind this separation narrative is well expressed by Elizabeth Shakman Hurd:

> The question is, *How* do processes, institutions and states come to be understood as religious versus political, or religious versus secular, and how we might ascertain the political effects of such demarcation? To define the boundaries of the secular and the religious is itself a political decision.
> (Shakman Hurd, 2008: 16 (original emphasis))

This chapter embarks on an examination guided by this approach. It investigates the French and Turkish Republics' tradition of ascribing a religious identity to particular individuals, an identity that ought to be 'transformed' if these individuals want to participate in political life. In other words, these individuals and their 'religiosity' have been central in delimiting the spaces and (re)producing the idea of boundaries between an active/public political life, in which religion is 'tamed' and a religious realm often conflated with a private and familial one. This process, as explored below, is far from being new. It has been key to the construction of the identities of both Republics, and to their definition of citizenship. Interestingly, secularism and its languages have, in both Republics, been part and parcel of the argument mobilized to justify contemporary intrusions into these subjectivities.

Paradoxes of the languages of *laïcité* and *laiklik*

While the languages of separation and neutrality are frequently understood as being central to the articulation of the discourse of secularism, it is important to note that these languages are deeply influenced by the historical and political contexts of the countries in which they are deployed. This explains some of the paradoxes and contradictions that these languages can carry. In the case of France and Turkey, contemporary articulations of these languages carry with them a tradition of heavy state interference in religion and religious subjectivities.

For instance, as Bowen reminds us, the French model of religious governance has been deeply influenced by a *gallican* tradition going back as far as the rule of Philippe Le Bel (1268–1314) (2007b: 1008). Already at that time the French state asserted its control over the church by establishing a national church that maintained a certain level of independence from Rome. This model has continued to shape the relationship between the French state and religions. It influenced, for instance, the *Concordat* (1801–1905) put in place by Napoleon Bonaparte. At that time, the state recognized four religious traditions – Catholicism, Reformed, Lutheran, and Judaism – employing their ministers, owning their religious buildings, requiring full subordination of their clergy to the Republic, and having a say in the form and shape these religions took.

A similar process took place in the Ottoman Empire where, as early as the sixteenth century, Ottoman officials saw the diversity within Islam as a possible cause for the fragmentation of the Empire. They therefore deported heterodox groups to the corners of the Empire, dealt severely with religious movements that escaped their control, and created a religious elite as well as an educational system supervised by these elites, both of which were put under state control (Mardin, 1993: 349). This control over Islam continued and became quite explicit in the nineteenth century when the Ottoman Empire went through a wave of centralization reforms and where several attempts to limit and regulate the power of Ulemas were at work. Sultan Abdülhamid II (1876–1909) understood very well the challenges at hand, while he saw centralization reforms as necessary to develop a strong state – the legitimacy of the Empire still lay in Islam. This is why he used Islam to legitimize his craft and foster a social cohesion of some sort. For Zürcher and van der Linden his rule led to unprecedented state interference in religious affairs, both with 'the content and the spread of the faith' (2004: 100). In other words, he was crafting an Islam that was manageable and loyal to the modern state project, in which the state gave, for instance, directions 'for publishers of the Koran, for religious education at schools and for sermons in the mosques' (ibid.). In his endeavour he tried, not unlike his predecessors, to create a homogeneous form of Sunni orthodox Islam, repressing other heterodox forms of the faith (Deringil, 1993: 28).

In other words, attempts to control and regulate the religious started early in both our cases. This is not to say that the reasons for doing so were not different and influenced by historical specificities. As discussed, Sultan Abdülhamid's policies, for instance, were marked by matters of his time. Yet these trends are worth keeping in mind in order to highlight the specificities of the modes of secularism in both countries today. Laborde, speaking on the French case notes, for instance, that despite the separation law, passed in 1905 and that officially established a legal separation between 'church' and state,[1] a tension between separation and regulation continues to haunt the French model of religious governance:

> One of the paradoxes of French *laïcité* is that, for all its commitment to the separation of church and state […], it has always, out of necessity, relied on state recognition of centralized religious authorities […]. The neutral state, therefore, is not totally indifferent to the structure of religious communities or to the content of their doctrines.
>
> (Laborde, 2005: 321)[2]

Because the secular Turkish Republic does not have such a separation law, this contradiction seems to be less explicit. Mustapha Kemal's Republic did officially cease to find its legitimacy in Islam, but the importance of a homogenous and regulated Sunni Islam has remained important, to different extents, throughout the life of the Republic. In fact, while great efforts were made in the early days of the Republic to limit the 'independent' powers and intrusion of Islam (through, for instance, the abolition of the Caliphate and religious courts (1924) (Davison, 2003: 337)),[3] the state established at the same time a Directorate of Religious Affairs (*Diyanet*) responsible for the administration (including financial) of mosques and Dervish monasteries, for the training and nomination of Imams and religious clerks, and for providing suggestions on the content of sermons (Zürcher and van der Linden, 2004: 103). Commenting on this situation, Davison (2003: 338) argues that, ironically, although the Caliphate and Sharia were dismantled by the secular Republic, the state at the same time created a new structure regulating and promoting the diffusion of an official Republican and homogenous version of Islam, a structure which had more religious authority than the Ottoman Sultan Caliph himself.

To put it differently, a commitment to official separation, like in the French case or to 'pushing out' from state affairs 'particular'/'independent' manifestations of religion as in the Turkish case, has not been antonymic with state intervention in religious affairs. On the contrary, in both cases these two processes go hand in hand – state elites have been deeply preoccupied with the importance of crafting religions that would fit within the boundaries of the Republican canvas, and at the same time identifying religious practices that were not deemed compatible with this canvas and collective life.[4]

This need to regulate the religious explains, as well, the tensions found within the language of neutrality. While this language can be understood, in a similar fashion to the language of separation, as implying a requirement for state neutrality and non-interference in religious subjectivities, in many instances both Republics have interpreted this neutrality as being possible only when citizens are considered not to be overtly determined by their differences – that is, when they are themselves considered to be neutral (or homogenous). This sheds light on why both states have been intervening actively in selected subjectivities. They seek to ensure that these individuals learn to make an abstraction of their differences (including religious and gender differences), so that they are deemed 'fit' to participate in the life of the Republic.[5] In this process, selected religious practices and differences are located in private/intimate spaces, separated from, and thus 'making room' for, public spaces[6] (this does not mean that public spaces are a-religious, rather that they are purged of specific religious traits deemed at a particular point in time 'incompatible' with the morality of these spaces). This, ultimately, has consequences for the 'content' of selected religious doctrines, as states require that aspects of these become invisible and/or not practiced in the public realm.

It is through a subtle analysis of this language of neutrality that one becomes aware of how this concept is mediated by both gender and religion. In effect, in many instances believers are asked to modify/reform aspects of their faith related to its vision of gender relations. Women, because of their role as 'border-guards', are, in this process, often the first to be targeted by these requirements (Yuval-Davis, 1997a). Not surprisingly, therefore, as discussed briefly in this chapter and at greater length later in the rest of the book, gender equality becomes a key language of secularism starting in the early twentieth century in Turkey and later in that century in France – a language deeply pervaded by a concept of neutrality that leaves little space for individual differences.

Some individuals, identified as being dominated by their personal ethic, are therefore more vulnerable to this process of intervention and homogenization than others. To illustrate this point, the next sections explore the historical intervention of both Republican states in the fashioning of the subjectivities of religious minorities and women.

France: 'regenerating' or excluding religious minorities

Although one of the aims of the French Revolution was to liberate citizenship from religious allegiances, vivid debates sparked over whether citizenship rights should be given to Jews – rights which they received in 1791. Yet the Jews continued to be the subject of suspicion, as they were considered to be a minority belonging first and foremost to a religious community (Baubérot, 2004; Benbassa, 2004). They had to constantly prove that their first allegiance was to the Republic, and not with another project. Baubérot recalls that at the time of the 1789 Revolution, increased demands were put on Jews to pledge publicly their loyalty to the Republican project through public citizenship pledges (2004: 189). Many feared that Jews would create a nation within the French nation, and underlined the importance of accepting them only as individuals:

> We need to refuse everything to Jews as a nation […] and allow everything to Jews as individuals […] they cannot form a political group or order in the state, they have to be individual citizens. But you will tell me what if they don't want to be. Well if they don't, they should let us know and they shall be banned [from the Republic].
>
> (Clermont-Tonnerre, revolutionary MP, 24 December 1789, cited in Philippe, 1997: 143)

To address these fears, a considerable amount of effort was put into trying to harmonize Jewish laws, in particular personal status laws, with French laws. This was done through different means. Napoleon Bonaparte tried to push for the establishment of a body that would 'represent' Jews and thus succeed in imposing the French civil code. Accordingly, in 1806, one of his first attempts was to establish a body that mimicked the shape of the political-religious rabbinic assembly that existed in ancient Palestine, empowered to rule on Jewish law. His hope was that this body, known as the *Grand Sanhedrin*, would have enough authority to reform Jewish family laws (Schreier, 2007).

Along similar lines, in 1808, a body known as the *Consistoire* was established, modelled on the organization representing the French Protestant community. In practice, this meant that a central *Consistoire* was put in place, as well as a series of departmental *Consistoires* in each department that had more than 2,000 Jews.[7] The functions of these bodies were to facilitate the 'regeneration' and moral improvement of Jews through education. Special emphasis was put on ensuring that they respected French civil family law; that is, on ensuring control over sexuality and family life. In other words, as Benbassa notes, besides having religious functions, these bodies were also directly serving the state's interests as they ensured that these citizens would be productive, not 'overtly' consumed by their faith, and that their intimate lives be governed by rules defined by the French state. 'In their eyes [Republicans] Jews were primarily an incarnation of non-enlightened thought, responsible for obstructing the authority of reason in western culture. The first minority to undergo rationalist absolutism was the Jewish one' (Benbassa, 2004: 119–20).

Accepting French family law was also set as a prerequisite to giving full citizenship rights to Jews and Muslims in colonial Algeria. At that time, a distinction was made between French citizens who benefited from all civil and political rights, and indigenous Algerians who were French nationals but not fully-fledged citizens because they continued to follow their own personal status law. In 1865, these subjects were given the option of renouncing their personal status law and, in return, acquiring full French citizenship. However, few of them chose that route as they considered it to be an act of apostasy.[8] Schreier explains that another solution devised to address this problem was to 'export' the *Grand Sanhedrin* to colonial Algeria. In fact, Flandin, an advisor of Napoleon III, commenting on the situation of Muslims in Algeria in 1865, explicitly traced a parallel between the situation of these individuals with the one of Jews in France in the early 1800s.

> In 1806 the Jews wished to become French citizens; at the time, they were governed by the Talmud, which, like the Qu'ran, sanctified polygamy, repudiation, and so forth. Napoleon I wanted to separate faith and law. He convoked an assembly of notable Jews, he constituted a great court of the Jewish nation, and on March 2, 1807, the Grand Sanhedrin … rendered a doctrinal decision in conformity with the emperor's thinking. The Jews then became French citizens.
>
> (Flandin, *Conseiller d'Etat*, cited in Schreier, 2007: 100)

Ultimately, while Algerian Jews were forced to accept the hegemony of French law through the *Crémieux decree* in 1870s, the situation of Algerian Muslims remained unresolved until the end of French rule, keeping them excluded from full citizenship but not immune to further efforts to organize their faith and control their morality. Consequently, at a time when the state was implementing the 1905 separation law in mainland France,[9] it backed a form of official Islam in colonial Algeria. In 1907, a decree was issued that introduced a modified version of the separation law for Algeria, in which the state continued to remunerate Imams in Algeria (Maussen, 2007: 984). In 1950, in response to attempts to render Islam more independent from the colonial state, the French Ministry of Interior issued a note explaining that full freedom of religion and implementation of the 1905 Law would undermine the stability of colonial rule. The same note recalled that Muslim believers supported concepts of a theocratic state, where no separation between the temporal and the spiritual existed, a vision that justified continual state intervention in religious affairs (Achi, 2006: 250 and Maussen, 2007: 984).[10] To sum up, Muslims, like Jews, had to be 'brought' into the frame of *laïcité*. This narrative explains why the 1905 Law could not be fully applied to this community (Geisser and Zemouri, 2006: 20).

This historical legacy is important in understanding contemporary French attempts to regulate Islam in mainland France in order to create an 'Islam of France' as opposed to an 'Islam in France'.[11] In effect, the French state has continued to intervene in the organization of Islam by providing support for, among other things, the creation of a body that would 'represent' this 'Islam of France' (Caiero, 2005: 79). For instance, prior to being able to participate in the consultations that would eventually lead in 2003 to the creation of a representative body, known as the *Conseil Francais du Culte Musulman* (CFCM), Muslims associations were asked to sign a founding text (Ministry of Interior, 2001). This text laid out the rights and obligations of the Muslim faith in France, including that believers respect principles of non-discrimination based on gender, religion, ethnicity, mental or physical health that are central to French secular law. It was meant to be, at the same time, a confirmation of adherence to the *laïc* (i.e. secular) character of the French Republic, as established in the Constitution and in the 1905 Law.[12] Here again, not unlike Jews who had to renounce their personal status law (in 1806) more than a decade after they had been accepted as citizens (in 1791), Muslims in contemporary France were asked to pledge their loyalty to the Republic and its values, despite the fact that they were already French citizens (and, for some of them, for more than two generations).

This discussion points to how membership in one community can influence access to full citizenship rights in another (Yuval-Davis and Werbner, 1999: 5). Indeed, full access to the polity for individuals belonging to particular faiths is dependent on whether they pledge their loyalty to the Republican project, and more specifically to its models of gender relations. One becomes aware, therefore, that citizenship rights in France and the concept of neutrality have historically been deeply related to the ability of selected citizens to embrace the state's dominant model of gender relations and sexuality – allowing, in so doing, the state to penetrate the intimate lives of its citizens. Narratives justifying this intervention have evolved with time and political climates. As of the late nineteenth century, *laïcité* became one of these tropes, and continues to be mobilized today. One sees, already, in this brief analysis of the situation in colonial Algeria, how this trope can be given particular meanings as a consequence of the political contexts in which it is deployed and of the individuals, religions and practices it seeks to regulate. This will become even clearer in the last part of this chapter, which discusses how *laïcité* has been used to regulate the place and morals of women in the early 1900s.

Turkey: 'regenerating' or excluding religious minorities

As underlined a bit earlier, the founders of the Turkish Republic and their successors attempted to promote a Turkified Sunni version of Islam that would unite citizens. Although the Kemalist state praised itself for having established a universal secular and civic Republic, this 'universalism' was based here as well on particularities. In this case it was based on an implicit ethnic and religious understanding of citizenship – where a full-citizen was understood as being a Sunni Hanefi Muslim, speaking Turkish and not overtly religious (Kirişci, 2000: 18; Houston, 1997: 3). This reading of citizenship explains the ways in which the secular state has perceived non-Muslim and Muslim minorities, and can shed light on its attempts to actively interfere in these subjectivities.

A distinction needs to be made between Muslims and non-Muslim minorities. As long as individuals of Muslim backgrounds have shown a willingness to 'tame' their subjectivities, they have been able to aspire to become fully-fledged citizenship. This has not been the case, however, for non-Muslims (Kurban, 2004/5: 346). In a sense, the exclusions of the latter group of individuals from full citizenship has helped the secular Turkish state delimit the boundaries of Turkishness, drawn up, paradoxically, on the basis of religious belonging (Kurban, ibid.).

This explains why demands made by individuals of a Muslim background to continue to practice specific religious rituals (e.g. sufi rituals) or for language and ethnic recognitions (e.g. Kurds) were characterized in the early days of the Republic as 'backward primitivism' and 'parochial particularism' (Houston, 1997:3). 'To be Kurdish (or anti-secular Muslim) was immediately inscribed as being anti-progress/modern and hence morally i.e. ontologically deficient' (ibid.). That is, in return for suppressing all distinct cultures, languages and histories, Muslims were able to actively take part in the life of the polity (Kurban, 2004/5: 346).

One understands why the Turkish state has had, throughout its contemporary history, difficulties in recognizing Alevis' identity and faith, why they have systematically been treated as Sunni Muslims. For instance, students belonging to the Alevi faith have been obliged to follow state-sponsored religious classes in public schools: 'The classes are instructed on the basis of the Sunni interpretation of Islam, and thus are particularly discriminatory against Alevi and Caferi pupils' (Kurban, ibid.: 362).[13] Alevis have also not been represented in the Directorate of Religious Affairs, which means that while the state has been paying for the construction of mosques, Alevis have been responsible for financing their own places of worships (cemevi) – places of worship which have not been considered legitimate by the Directorate. For Kurban (2003: 189), Alevis' communities have been a 'non-existing entity, an absence' in Turkish law, facing intense pressure to transcend their particularities for the good of the nation. Kurds have been subject to similar homogenization policies, including, for instance, been forced in the 1930s to resettle in predominantly Turkish areas to facilitate their assimilation. This process continued throughout the twentieth century. For example, after the 1980 military coup, the Kurdish language was banned throughout Turkey, and active attempts to change the names of Kurdish towns and villages were initiated. The situation has been changing over the past two decades, in part due to the EU accession process and political liberalization. Kurds have, for instance, been able to publish their newspapers and broadcast radio shows in Kurdish. However, despite these reforms, this tradition of state interference remains difficult to unsettle:

> In late 2001, at a time when the Turkish Parliament was passing constitutional reforms towards meeting the political criteria for accession with the EU, the Interior Minister sent out a circular requiring provincial governors to ensure that parents name their children '[i]n a manner appropriate for our national culture, moral values and customs' as required by the Civil Registration Law.' Thus, the Ministry granted governors wide discretion in implementation, essentially telling them to ban Kurdish names.
>
> (Kurban, 2003: 196, citing Human Rights Watch, Questions and Answers: Freedom of Expression and Language Rights in Turkey (Apr. 2002))

The situation has been different for non-Muslim minorities. Although they are formally considered to be citizens, in practice it has been even more difficult (if not impossible) for them to have full access to their rights. First, only the non-Muslim minorities mentioned in the Lausanne Treaty (1923) are recognized in Turkey; that is, Armenian Orthodox, Jews and Greek Orthodox. All the others, including Assyrian Christians, Protestants or Baha'i, do not legally exist (Smith, 2005: 445).[14] Although the Lausanne Treaty had been designed to protect the rights of the aforementioned minorities, it ended by creating a situation where 'non-Muslims were no longer the authentic components of social imagination, but rather "additional" elements attached to the state through international law' (Kurban 2004/5: 348). In other words, the legal distinction between non-Muslims and Muslims has been understood as marking the supremacy of one group over the other. Non-Muslims have, in fact, been considered to be 'foreign elements' (Kurban 2004/5: 348) having allegiances outside of the Republic, and therefore threatening national cohesion. As a result, they have been subject to a series of discriminatory laws throughout modern Turkish history. Between 1942 and 1944, for instance, a capital tax was established with the aim of 'Turkifying' the economy, where non-Muslims were taxed as much as ten times more than their Muslim counterparts (Smith, 2005: 448). Likewise, they were not allowed to join the military or work as public servants, and minority foundations saw many of their properties confiscated throughout the twentieth century.[15] This entrenched discrimination resulted in a slow homogenization of the population.[16] While in 1906, nearly a fifth of subjects living in Turkey were minorities, in 1927, non-Muslims comprised only three per cent of the population and today they represent one-quarter of one per cent (Smith, 2005: 448–49). Here again, even if non-Muslims are subject to less overt discriminations today, they continue to be subjected to restrictions. This is translated, for instance, through the implementation of policies prohibiting the training of Christian clergy in Turkey, putting restrictions on the elections of heads of religious communities, making it difficult to manage and own religious buildings or other real estate properties, requiring headmasters of non-Muslim minority schools to be Turks, and so on (Kurban, 2004/5: 352 and Smith, 2005: 449).

One can therefore see from this analysis that in the Turkish case, also, there have been active attempts to homogenize citizens. For Kirişci (2000) this programme is even visible in immigration and refugee policies of the last decades that have favoured individuals of a Sunni Hanefi religious background over others. These attempts shed light on how, in this case, the foundations of the 'universal' secular public ethos are based on a certain understanding of Sunni Islam. One also realizes that, not unlike the French case, there is a repeated tradition of state intrusion into the lives of selected individuals requiring them to transcend their particular characterisitics in order to participate in the collective life. While individuals in the Turkish case have been asked to embrace an 'enlightened' vision of Islam, in the French case a strong emphasis has been put on their ability to adopt the laws and morality of the dominant culture. The analysis of both of these cases exemplifies the deep-seated paradoxes inherent in requiring a certain level of homogeneity (neutrality) among citizens. While theoretically this is supposed to facilitate equality, one realizes that it does so to the benefit of the individuals understood as belonging to the dominant culture, and at the expense of those understood as having different and/or multiple identities and allegiances.

Women and the nation-state in the nineteenth and early twentieth centuries

Women in both countries have also been particularly prone to state intrusions into their subjectivities, either excluding them entirely from participating actively in the life of the polis or including them on the condition that they embrace full-heartedly the secular ethos. One of the key differences between Turkey and France, is that in the Turkish case the 'image' of a modern women has been, since the early days of the Republic, identified as one of the symbols of the Republican state and as exemplifying access to equal citizenship. In the French imaginary, on the other hand, women have for a long time been considered incapable of ever becoming neutral, to make abstraction of their 'natural' differences, and have, thus, been excluded from participation in collective life. In both cases, however, as we will see, a secular rhetoric, in particular the language of neutrality and equality, has been mobilized to justify these different positions. Thus, women's bodies have been used here, as well, to mark and differentiate spaces.

France: the historical exclusion of women unable to become neutral

Not unlike religious minorities, acquiring full citizenship rights has been harder to attain for French women. What is interesting for our purposes is not only the fact that women have been subject to an exclusionary process, but that this process has been justified by the mobilization of secular narratives. Women have been described, for a long time, as being a tangible threat to the Republican project and have therefore been kept out of many of the activities of the polis. In that respect, at the time of the French Revolution a similar distinction to the one made for minorities was applied to women. Women were understood to be socially dependent and therefore not able to be active rights holders identified as 'individual agents, capable of making moral choices, exercising liberty, and speaking on their own behalf' (Scott, 1996: 34). Women were described as being inherently emotional, defined by their sex, and incapable of altering their particular nature to transform themselves into universal citizens[17] – 'The male is only male at certain moments, but the female is female throughout her life' (Dr Moreau, 1793).[18] This female nature, it was argued, led them to be socially and financially dependent on men as their 'natural' responsibility was to take care of their home. This natural order was considered to preserve order in society – 'The private functions for which women are destined by their very nature are related to the general order of society' (André Amar).[19] Women were thus not given the 'universal' right to vote until 1944, while men received it in 1848. Interestingly, during the Third Republic, arguments justifying the exclusion of women started to be based on the fact that they were not secular enough. They were believed to have a propensity towards religiosity that led them to give their soul to priests during the catholic ritual of confession, betraying the spirit of the Republic:

> While we are calm and happy partaking in our daily activities, our women fascinated by these men of lies are drawn to the confessionals and without telling us they betray all our life secrets […] While we believe that we were able to put our loved ones on the path of truth, we are despicably deceived because our work is destroyed […] by the tale of these deadly men: they are stealing the conscience of our wives.
>
> (a socialist leader, cited in Baubérot, 2004: 196)

Women were considered at this point in time to be too pious and submissive to priests, and therefore a threat to the political community. On this point Scott sensibly argues that tropes describing women as determined by their sexuality or as religious fanatics were similar in the sense that they were both depicting them as non-autonomous subjects, lacking the rational discipline to control outside influences or to give precedence to the common good. 'Even at home, a woman might be an agent of priestly subversion, but in the political realm the damage she could do was much greater' (1996: 103). Scott's account resonates well with Pateman's argument about the gendered dimension of citizenship, and of public and private spheres (1988), in which women have been constructed as belonging to an 'a-political', 'familial', 'sexual' and 'religious' private realm whereas white bourgeois men belong to the public realm. With respect to our discussion, one sees how secular narratives have been used as early as the nineteenth century to create and delimit space through restricting access to citizenship. While Jews and Muslims were unable to access their rights in the political realm if they did not embrace secular laws and thus reform their model of gender relations, women were considered de facto excluded from that realm because of the gender differences that made them overtly influence-able to religious dogmas.

Looking once again at colonial Algeria and how *laïcité* was applied to Algerian women is interesting in light of the above as it provides us with another example of how meanings given to *laïcité* can change as a result of different times, political climates and geographical locations. Indeed, while it was mobilized by Republicans to justify the exclusion of women from collective life in mainland France, it was at the same time used to favour Muslim women's 'emancipation' in colonial Algeria. Paradoxically, French feminists fighting male Republicans at home, and asking for a modification of the civil code so that it would allow them to enjoy full citizenship rights, embraced the colonial project and fought for the enforcement of this same code in Algeria, which in their eyes would ensure that women would be 'liberated' from the patriarchal grip of religion and the Muslim men enforcing it. Through its encounter with Islam, *laïcité* and the civil code it was thought to enable became synonyms in a specific geographical area for equal treatment.[20]

> Though at home in France, feminists, and particularly lawyers, voiced severe criticism about the shortcomings of the Civil Code [French civil code], they advocated that it replace Muslim law in Algeria […] their idea of citizenship was predicated on the assumption that profound religious and cultural differences must be de-emphasised to permit the possibility of equal treatment.
>
> (Kimble, 2006: 125)

This colonial legacy shares some parallels with the current situation in France. While women have fought for their formal inclusion in the polity, gender equality has only recently become an explicit language of *laïcité,* as a result, partly, of the growing presence of Islam in France – a presence which is the consequence, among other things, of the immigration of former colonial subjects after the colonial wars of independence. This new focus on gender equality is illustrated in the series of petitions, public speeches and reports in favour of the passing of the March 2004 law banning visible religious symbols in public schools.[21] These focus on the headscarf as *the* problematic symbol that ought to be prohibited, basing their rhetoric in the argument that it transgresses gender equality – an equality that is precisely protected by the implementation of *laïcité* in schools. Not unlike colonial times, this link between gender equality and *laïcité* has led to the creation of unforeseen alliances between Republicans and feminists, exemplified by a petition addressed to the French President signed by several well-known French feminists in the French edition of the magazine *ELLE* in favour of the March 2004 law. For Göle (2007: 186) this alliance is particularly noteworthy inasmuch as it would have been the subject of severe criticisms by radical feminist movements in the 1970s, especially since the petition was addressed to the male leader of the Republic and through a medium where women's bodies are commercially marketed. Yet the author stresses that the understanding of *laïcité* that has emerged at this particular point in time has been able to take over those feminist priorities, casting a veil on the patriarchal tendencies of French society.[22]

This discussion reveals, in line with Najmabadi's (2006) findings, the importance of considering the colonial history of the encounter between Islam and secularism. Doing so not only sheds light on the multiple meanings given to *laïcité*, but also on how gender equality and the 'emancipation' of Muslim women have come to occupy an important place in secular tropes. As such, it complements our understanding of the gendered dimensions of secular discourses. While *laïcité* was mobilized as a justification for excluding women from full citizenship rights in the Republic in the early 1900s, as they were deemed incapable of ever becoming neutral, today only 'sufficiently' secular women are able to fully participate in secular spaces. Those constructed as being 'too' religious or 'too' submissive are being pushed out of this imaginary and deprived of a number of their rights. The dichotomy between autonomy and submission is (re)produced once again, yet it is located this time within the category of 'women' itself. This is a reminder of the vulnerable position of women, where in this case secular women are constructed as the 'border-guards' (Yuval-Davis, 1997) of secular spaces, while women wearing headscarves become 'civilizational "others"' (Kandiyoti, 1997: 117) whose affiliation to one community is incompatible with their inclusion in the other. Thus, the 'condition' of women continues to be central to delimiting the boundaries of the secular ethos, the exclusion of devout women becoming essential to the making and (re)production of secular spaces.

Turkey: the importance of including particular 'types' of women in nation-building

As mentioned briefly earlier, throughout the nineteenth century the Ottoman Empire went through a wave of centralization efforts resulting in an expansion of state bureaucracy. These led to major reforms (e.g. *Tanzimat* reforms) where, among other things, the *awaqf* – religious endowed properties – were put under state control and the legal system, based mostly until then on Sharia law (Islamic law), was restructured. While new commercial and penal codes were established respectively in 1850 and 1858 (Davison, 2003:44), Sharia law became associated with family law, and this remained the case until 1917. This is interesting as it is indicative of the influence of modern narratives in which religious and family life are located in the same realm – i. e. a 'private' realm – differentiated from 'secular' politics. It is also symptomatic of the position of women and family relationships, which became central in the agenda of the Ottoman polity around the times of the *Tanzimat* to express deep anxieties with respect to preserving cultural integrity vis-à-vis European influences (Kandiyoti, 1991b: 23). Women became the barometers of the moral 'health of society', a moral health which varied in accordance with political transformations and positionalities. 'From Islamists, who advocated a return to the unadulterated application to the Shari'a to Westernists who favoured a radical break with Islam, all used the condition of women as an indicator of the moral health of society' (Kandiyoti, 1997: 124).

Thus, the status of women was already set as a key indicator of the morality of political projects at the end of the Ottoman Empire (Kandiyoti, 1991b: 23). As a result, unlike France, the image of a 'modern' woman became a key symbol of the new Turkish Republic. This 'new' woman 'liberated' by the secular Republic was constructed as marking a break with the Ottoman past, in which women were depicted as subdued to religious forces (ibid. 1991b: 41, 43). *Laiklik* was conceived as being hand in hand with women's 'emancipation'. Yet this emancipation was less about giving autonomy to women, and more about a state acting as a 'benevolent' patriarchal figure setting the rules of conduct that women had to perform when participating in the polis. In other words, even if citizenship was defined through their active participation in the public realm, this participation was subject to particular rules and regulations. For instance, while women were highly encouraged to de-veil, they were at the same time responsible for protecting their honour and had to develop new types of 'puritanism', signalling their sexual modesty (Kandiyoti, 1997: 126). Equality here was based on the ability of women to perform a 'neutral' identity, a 'neutrality' requirement defined in accordance with masculine norms:

> This new woman was supposed to march in official parades, hold a Turkish flag, and wear a school or military uniform […] Turkey had a new 'un/veiled', urban, educated, 'modern' woman representing the new nation-state with her body in dark suits, with short hair, no make-up on her face, not tiny clue pointing out her sexuality. Public, in this sense, was presented like a shop window and women's bodies (as political texts) were its assets.
>
> (Kejanlioğlu and Taş, 2009: 427)

The performances of women were, therefore, from the start of the Republic, key to indicating how the nation was to be imagined. Little space was left for individual initiatives or differences. This explains one of the paradoxes of this 'emancipation', which is that despite the fact that women's participation was encouraged it was also limited by a 'glass ceiling'. As a consequence, women remained seriously underrepresented in high-level positions, including in politics, and their ability to engage in independent activism was strongly curtailed (Arat, 2005: 17).[23] It is, moreover, noteworthy that their performance and bodily appearance were also set as markers of the private and public realms. While they were asked to embrace this neutrality requirement in public life, they were required to perform another type of femininity defined this time in term of their role as mothers, wives and daughters in the private realm. In so doing, not unlike their French counterparts, they participated in the (re)production of a private sphere that was identified with family and deep gender inequalities.

> In the private domain […] differences between men and women were rearticulated and the hierarchic relationship that had traditionally defined male-female relationship reproduced. Even though women were encouraged to be educated and assume professional roles, they were encouraged to play traditional role as well.
>
> (Arat, 2005: 18)

In short, the ability to fully participate in Turkish public life has been mediated since the early days of the Republic by gender and religion.[24] While Turkish women, unlike their French counterparts, were considered capable of abstraction, their bodies and performance have, like in the French case, been intimately linked to the making of space.

The importance given to women's bodies and women's performance has prevailed in Turkey, and has become ever more significant from the 1980s onwards, with the growing presence and signs of permanency of Islam in urban centres. Women's bodies have become one of the symbols of the power struggle taking place between Kemalist's elites, promoting a certain reading of *laiklik* and morality that comes with it, and a conservative religious elite who have been challenging aspects of this morality. In this respect, Navaro-Yashin argues that the emphasis put by Kemalist elites on women's bodies is one of the reasons explaining why these also became key to the Islamist struggle (2002: 27). In fact, the rise of Islamic parties starting in the late 1980s, along with the growth of a new Muslim bourgeoisie, gave a new visibility to women wearing headscarves. The image and presence of these women in the ranks of Islamic parties, such as the Welfare Party in the 1990s, became central to their rhetoric. This signalled the difference in the ideologies of the Islamic parties involved in disputing the rules of the Republic, notably the requirement to erase sexual differences in the public realm.[25] In a sense, therefore, women who represented this movement were also constructed as 'border-guards' – protecting and performing this time not the values of the Republic, but of a more religious *nomos*. Yet, not unlike the role imagined for women by secular elites, these new possibilities offered by the Islamic elites have been circumscribed by specific rules. Women have been asked to contribute to the cause, but little space has been given for them to take individual initiatives. They have, as well, as will be discussed in greater details in Chapters 3 and 5, been faced with a glass ceiling which has prevented them, for instance, from accessing high-level positions in politics (Arat, 2005: 66). In their study of the Welfare and Virtue Party,[26] Arat (2005) and White (2002) show that the preferred place for non-educated and poor women continued to be the household. While the situation of educated women is described as being more complex, as they were encouraged to participate in the life of Islamic parties, the prevalent idea remained that their first priority should be with their family and that they had to be protected by men.

> The paradox of veiling lies in two sets of superimposed meanings: first, the Islamist challenge the status-quo; second, Islamist support for the principle that woman's place is in the home and her role is to take care of husband and family.
>
> (White, 2002: 213)

While looking in detail at the position of women in Islamic circles is not the focus of this work, the above discussion is nevertheless relevant to understanding the complexities of the devout women's struggles discussed in the next chapters. While the headscarf is understood by some as an important symbol in disturbing the status quo, it continues to be very much associated with family, motherhood and homemaking as well (White, 2002: 223). In other words, here also the relationship between gender and religion continues to play an important role in the (re)production of spaces.

Conclusion

In the mid-1900s, Reformist Ulemas in colonial Algeria were already choosing to ask for more autonomy from the French state by making reference to *laïcité* and its languages. They found in the 1905 Law, which was being implemented at the time in France, a resource to challenge the French state's tutelage over their religion and to ask for a 'complete' implementation of the separation law.

> We cannot explain the reasons why with the French government being secular, and secularism prohibiting state interference in religious affairs, Islam is the only religion in which the administration has the right to interfere […] The 9 December 1905 law on the separation of religion and state was promulgated, yet it has never been applied to the Muslim faith.
>
> (Association of the reformists, Ulemas, 1947, cited in Achi, 2005: 73)

This is representative in many ways of what has been discussed in this chapter. I have started to unravel the tensions that exist within the languages of secularism in both countries. To do so, I have pointed to the importance of taking into consideration historical legacies. Doing this allows us to better situate and understand the meanings ascribed to secular languages. As such, this chapter has investigated how both the French and Turkish states have had a tradition of heavy interference in subjectivities, an intervention in which religion and gender have played a key role. Since the early 1900s, the languages of secularism have been used to justify this state interference. The language of separation has, for instance, been used to locate, regulate and control particular religions and religious subjectivities. In this story, regulation has been considered necessary in order to 'prepare' these religions for 'full' separation. The study of the French case points to the fact that this intervention has been done regardless of the religion, as not only Muslims but also Jews and other believers have faced interventions in the organization of their faith, and in their religious dogmas and practices.[27] This echoes criticisms of the thesis justifying state intervention in light of the 'nature' of Islam (e.g. Lewis, 1993; Huntington, 1993). However, despite the incoherence of this thesis, one realizes that it remains quite powerful, as it continues to this day to be used to justify interventions in the Islamic faith.

This chapter has also discussed how secular tropes are intrinsically linked to discourses of modernity, in which family and sexuality have come to occupy a key role. Indeed, the regulation of the religious justified by the languages of secularism has led to a regulation of family relations. In this process it is interesting to note how 'secular values' are articulated repeatedly through the image of 'civilizational "others"' (Kandiyoti, 1997: 117), which is represented, in both cases, by religious family laws carrying defective and patriarchal norms, and by women considered as consumed by their faith – 'victims' of these norms and unable to (re)produce the 'modern' boundaries of the nation-state. While the connection between secular tropes, women's bodies and space will be examined at greater length in the next chapter, the above discussion already points to how the (re)production of space is central to the articulation of the languages of secularism. It fact, looking at the spatial workings of the languages of secularism is perhaps the best entry point to understand the intimate relationship that exists between these languages, and gender and religion.

Finally, as indicated in the quote from the association of reformist Ulemas, cited at the beginning of this conclusion, this chapter has begun to unravel the multi-vocal character of the languages of secularism – languages that are contingent and which shift in accordance with political situations and/or the actors who are making reference to them. If we take the language of separation, we realise that, in the French case, the dominant meaning given to this language, and the level of state interference it conveys, has been the source of vivid debates among French elites as early as the Third Republic. For some, the 1905 Law lays out a clear separation between religion and the state – a separation that requires a certain level of impartiality from the state and that does not mesh with heavy state intervention in religious affairs. For others, however, achieving this ideal of separation requires interference in selected subjectivities. In other words, one becomes aware of the difficulty of reaching a consensus over the interpretation of this separation principle, and the role religion should play in the public realm. This is relevant as it makes apparent the tensions and contradictions found within the language of separation – contradictions that were, and continue to be, used as a resource for arguments by religious activists. The lack of such a legal framework in the Turkish case renders these contradictions less explicit. Indeed, a separation between Islam and the state, in which the state would formally cease to interfere in religious affairs, has until now been ruled out or at least postponed until a distant future. This sheds light, as discussed later in the book, on why religious activists use the alternative resources at their disposal to frame their claims.

To sum up, through this comparative analysis, one understands the importance of unravelling the different layers of meaning given to the languages of secularism – meanings that are the product of specific histories and that influence both the content and form taken by the (re)articulations of these languages. The tensions within these languages point, also, to the usefulness of understanding secularism as a hegemonic process – a hegemony which does not only 'passively exist' (Williams, 1977: 112), but which is being continually altered, challenged, and renewed.

Notes

1 The 1905 Law is considered to be one of the legal pillars of French *laïcité*. This law, without referring explicitly to the concept of *laïcité,* is considered by the *Conseil d'Etat* (the highest court in France) as putting in place *laïcité*'s two main legal pillars: freedom of conscience and the principle of separation. Through its first article, the law affirms freedom of conscience and, by correlation, religion. The second article recognizes the principle of the separation of church and state, where not only is religion not allowed to interfere in state affairs, but where the state is also required to be neutral towards all beliefs and refrain from interfering in religious affairs. For more information, as well as a full reading of the law, see Conseil d'Etat, 2004c: 258–60 and 405–15.

2 This necessity to have central bodies that represent particular faiths is influenced by Christianity, and more particularly Catholicism organized in a hierarchical manner. For a discussion of this point, and its implications for faiths that are not organized in the same way, see Silvestri, 2007.

3 These reforms included a change in the alphabet from the Arabic script to the Latin one, and a ban on the wearing of the fez (the head covering worn by men). Great efforts were made, at that time, to centralize the school system and make education a monopoly of the state. This bears similarity with our French case, in which, under the Third Republic, laws were put in place to establish secular, mandatory and free education (e.g. Jules Ferry Laws (1881–82)) and banning Catholic congregation members from teaching activities (e.g. anti-congregations laws (1904)) as they were not considered fit to participate in the 'making' of future citizens (see Baubérot, 2004: 83–84).

4 The notion of collective life corresponds to the notion of *vivre-ensemble* in French. It is often used in reference to the ethic prevailing in a space in which citizens interact with each other. *Laïcité* and *laiklik* are often understood as setting the rules of collective life. Yet, those rules are not fixed but vary as a consequence of the understandings given to these terms.

5 Shakman Hurd (2008) and others (e.g. Connolly 1999) document how this particular interpretation of secularism and neutrality are influenced by the philosophy of Kant and his idea of universal morality ([1793] 1979), which requires citizens participating in public life to learn to live their personal convictions in a 'rational' and 'autonomous' manner in order not to be blinded by dogmas, fanaticism or to be locked into their personal frame of reference. This is thought to enable the creation of a 'universal' public sphere, in which citizens can live together peacefully, united by their commonalities (for further discussion on the influence of Kantian philosophy see Shakman Hurd, 2008: 25 and Connolly, 1999: 29–36).

6 The expression 'making room' is borrowed from Deutsche, 1999.

7 This meant that 7 *consistoires* were established in mainland France, and this system was expanded when Algeria was colonized in 1830 for Jews residing there (Benbassa, 1997: 144).

8 Schreier notes that between 1865 and 1870 only 142 Jews out of 33,000 chose that option. The numbers were also low for Muslims, as in 1878 only 435 Muslims out of 3 million decided to renounce their personal status law (2007: 100).

9 It is relevant to note that in mainland France the passing of the 1905 Law had an impact on the organization of religious communities. For instance, the Jewish *consistoires* became faith-based associations, ceasing to receive state financial support. For further discussion on this issue see Benbassa, 1997: 149 and Benbassa, 2004: 53.

10 As mentioned in the introduction, it is relevant to note how this narrative, in which Islam is seen as a religion that needs to be controlled by the state, has been used repeatedly by policy makers and scholars throughout the twentieth century to justify the differences in governance between Islam and Christianity.

11 These expressions have been used by French politicians, notably Nicolas Sarkozy (2004: 100).

12 This consultation process, known as the *Istichara* process, was launched by Jean-Pierre Chevènement, when he was interior minister (1997–2000). For further discussion of this document see Ferrari, 2005: 16–17.

13 A case was brought to the ECtHR by a member of the Alevi faith on this issue. The court ruled that making these classes compulsory was a violation of article 2 protocol 1 (right to education). For further information see: Zengin v. Turkey, 2007.

14 This creates several problems with regards to their freedom of religion, including having a place of worship (Kurban, 2003: 173–74).

15 For more information see Kurban, 2004/5: 350.

16 Smith (2005: 448) and Kurban (2004/5: 352) provide further information on this homogenization process. They stress, for instance, that in 1948, 30,000 Turkish Jews emigrated to Israël. Moreover, while there were still 100,000 ethnic Greeks in 1950s, the 1955 anti-Greek riots in Istanbul, the expulsion of dual citizens in 1964, and frictions over Cyprus reduced the community to 3,000 individuals.

17 It is important to note that at the time of the Revolution, universal suffrage had not yet been implemented but women were deprived of other civic and political rights, such as creating and participating in societies and clubs, participating in parliamentary debates, and so on (Scott, 1996: 64).

18 Dr. Jacques-Louis Moreau, 1793, cited in Scott, 1996: 49. This citation is making reference to the widespread idea at the time that because a woman's genital organs were located inside her, she was intrinsically dependent on her 'female nature'.

19 André Amar, Representative of the Committee on General Security, 1793, cited in Scott, 1996: 48.

20 Ahmed argues that a similar paradox was present in colonial Egypt, where the champions of unveiling in Egypt were fervently opposed to the suffrage of women at home. She unravels how feminism could be both fought at home and used in a colonial context to promote the dominance of the 'white man' (1992: 154).

21 These petitions include Kintzler *et al.* 2003; Vigerie and Zelensky, 2003; Union des Familles Laïques, 2003; Elle, 2003.

22 The fact that several feminist groups were co-opted by this new secularist narrative led to divisions within feminist ranks. Groups such as the Collective Feminist For Equality (CFPE) were created to express their worries about the new 'anti-Muslim' turn taken by mainstream feminists. They considered this turn to be exclusive and patriarchal, as it failed to 'listen' to women and imposed on their bodies a certain set of values. This new Collective is the first initiative where both pious Muslim women and non-religious French feminists have been working together with the aim of creating a space facilitating dialogue and joint actions. This group and some of its actions are discussed in Chapter 4.

23 Women were, for instance, restricted from creating independent organizations, such as political parties or federations (Arat, 2005: 17).

24 Class was also important here, as the ability of poor, uneducated, and rural women to partake in the activities of the polis was equally limited. In this regard, Kejanlioğlu and Taş note that this class bias was articulated in narratives produced by the Republic, in which this 'new' woman was expected to act as a model for the '"traditional", rural, "backward", "ignorant", women' (2009: 427).

25 The Virtue Party even considered using the headscarf as one of its official symbols. This idea was not pursued because it was still considered to be too 'feminine' (Recai Kutan (leader of the Virtue Party), cited in Çınar, 2005: 85). One realizes again here how feminity continues to be constructed as being more of a passive carrier of tradition in contrast to masculinity which is viewed as the motor of political agency (ibid).

26 Both the Welfare and Virtue Parties were political parties with an Islamic leaning. The Welfare Party, also known by its Turkish name as the Refah Partisi, took office in 1996 and was closed down in 1997 as a consequence of the 1997 soft coup. The Virtue Party, known by its Turkish name as the Fazilet Partisi, is the successor of the Welfare Party. It was founded in 1998 and outlawed in 2001. For more information on these political parties see Chapter 5.

27 Although this has not been discussed, the French state, particularly during the Third Republic, intervened heavily in the organization of the Catholic faith in order to limit its control over education and other areas of life. Constraints were also put on the possibility of priests and congregation members teaching in public schools. For more information see note 3.

LAÏCITE
HELP
HELP
HELP
vanlo . A

3 The slow exclusion of pious women from French and Turkish societies

(Re)producing spaces

> Women are sent back in their homes – they are refused in public spaces, in education and at work.
>
> (activist, Paris, 2012)

In an interview given by Marine Le Pen (head of the French Far Right party, the Front National) to the daily newspaper, Le Monde, in September 2012, the politician was asked if she was in favour of the prohibition of the headscarf in public spaces (*espace public*). She responded: 'Yes in shops, transports, the street' (Le Monde, 2012). While her remarks have to be understood as part of a Far Right narrative, they are nevertheless representative of a trend, which has become more apparent over the last decade, where women wearing headscarves are being excluded from different spaces. A similar trend has also marked in different ways Turkish contemporary history.

This chapter looks into how this phenomenon contributes to the creation and (re)production of secular spaces in both states. It posits that what is particularly noteworthy about this process is that these spaces and the criteria that define them are far from being stable. They shift in accordance with the understandings given to *laïcité* and *laiklik*, and can even blur the 'traditional' dichotomies understood as being central to the organization of secular narratives. This reality was well expressed in the comments of a friend of mine to whom I was explaining, over coffee, the recent attempts by French politicians to extend headscarf bans to nannies working from their homes. Quite astounded by this new situation, she remarked that this was opening a Pandora's Box as these exclusions were not respecting the public/private distinction that had been part of the secular rhetoric. I would argue, in fact, that closely documenting the shifts of secular narratives helps us in understanding how spaces and boundaries (e.g. public/private or secular/religious) are constructed and evolve with time and in accordance with the meanings given to *laïcité*.

What seems to remain a constant, however, is the central place given to women and gender relations in the formation of secular narratives. As discussed in Chapter 2, women have been central in the construction of secular narratives and spaces since the inception of both Republics. This continues to this day, as space is being organized around the partial or full exclusion of devout Muslim women and the gender relation model they are thought to represent. Thus, by highlighting this constant, this chapter points to the importance of understanding secular narratives, and their impact on space, as gendered processes.

The exclusion of pious Muslim women and the making of spaces

The comparison between France and Turkey has become quite fascinating over the past decades. Indeed, the need for a woman of Islamic faith to transcend her dependence on religious authority – to become 'autonomous' – has become central to the articulation of *laïcité* and *laiklik*. Nonetheless, it is important to note that, generally, tensions have not been triggered by women wearing headscarves per se, but rather by the precise fact that they have been wearing it while demanding active participation in the life of the polity and to be fully-fledged citizens. In other words, the wearing of the headscarf by first generation Algerian mothers – who are perceived as not speaking fluent French, not working and confining themselves to their home – is not considered to be that problematic. Likewise, poor Turkish women living in rural Anatolia and wearing a headscarf are not intimidating.[1] Both figures, in fact, feed and legitimize the 'either/or' structure of dominant secular narratives, as they exemplify the 'non-emancipated' religious other who needs to be saved by a secular polity. On the other hand, second or third generation French women raised and educated in French schools – who continue to wear a headscarf while still aspiring to partake fully in the activities of the polis – have been perceived as more troublesome. One finds a parallel phenomenon in Turkey, where, with the rise of a new pious bourgeoisie, the presence of women wearing headscarves has increased in urban circles that were previously 'reserved' for secular women. Not only have these pious women been demanding access to higher education, but they have also been aspiring to be active in the workforce (e.g. lawyers, professors), practice sports, and even become members of Parliament. This trend is challenging aspects of the model of citizenship imagined by secular elites – a model characterized by a 'neuter' woman emancipated from her differences, and by an inherently dualistic thinking where religion (or particular religious expressions) are understood as being opposed to the secular (and by correlation secular spaces). Thus, the idea of a woman who is both modern and pious, aware of her citizenship rights and duties and asking to exercise them, openly blurs the sense of boundness central to the geography of dominant interpretations of secularism (Göle, 2010: 256). Notice, as well, the role played by class in these narratives, as women who are not members of the bourgeoisie, or who do not aspire to earn a living, are considered to be less of a disturbance (on this see Kavakçı, 2010: 23).

To put it differently, by wanting to take part in the life of the polis, women wearing headscarves in both countries have been imagined as transgressing a public/private dichotomy central to the articulation of the secular Republican ethos. Yet, at the same time, their presence, or the idea of their presence, in these different public spaces becomes essential to creating and maintaining the fantasy that these are 'equal', 'neutral' and 'stable' environments (Deutsche, 1996: 278).[2] That is, it is essential to the idea that such environments can exist if these women are reformed or expelled from these spaces. As such, these women, their religious practices and their aspiration to gain social and economic capital, play an essential role in the (re)production of spaces. Needless to say, the boundaries of these spaces are not stable, as they shift with time – a reality that often has direct repercussions on the lives of these women.

To restore the 'stability' of public spaces, or to simply mark them as secular and thus modern, a renewed importance has been given, in both our cases, to implementing secularism and its language of neutrality. As the reader will come to realise, the language of neutrality has been intimately linked with the language of gender equality.[3] In effect, the neutrality requirement in a particular space is considered here to be key in cultivating a gender-equal environment. This neutrality requirement has first been evoked, as will be discussed, to regulate the bodies and practices of providers of public services (i.e. public servants). These citizens, more than others, have been asked to show that they can abstract themselves from their religious practices, as they represent the state and its secular ethos. Yet, this requirement has also been slowly extended in formal and informal ways to different users of public services. This chapter discusses how, more surprisingly perhaps, this concern for neutrality affects individuals working in spaces that are considered to be 'private'. This is becoming quite explicit in France, as spaces previously labelled as private are increasingly being identified as 'common' spaces contributing to the common good. They are described as spaces where secularism ought to be implemented to preserve social peace and cohesion, as well as productivity. In the Turkish case, also, this neutrality argument affects in different ways the position of devout women working in private businesses. For instance, their presence is frequently narrated as disturbing the modern image of companies.

Thus, the problem is not just about a few persistent women, but has become, de facto, about the limits of this neutrality principle (that is the limit of where the secular ethos should/could be implemented). Should it only be applied to providers of public services? Or also to users? Should it limit itself to public services, or should it be extended to everyone inhabiting public spaces? And if so, how should the boundaries of this public space be defined (e.g. roads, day cares, etc.)?

'Making room' for public spaces

The neutrality of public servants

In both countries, the neutrality of public servants has become a quasi, non-negotiable requirement of secularism. This is because public servants are understood as representing the state, and are therefore responsible for protecting and (re)producing the values of collective life. This means, in concrete terms, that their personal right to religious freedom can be curtailed so that they are not perceived as endorsing a particular ethic (aside from a secular one) that could affect their ability to treat citizens in an equal manner. 'The state can ask civil servants to abstain from all and every act that could result in doubts about [its] [the state] neutrality' (Conseil d'Etat, 1950). As such, public service providers have been, in both countries, the first to be affected by restrictions on the wearing of religious symbols. Yet these have not always been systematic and have in recent years been extended to new types of 'providers'.

The French case

While the importance of the neutrality of public servants had already been prevalent during the Third Republic (1870–1940), when members of congregations or priests were denied the right to teach because of their allegiance to Catholicism, Salton argues that at the time the interpretation of *laïcité* that had led to their exclusion was understood as circumstantial, and could therefore change with time (2007: 208–10). He illustrates this point by drawing on a case brought in front of the *Conseil d'Etat* in 1912 concerning a priest (Abbé Bouteyre), in which the *Conseil* had ruled that preventing an individual from becoming a secondary school teacher was justified by *laïcité*. Yet, judges also noted that this could be subject to change once the trauma of church-state separation was attenuated (2007: 209). This position seemed to be the one embraced by the *Conseil d'Etat* in the 70s, when it ruled that a secondary school teacher, who had become a priest after being admitted as a public school teacher, could not be dismissed from his position.

> While it is true that constitutional provisions that established the *laïcité* of the State and of public education impose the neutrality of public services and particularly of public education towards all religions […] they are not in themselves an obstacle to the possibility of devolving some of these [educational] functions to a member of the clergy …
>
> (Conseil d'Etat, 1972, cited in Salton, 2007: 209).

From the late 1980s onwards, in part because of the increased presence of visible forms of Islam in France,[4] the wind changed and a more restrictive concept of neutrality started to emerge. This was concretized through different ministerial directives and the opinions of the *Conseil d'Etat*. The *Circulaire Jospin* (1989), for instance, stressed that teachers had the duty to be neutral and could not display their religious convictions publicly. Judges in the Kherouaa Affair in 1992 based their ruling on similar arguments, and the *Conseil d'Etat* in the *Avis Marteaux* (2000) ruled that a school instructor, who had refused to take off her headscarf in school, had been legitimately laid off.

> [T]he fact of a civil servant assigned to public education manifesting, at work, his or her religious beliefs, particularly by wearing a sign with the purpose of displaying his or her belonging to a religion, represents a violation of his or her [professional] obligations
>
> (Conseil d'Etat, 2000, cited in Salton, 2007: 210)

The *Avis Marteaux* confirmed that the wearing of visible religious symbols by public servants was incompatible with the ethos of *laïcité*, and, although it was only a piece of jurisprudence, the broad way it was formulated, and the fact that it was a judgement from the highest court in France, has given it an almost law-like status. From then onwards, the neutrality requirement of public servants has been considered a non-negotiable requirement of *laïcité* and has almost never been questioned. This is well conveyed in the series of reports on *laïcité* published over the last ten years, including in the Stasi report (2003),[5] the Rossinot report (2006) and the Gerin report (2010).[6] This application of neutrality to public servants has, however, opened the door to other sets of questions, including who should/could be considered a public servant; that is, whether someone not paid by the state but who offers a service to a public institution is required to follow the rules set out for public servants paid by the state.[7]

In effect, in 2006, the Rossinot Report suggested that the responsibilities of public servants be extended to individuals doing temporary work for public services, such as jury members, voluntary workers or to private companies' employees sub-contracted by the public sector (2006: 33, 49). This point is reiterated in one of the recommendations made by the High Council of Integration (HCI)[8] in its *Avis* published in 2010 on *laïcité* in public spaces. Recommendation 4 of this document reads as follows:

> Reaffirm *laïcité* in public services by the adoption of legislative measures so that the principle of *laïcité* is respected by all occasional collaborators of public services (this is already the case for juries in assize courts, jury members for public services exams, but not, for example, for individuals who accompany public schools, middle school and high schools outings).
>
> (HCI, 2010)

The last part of this recommendation makes reference to attempts to restrict mothers of students wearing headscarves from participating in public school events or from accompanying their children on school outings. Individuals who have positioned themselves in favour of such restrictions have argued that these parents ought to be treated as temporary employees of public services. Although the High Authority for the Fight Against Discriminations and Equality (HALDE) ruled in 2007 against extending this neutrality requirement to parents (HALDE, 2007a),[9] this decision did not put an end to the debates. Rather, politicians and intellectuals continued to argue for this extension. Their struggle was finally successful as the possibility of this restriction was included in a ministerial circular released in March 2012 giving guidelines to all public schools for the 2012–13 school year (Ministry of National Education, 2012).

Although the neutrality requirement for public servants has been framed as affecting all visible religious symbols, it is important to note that most of the jurisprudence since the 1980s (including the aforementioned HALDE decision) has been about women wearing headscarves. Likewise, most of the reports on this issue, including those mentioned in this analysis, and public debates accompanying particular measures, such as the exclusion of mothers from school outings, referred to the headscarf as the 'problematic' visible religious sign. In a sense, therefore, one could argue that women wearing headscarves, not unlike priests or religious minorities who refused to renounce their personal status law under the Third Republic, are today slowly being excluded from 'providing' any type of public service – they are considered unsuitable to represent, foster or promote Republican values. Note here that one of the reasons for this treatment is that, like minorities in the past, the fact that they refuse to take off their headscarf is associated with a refusal to embrace the dominant model of gender relations (Scott, 2007: 171–73). Through these evictions, public services are set apart as a 'public space' representing, (re)producing and fostering *laïcité*. While the 'special' status of this space is marked first and foremost by the strict and non-negotiable implementation of the principle of neutrality to providers, it is being extended, as discussed later in this chapter, in a formal and informal way to users of this space.

The Turkish case

> In the 2000s, more than one hundred thousand students, one thousand civil servants, and three hundred primary and secondary school teachers were forced to leave their positions because the Turkish government implemented the ban – a policy proclaimed as 'zero tolerance for the headscarf'.
>
> (Elver, 2012: 20)

The first legalization on dress code for civil servants in Turkey was put in place during the Republican period in the 1920s, as part of Mustapha Kemal's reforms. It banned the fez worn by men and required civil servants to dress in a modern and 'westernized' fashion. Yet, at that time, no legal regulations were put in place targeting the dress code of women specifically. This lack of formal rules continued until the late 1970s. Özdalga (1998: 41) explains that one of the reasons for this was that the constitutional principles of secularism were interpreted as already requiring an implicit ban on religious covering in public offices and schools – an interpretation which is in line with the requirement of neutral identity discussed previously. Formal regulations were enforced when this 'unwritten' settlement started to be challenged by a growing number of women wearing headscarves in public spaces in the 1980s. At that point, the military regime officially prohibited civil servants from wearing a head covering, noting that it considered the headscarf to be the carrier of a 'certain ideology' (Aydin, 2005: 43). In 1981, the first piece of regulation on dress in higher education was released, requiring staff and female students to wear 'ordinary, sober, modern dress', and prohibiting women from wearing the headscarf (McGoldrick, 2006:135). Although this neutrality requirement became an official policy, its implementation up until the 1997 'soft' coup was left to the discretion of each institution. This changed after that point when secular elites attempted to purge public space of visible Islam.[10] Following this, the Turkish faith-based rights organization AKDER reported accounts of secondary school teachers in religious schools (*Imam Hatip* schools) and public servants, who had been working with their headscarf for several years, who were suddenly put under investigation or dismissed (AKDER, 2004). To sum up, one can see how this coup, much like the March 2004 Law, marked a shift in the dominant understanding of secularism, where headscarves became de facto incompatible with this framework and the values it contained.

The Turkish case is insightful, as well, as this interpretation of secularism has been the source of intriguing extensions. First, not unlike the situation in public French schools, mothers of university students have been prohibited from participating in graduation ceremonies or other events on the grounds that their head covering challenges the neutrality of these spaces (e.g. Kavakçı, 2010: 106). In other instances, in some public services the headscarf ban has been extended to employees who replaced their headscarf with a wig.[11] Although the wig is not a formal religious symbol, it has been considered in this context to be an expression of religiosity carrying anti-secular connotations (AKDER, 2004). Merve Kavakçı in her book discusses other cases, where the principle of neutrality was extended to civil servants outside their workplace (Kavakçı, 2010: 81–82, 88–89).[12] In 2005, for instance, under the rule of the AK Party, the Council of State[13] confirmed that a schoolteacher could be deprived of promotion because she wore a headscarf outside school premises, even if she took it off when she entered the premises. She had to keep it off, to set an example, on her way to and from school (Kavakçı, 2010:107). Again, similarly to France, these extensions are not systematic but vary according to internal regulations or particular individuals heading these institutions. Thus, one sees here also how the principle of neutrality is used to regulate different aspects of the lives of individuals. On the premise that public servants are representing the state and its ethos, this requirement extends its tentacles beyond the boundaries of public services per se into the intimate life of citizens.

Extending the neutrality requirement to users of public services: setting apart educational spaces

The French case

One of the recurring comments made by scholars about the March 2004 French law has been that with this law the neutrality requirement was extended to students (Göle, 2007; Bowen, 2007a; Salton, 2007). Until then, students, considered to be users of public services had, because of this status, enjoyed relative freedom to practice and express their religious convictions. Thus some argued that this law would set a precedent and be used to justify interventions in the subjectivities of other users, as well as citizens. And in effect, this is what has been happening.

The rationale behind extending the requirement of neutrality to students is explained in the Stasi report that recommended the passing of the 2004 Law. In this report, schools are set apart as neutral spaces with the mission of educating students who are described as being 'destined to become enlightened citizens' (2003: 56). Former President Chirac, in a speech where he presented the Stasi report, compared this space to a 'Republican sanctuary' whose peaceful environment had to be 'defended' (Chirac, 2003). The headscarf worn by students has been understood here as infringing on this educational mission, as it is a reminder of outside pressures, pressures that carry a proselytizing message not compatible with Republican values and that have the potential of intimidating other students (especially female students).

> For the educative community, the wearing of the headscarf is too often a source of conflict, divisions and even suffering. The visible character of the sign is felt by many to be against the school's mission, which is to create a neutral space, and a place fostering the awakening of critical consciousness. It is also an attack on the principles and values that the school must teach, particularly equality between men and women [...] The Republic cannot stay deaf to the desperate screams of young girls [girls pressured to wear the headscarf]. The educational space needs to remain for them a place of freedom and emancipation.
>
> (Stasi, 2003: 57, 58)

Through this narrative one sees yet again the role played by the presence of women wearing headscarves in enabling the production of neutral spaces, spaces that protect and (re)produce a particular reading of neutrality and thus equality.

Prior to the passing of the 2004 Law, the state and courts dealt with students wearing headscarves in schools on a case by case basis, evaluating each time if the actions of a particular student was disturbing public order. By implementing a systematic ban, the state ensured that schools automatically offered a 'peaceful' environment not subject to 'divisive' tensions. In the process, it has also been delimiting the boundaries of the religiously acceptable. While in these accounts the headscarf has clearly become incompatible with secular values, on the other hand small hands of Fatima (i.e. amulets worn on a bracelet or a necklace to protect against the evil eye) have been defined as acceptable expressions (Chirac, 2003). This reading assumes that a religious expression can be easily modified or replaced by one more compatible with Republican values – even if the latter one carries for some a cultural and not a religious connotation.[14] This process bears resemblance to past attempts to 'regenerate' minorities – one could argue that the Republic is actually engaged in a contemporary 'regeneration' project.

The Stasi report, in 2003, notes that the situation remains different in universities because students are adults and therefore free to express their religious convictions. Yet it also clearly warns that these expressions should not in any way disturb or transgress the peaceful organization of university teaching. A few years later, the HCI, along similar lines, stressed that because the tradition of freedom of expression is key to the functioning of universities, neither a professor nor the content of their teaching should be subject to the neutrality principle. It highlights, nevertheless, that proselytising should be prohibited and that co-ed education and respect for equality between men and women should be preserved (HCI, 2010). Since neither documents give concrete examples of what is meant by 'transgression', 'proselytism' or 'respect for equality', one wonders what practices could fall into these categories – could wearing a sign that could be perceived by some as having a proselytizing character or questioning gender equality be considered a transgression? Or could it become one? In fact, as of 2011, the *burqa* (the veil that covers the entire face of the wearer) and *niqab* (the veil that covers all the face of the wearer except for her eyes) have been considered transgressions in public spaces (including all public services (e.g. higher education facilities)). Likewise, some of the interpretations given to the headscarf discussed above could be considered to 'disturb' the peaceful organization of universities. In effect, different public and private higher education facilities, using this type of argument, have inserted in their internal regulations a clause prohibiting the attendance of students wearing a headscarf in their facilities. Although this type of clause has no legal basis, it remains up to individuals to challenge their exclusions.[15]

The Turkish case

In Turkey, bans have affected, and continue to officially affect, students in public schools. They also affected universities until 2010, when they were slowly relaxed. Like bans targeting public servants, these were first implemented in the 1980s, but became more widespread and systematic in the late 1990s, after the 1997 coup.[16]

The period between 1980 and 1990 was marked by a general indecisiveness around headscarf regulations in universities. In 1981, the National Security Council followed by the Council of Higher Education (YÖK) prohibited students from wearing headscarves in universities leading to large protests (Özdalga, 1998: 41). After a change of government, YÖK relaxed this ban by accepting that students wear a '*türban* in a modern way' (Kavakçı, 2010: 53).[17] What exactly was included in the category *türban* remained unclear, but it was generally understood as a headscarf that covered the head but not the ears or the neck of the wearer (Özdalga, 1998: 42) – a move that delimits once again the boundaries of acceptable religiousness.[18] 'The general public view was that it was supposed to be more modern looking than the *başörtüsü* [scarf that covered the neck and ears] […] maybe somewhat similar to that of the French bonnet' (Kavakçı, 2010:53).

President Evren, in 1986, in dissension with Prime Minister Özal, tightened the rules in universities. As such, in 1987, YÖK revised its earlier provisions and banned the *türban* in universities – the underlying meaning of the *türban* started to change from that point onwards and became associated with a religious expression threatening the Republican project (Kavakçı, 2010: 54). This back and forth between permitting certain types of head covering and then outlawing them continued for a couple of years. Again, in 1988, a law was passed allowing students to wear a headscarf out of personal conviction and said that 'Modern dress or appearance shall be compulsory in the rooms and corridors of institutions of higher education, preparatory schools, laboratories, clinics and multidisciplinary clinics. A veil or headscarf covering the neck and hair may be worn out of religious conviction' (Law no. 2547, Higher Education Act, cited in McGoldrick, 2006: 135).[19] This piece of legislation was annulled by the Constitutional Court, who argued that it was a breach of *laiklik* (Ozdalga, 1998: 46). McGoldrick notes that the court found that this law could not be reconciled with the principle of sexual equality central to Republican values. Similar to the French narrative, *laiklik* was understood as enabling a space in which individuals could emancipate themselves and become equal and autonomous citizens.

> Secularism is the civil organizer of political, social and cultural life, based on national sovereignty, democracy, freedom and science. Secularism is the principle, which offers the individual the possibility to affirm his or her own personality through freedom of thought […]
>
> (Constitutional Court Judgement, March 7 1989, cited in McGoldrick, 2006:136)

It is relevant to note that this judgment came out in the late 1980s, around the same time as a Turkish-Islamic synthesis programme was being enforced.[20] That is, while the secular state was promoting a state-controlled Islam to create a sense of national consciousness, the wearing of the headscarf was already considered at that time, to be outside of those boundaries. This stand became even clearer after the 1997 coup, as the headscarf came to be systematically associated with political Islam, regardless of the wearer's actions or beliefs.[21]

In the mid-2000s, some universities and university professors tried, once again, to be more lenient towards the ban. Yet, these attempts were reversed when the ruling AK Party attempted to lift the ban in universities by making constitutional amendments. These amendments were used as the basis to file a closure case against the AK Party in March 2008, as well as file a case denouncing these changes as incompatible with the constitutional principle of secularism. Ultimately, although the AK Party was not closed down, the amendments were annulled by a decision of the Constitutional Court in October 2008. From then onwards, the AK Party has avoided tackling the headscarf issue directly. Indeed, when university bans were finally relaxed in late 2010, this was a result of the change in attitude of the secular Republican People's Party (CHP), which was eager to attract religious voters ahead of the following year's election.

Extending the neutrality requirement to users beyond schools and universities

As already discussed, there have been various attempts to extend headscarf bans to temporary civil servants and their families, as well as to women attending higher education facilities. In addition, non-systematic extensions to users of public services in spaces providing public services (e.g. city halls, administrations, political parties and so on) have also been recorded. These extensions often depend on the individuals enforcing them. For instance, in April 2008, a referee at an inter-regional ping pong tournament in Bolu, Turkey, decided to prohibit a player from participating because she was wearing a headscarf (AKDER, 2008). He argued that she could not be wearing it during the tournament, a tournament which was marked, through her expulsion, as being a neutral and public space. This is interesting, as it is yet another example of how the notion of public space is flexible. It also exemplifies how the (re)production of space is far from being only a matter for bureaucrats – 'concerned' citizens are actively involved as well in this disciplinary process on a daily basis. They take it upon themselves to 'enact', 'protect' and 'foster' particular rules delimiting where the secular ethos should be performed. The fact that these individuals feel responsible for ensuring that a certain understanding of the polity prevails resonates vividly with Kandiyoti's reflection on state-sponsored religious fundamentalism, in which she notes that 'the exercise of patriarchal authority may be extended to unrelated men, like the clergy, the police or "concerned" citizens, who are given free hand in monitoring women's dress and conduct in public places' (Kandiyoti, 1991a: 440).

France and the charter of laïcité: a daily pledge to collective life

Ad hoc extensions enforced by mayors and other policy makers and affecting a wide range of users have been reported over the last decade in France. These ought to be understood as being part of a larger effort to advocate for a stricter implementation of the neutrality requirement to users of public services.[22] They set apart public services as spaces that symbolize the ethos of the Republic, and thus where the neutrality of both users and providers becomes non-negotiable. While restricting the wearing of visible religious symbols is one of the first signs marking the neutrality and non-negotiable dimensions of these spaces, other demands such as special dietary requests or the need to be seen by a doctor of the same sex are, also, frequently considered to be out of bounds.

The Rossinot report, for instance, calls on hospital patients and other users of public services to respect the Republican principles carried by *laïcité*. The report does not explicitly forbid religious symbols – it does, however, argue that proselytizing activities and behaviour that encourage gender segregation are incompatible with these principles (2006: 8–9). In this discussion it makes reference to the March 2004 Law and notes that the majority of Muslims fulfilled their citizenship duties by respecting it. 'Practicing Muslims, have, in the vast majority accepted its implementation [i.e. the law] and respected its requirement proving therefore their civic participation and their will to adhere with loyalty to the principles that rule our society' (Rossinot, 2006: 9). The Gerin report is more explicit in suggesting that all women wearing a *niqab* or *burqa* be prohibited from entering hospitals or other public services, as these veils are considered to transgress the values that these spaces promote and foster (2010: 204). Once again, being a 'good' citizen, respectful of Republican values – or perhaps simply having the privilege of being included in the category citizen – implies that individuals, and more specifically women, should be ready to reshape their religious practices.

As a matter of fact, policy makers have thought of a way to remind citizens of the values that ought to be protected and fostered by public services. They have proposed developing a charter of *laïcité* that would be distributed and posted visibly in all public services, as well as given out at each important stage of a citizen's life. 'The Charter […] could also be given at key civic occasions (citizenship ceremonies, when identity cards or electoral cards are sent or collected, during civil weddings, or during civil defence days …)' (Rossinot, 2006: 43).[23] In a sense, therefore, this charter would not only indicate the special 'status' of public services, but its diffusion would become a ritual, as it would be distributed during key rites of passages in the life of a citizen.

Building on these recommendations, the HCI drafted in 2007 a sample charter entitled 'Charter of *laïcité* in public services'. This charter was then transformed into a poster and distributed widely throughout public services in 2010 (HCI, 2011a). The preamble to the charter notes that while the March 2004 Law is only applicable in schools, a 'gentleman's agreement' should be implemented in other spaces (2007: 38). This 'agreement' implies that users of public services are free, but that this freedom should not be confused with laisser-faire. In fact, users, as citizens, have moral obligations to follow the rules of 'reasonable behaviours' (ibid.), which are clearly spelled out in the charter:

> Users of public services have the right to express their religious convictions in the limits of the respect of neutrality of public services, its good functioning, and of imperatives of public order, security, health and

> hygiene. Users of public services have to abstain from any form of proselytizing. Users of public services cannot refuse a public servant or other users, nor require the adaptation of the functioning of public services or of a public equipment …
>
> (HCI, 2011a)

While the headscarf is not, for the moment, officially prohibited from these spaces, since it is understood to be a 'sign' whose compatibility with 'good functioning, public order, security, health and hygiene' is continually (re) assessed, it is not impossible to imagine that at another point in time it could be considered to transgress the rules of these spaces. Certainly some of the meanings that were conferred on it during the debates around the 2004 Law, and that continue to be applied to it by several commentators, would consider it to be incompatible with these rules.

Turkey: politicians subject to the neutrality requirement

THE MERVE KAVAKÇI AFFAIR

These rules of 'reasonable behaviours' do not only affect women who 'use' public services, but also those involved in political life. In France, for instance, women wearing a headscarf have faced difficulties when they have sought to participate in city councils, vote or become members of political parties.[24] Remember the example of Ilhem Moussaid discussed in the introductory chapter. In February 2010, the presence of this young woman wearing a headscarf on the electoral list of the NPA created weeks of vivid debate. Many politicians considered her presence to be an outrage to the Republican ethos. Likewise, one finds similar examples in Turkey, where, for instance, under President Sezer (2000–2007), wives of politicians wearing headscarves were not invited to the President's residence, an act which marked the public character of this space.

> […] Secularism is the basis of the Republic and Presidency is a public realm […] The presidential residence where the Republic is represented, and the reception that is hosted by the President are both public spaces and wearing *başörtüsü* [headscarf] cannot be permitted.
>
> (Sezer, cited in Kavakçı, 2010: 87)[25]

The Merve Kavakçı case is a good illustration of this phenomenon. Kavakçı, a 31-year-old engineer, was the first woman with a headscarf elected in Turkey, running for the former Virtue Party in 1999. When she entered parliament to take her oath she refused to conform to the implicit dress code of the space, structured around the neutrality principle. Although this code did not explicitly mention the ban, the non-religious parties understood this move to be an offensive challenge against the secular roots of the Republic. She had challenged the unwritten rules of parliament. This led to strong reactions from other politicians. While another MP who had been elected with a headscarf, but had agreed to remove it when seating in parliament, was applauded when she entered parliament, Kavakçı was confronted by a shouting crowd who demanded that she get out (Shively, 2005: 52). She was eventually prevented from taking her oath, thrown out of parliament and later deprived of her Turkish citizenship.[26] The closure of the Virtue Party followed soon after.

Politicians' comments on the Kavakçı affair are particularly revealing. Bülent Ecevit, the future Prime Minister and leader of the Democratic Left Party noted that:

> Everyone in Turkey has the right to wear whatever they like in their private lives. But the General Assembly of Parliament is not within the bounds of anyone's private life. Those in state life should obey the rules and regulations of the state. Parliament is not the place to challenge the state.
>
> (Ecevit, cited in Çemrek, 2004: 56)

He also added that Kavakçı should 'know her limits' (Ecevit cited in Shively, 2005: 52). The President of Turkey at that time, Süleyman Demirel, issued a statement where he called Kavakçı an 'agent-provocateur' working for foreign powers such as Iran and Hamas (Kavakçı, 2010: 110). And even the Chair of her own party, Recai Kutan, criticized her for 'exposing the party to condemnation and suspicion' (Shively, 2005: 52). In her book, Kavakçı notes with respect to that last point that:

> These protests [protests from other politicians] were sufficient for the FP administration [the Virtue Party's administration] to withdraw its support. That day, I was not permitted back in my party for a second attempt to take the oath. After a few politically correct statements, I was left on my own to deal with the challenges to come.
>
> (Kavakçı, 2010: 77)

Even though, after this event, Kavakçı held a press conference where she stressed that it was her choice to wear the headscarf, politicians continued to argue that her aim was to import Islamic fundamentalism into Parliament.

Many aspects of this case are telling. First, as Shively points out, it shows how tensions came from the fact that Kavakçı did not respect the rules and not from the fact that other politicians from the Virtue Party, including women who were not wearing a headscarf or had agreed to take it off, were taking part in parliamentary life (Shively, 2005: 52). Second, the story of Merve Kavakçı is a good example of the 'alienation' that one is faced with when national scripts are not properly narrated, 'alienation from the shared meanings which constitute a language of identity, affiliation and loyalty'

(Kandiyoti, 1991a: 433). Finally, the reader is made aware that little space was given to women's individual agency. Politicians (male politicians in this case, including members of Kavakçı's own party) were speaking for her, were discussing her motives, and were overlooking what she actually had to say. They seemed, in fact, to be blinded by a dualistic way of thinking, in which women's visible piety could not be associated with individual sovereignty.

THE AK PARTY AND WOMEN WEARING HEADSCARVES IN PARLIAMENT

With the dominance in the political landscape of the AK Party starting in the mid-2000s, one would perhaps expect this situation to change. Yet, in the June 2011 elections, almost ten years after the AK Party first came to power, there was still no woman wearing a headscarf on any party's list, including the lists of the AK Party, and this despite active efforts by devout women to figure on those lists.

In this respect, the reactions of the AK Party to one of the campaigns launched by a devout group of women are noteworthy. In the spring 2011, a group of activists organized a campaign, known as the 'no headscarf, no vote campaign', in which they asked all political parties to consider putting women wearing headscarves on their lists. While they expected secular parties to condemn their campaign, the harshest criticisms came from the AK Party and conservative politicians (Akyol, 2011).[27] In the autumn of 2011, the AK Party, successfully re-elected, refused once again to change the bylaws regulating the dress code in parliament, a move that would have abolished any informal regulations not permitting women wearing headscarves to become members of Parliament (Zıbak Dişli, 2011). It would seem, therefore, that the AK Party's position ended up contributing to 'the expansive construction of the "new" public space and exclusion of *başörtülü kadınlar* from it' (Kavakçı, 2010: 88).[28]

While this reluctance can be explained in part because of Turkish history, marked by a series of coups and political party overthrows, it is important to note, however, that the situation in 2011 was rather different from the one in 1998. The AK Party had, by then, acquired unprecedented power, illustrated, for instance, by the fact that it was not closed down in July 2008 or by the change in attitude of secular parties with respect to women wearing headscarves in universities mentioned earlier. Moreover, observers have noted that nation-wide trials such as the Ergenekon trial, initiated in 2008 against alleged ultra-nationalist groups working to overthrow governments, have allowed the AK Party to acquire control over key institutions such as the military, judiciary and bureaucracy (Öktem, 2011).

Therefore, this position cannot be fully understood if we only look at it from a secular/religious powerplay. It is, in my opinion, equally important to include in the equation the particular role given to women in Turkish history in delimiting the boundaries of the nation, including the boundary between private and public realms. As has been argued, this role has been marked by distinct rules, where access to full citizenship has been mediated by religion, gender and class. In other words, while observers have frequently noted the new visibility of women wearing the headscarf since the late 1980s in urban areas, it is important to understand that this visibility remains circumscribed, to a certain extent, by heterosexual familial bonds. It would seem that devout women are invited to participate in activities in the public realm by conservative elites more as mothers, daughters, wives and sisters than as autonomous women. In so doing, while the presence of these women marks the growing hegemony of conservative elites, it does not seem, for the moment at least, to represent a deep challenge to the spatial workings of secularism.

Thus, paying attention to headscarf discrimination reveals the deep parallels that exist between the worldviews of conservative and secular elites, where similar dichotomies, central to dominant articulations of the modern, continue to be (re)produced and where women's bodies are key to this geography. This historical continuum can help us shed light on situations that might seem paradoxical, including the fact that conservative elites have been in favour of the inclusion of students wearing headscarves in universities, considered to be bastions of the secular Republic, while at the same time paying little attention to the need to lift restrictions elsewhere – a move that would, for instance, greatly facilitate devout women's access to jobs in both the public and/or the private sectors.

Extending the neutrality requirement to citizens in the 'private' realm

France and the multiplication of spaces

> The HCI considers that it is important to affirm that, in a private business, we have the right to want to work in a religiously neutral frame, individuals being preserved in that space from all communitarian pressures.
>
> (HCI, 2011b: 6)

> Until now, it was established that the manifestation of religious belonging was determined by a distinction between public and private sphere […] It seems today that the notion of public sphere needs to be questioned, notably when some evoke that outside public services, *social spaces* are part of a private space, like businesses. To which extent can religion manifest itself in public life? From which point does the freedom of the believer infringe on the one of the citizen?
>
> (HCI, 2010, author's emphasis).

While the 2004 Law applied the neutrality requirement to users of public services, the 2010 Law imposed this requirement for a particular type of head covering beyond those spaces. In so doing, the law opened the door to extending this neutrality principle to individuals outside public services. Building on this opening, the HCI in its 2010 opinion on *laïcité* in public services and in its 2011 opinion on *laïcité* in businesses, draws a distinction between three spaces. The first, identified as the 'public sphere', is defined as the space where public services are located and in which *laïcité* and its neutrality principle are applied strictly. This concerns, first and foremost, providers of public services, but can also be extended to users. The second space is labelled as a 'social space' and includes the public domain of circulation (e.g. roads, parks, etc.) as well as private businesses opened to the public. It is argued that because these are common spaces, freedoms can be limited in order to respect public order. In the third space, identified as the 'private domain', often conflated with the household, it remains possible, as long as the law permits it, to share religious, philosophical and political opinions.

The usage of the term 'social space' is noteworthy as it is has been used as a way to suggest that the neutrality requirement and *laïcité* be extended to private businesses that were until then not affected by this requirement. The possibility of this extension is clearly spelled out in the 2011 HCI opinion on *laïcité* in private businesses (HCI, 2011b). Indeed, the opinion considers that over the last couple of years businesses have been faced with a 'rising' number of religious demands.[29] While the opinion notes that it is concerned by all religious demands, it stresses that most of these have been formulated by individuals belonging to the Muslim faith (HCI, 2011b: 8). The wearing of visible religious symbols, including the headscarf, is considered to be particularly problematic as it is understood as being incompatible with employment, in which individuals are in contact with clients and represent the brand of a particular company (HCI, 2011b: 15).

To address these worries, and because the peaceful co-working of employees and the smooth functioning of businesses should not be infringed, the opinion suggests including in the work code of businesses two articles on *laïcité*. The first would allow private firms to put limits on religious demands, and the second would facilitate the implementation of the principle of neutrality in those spaces. The latter is formulated as follows: '[…] The principles of neutrality and impartiality facilitate […] the good functioning of businesses. The absence of manifestations of religious expressions, whether these be practices or visible signs, is therefore strongly recommended' (HCI, 2011b: 18).

Businesses are, in this new rhetoric, set apart as spaces where citizens cohabit together and where social peace ought to prevail – a peace that will ensure, among other things, that the productivity of these spaces will not be disturbed.[30] One clearly sees how *laïcité*, which was until recently being used only to mark the special status of public services, has now travelled to another space – the 'social' space. Not surprisingly, the same opinion suggests that respect for *laïcité* be included in the professional ethics of companies. Moreover, human resources are invited to develop courses on *laïcité* for their employees (HCI, 2011b: 19). It is almost as if *laïcité* is not only being mobilized during the different Republican rites of passages, but is also becoming something that ought to mark working life.

The boundaries of the 'private domain' are also shifting in accordance with where *laïcité* is extended and implemented. In the above-mentioned opinion of the HCI, it is now combined with the household. Yet this depends on the activities undertaken in this household. For instance, in 2012 the French Senate, building on a recent court ruling that confirmed that a childcare provider could be laid off from a private day care if she refused to remove her headscarf (Baby Loup, 2010, 2011), voted in favour of a law proposal that aimed at extending the neutrality principle to childcare providers in charge of children under the age of six. This included nannies working in their homes, regardless of the fact that they received funds from the state (Assemblée Nationale, 2012). In fact, article 3 of this law notes that if childcare providers do not stipulate in their work contract that they are unable to respect the neutrality principle, it is then assumed that they will not be expressing their religion when working.[31]

In my view, this law proposal should be understood as a continuum of what was discussed in the previous sections of this chapter. Indeed, in a similar way to the regulations that seek to extend the 'neutrality' principle to parents participating in school outings, it attempts to extend this principle to workers who are not public servants but who are exercising an educational activity – that is, this extension is necessary for the best interests of the Republican child. This intrusion of *laïcité* into the private realm is also justified by arguments grounded in the preservation of social peace, and the need to foster and cultivate a harmonious sense of living together (Richard, 2011: 28). This law proposal triggers a series of challenging questions. As a member of Parliament commenting on this proposal argued, the proposal failed to define precisely what it meant by 'religious expressions', leaving unanswered questions such as whether it would only be applicable to religious dress, or also to a 'representation of Mecca' in one's household or a 'way to prepare a meal' (Benbassa in Le Bars, 2012). Yet this lack of definition is far from being novel. It characterizes most of the proposals discussed previously in this chapter, and leaves open the possibility of interference in different types of practices depending of the context and political climate. Ultimately this proposal opens the door to direct interventions in the household of devout individuals and, more particularly, of devout Muslim women. Thus, under particular circumstances, a household is transformed into a 'social space' that can and should be scrutinized not only by the state but by parents as well.

Turkey and expansions of discrimination in the private sector

> Consider a journalist wearing the headscarf: If she wants to pursue political news, the settings she will be allowed to access will be limited as a result of the ban. Or consider a woman pharmacist who operates her own pharmacy: If she

will do business with government organizations, her presence in meetings as a headscarved woman will invite trouble.

(Cindoğlu 2011: 8)

Even if the ban in Turkey has officially only been applicable to public servants and students, much like in France, a spill-over effect has taken place over the last two decades (Elver, 2012: 32–33). Similar arguments to those in the French case, including those based on the modern and secular image of a firm, have been used to limit employment opportunities for women wearing headscarves. A recent Turkish Economic and Social Studies Foundation (TESEV) study, conducted by Cindoğlu, tackles this issue (2011). The study shows that one of the difficulties faced by women wearing headscarves working for private firms is the fact that they have to work and interact with government officials and in government settings where a ban on the headscarf continues to be enforced (Cindoğlu, 2011: 72). For instance, if a lawyer wearing a headscarf has her own practice, she will have to plead her cases in court, which will be difficult, if not impossible, when courts are considered to be secular spaces. She may therefore have to resort to quite extreme solutions where, for instance, she hires another lawyer just to plead her cases. This spill-over effect, affects mainly white-collar professions – in which many educated pious women seek to be employed (ibid. 72).[32] When women wearing headscarves succeed in getting employment they are, therefore, often relegated to back office jobs.

The report underlines that a related preoccupation for companies is their modern image – an image that is not compatible with narratives that equate the headscarf with traditions, family and non-secular values:

> Not all private companies hire headscarved women. An attire involving the headscarf and full body covering is considered unacceptable in the first place because it does not go well with the 'modern' company image, without regard to whether such attire has anything to do with job performance directly.
>
> (ibid. 87)

This is another factor explaining why headscarved women are frequently given positions where they remain 'invisible' or are asked to be invisible (i.e. asked to modify their headscarf or replace it with a wig) (ibid. 90). Even if the neutrality requirement of businesses is not spelled out as clearly as in the French case, these measures have a similar result as particular expressions of religion are rendered invisible – in other words, the neuter requirement around which the public sector is organized impacts businesses as well.

It is worth noting that while it is difficult for devout women to get employment in firms owned by secular elites for whom the headscarf is frequently understood as a direct attack on the Republic, they also face restrictions in firms owned by more conservative businessmen. They are, often, defined in these settings primarily in terms of their familial bonds (e.g. sisters, daughters, wives), and are therefore treated more as family members in need of protection by their employers than as equal employees (ibid. 85). Since their primary identity is considered to be with their family and since conservative employers often argue that they are doing these women a 'favour' by hiring them as their chance of getting a job elsewhere are scarce, the report notes that these women are frequently paid less than men or other women, and are often the first to be laid off (ibid. 88).

> 'Green' capital operates contrary to expectations: 'They [the headscarved women] need us, I'll pay the lowest wage and she'll work here, she can't go anywhere else, she's bound to do that'. Even that low-pay job is a backstage one. Like, not in a place where you're visible. If there will be two headscarved women in the secretariat of the newspaper I work at, they don't really like that, they say 'one wearing a headscarf and one who doesn't' or 'no headscarved women there'. It's as if they want to present the right image to outsiders, like a shop window.
>
> (Ayşe, in Cindoğlu, 2011:94)

To sum up, neutrality continues in this case also to be an indicator of the modernity and progress of different spaces, including businesses. While the sociological realities of France and Turkey are different, both countries are faced with a similar growing presence of qualified, devout women who wish to enter the job market. The fact that these women are affected by the neutral requirement in private businesses is yet again an indication of the precarious and unstable character of the public/private divide. The Turkish case, and the growing presence of a devout bourgeoisie, also reveals that this requirement transcends secular and religious divides. Conservative businessmen and politicians seem to be somewhat influenced by similar dichotomies that have haunted, and continue to haunt, secular imagination – associating women's visible expressions of piety with tradition and the familial realm, and neutrality with progress and modernity. This is revealing of the deep-seated character and complexity of secular narratives, marked by dualistic thinking. While the presence of women wearing headscarves in different public spaces seems, in the first instance, to partly challenge these secular narratives, if we analyse this phenomenon closely we realize that these women continue, in many cases, to be assigned one identity, which circumscribes quite rigidly their access to full and equal citizenship rights.

Conclusion

This detailed comparative analysis of headscarf bans might seem, at first, excessive. Yet I deliberately chose not to focus on one moment in time (e.g. the 2004 Law) or one country, in order to closely capture the shifting and unstable character of the languages of secularism and, in particular, the language of neutrality. Much as with what was explored in Chapter 2, this is important since these instabilities are used, as the reader will come to realise, by devout activists in both countries to frame and base their claims.

Moreover, exploring how exclusions unfold in multiple sites rather than analysing just one site (e.g. schools), invites us to become acutely aware of the intimate relationship that exists between secular tropes, the production of space and gender. While the boundaries of public space extend or retract in accordance with time and political climates, this is not without consequences for the lives of devout women. In effect, by documenting these movements, one is able to clearly realise their vulnerable position as they find themselves at the margin of spaces – their ability to enjoy their citizenship rights varies therefore in conjunction with these shifts. In a sense, this points to the fact that unstable boundaries are not to be confused with porous ones, as individuals experiencing these boundaries face direct hardships in their daily lives, and high hurdles when they try to transcend or disturb them.[33] Acknowledging this reality opens the door to exploring more normative questions related to conceptions of inclusive models of citizenship and plurality that acknowledge the productive role of disruption.

The systematic comparison offered in this chapter plays a triple purpose in my view. It helps to de-centre and put in perspective a discussion that otherwise stays focused on only one country. In so doing, the reader becomes aware of how secular tropes are deeply related to modern constructions of space (e.g. private vs public, political vs familial, secular vs religious) that have a global dimension. By positioning the French case next to the Turkish case, one also realises that it is not only secular elites who are involved in the (re)production of the gendered spatial workings of secularism. It is also being (re)produced, at least to a certain degree, by religious elites. This is interesting, inasmuch as it again helps us to go beyond a discussion that is often framed in terms of a religious vs secular dichotomy. In other words, these workings are ingrained in conceptions of modernity and citizenship that transcend this divide. Finally, the reader is invited to see how shifts in the languages of secularism shape the boundaries of what is religiously acceptable. A recurrent trend that flows throughout the discussion is that it is embodied practices that travel between the acceptable and the non-acceptable. On the other hand, beliefs that stay in one's conscience are not challenged – they remain within the boundaries of what is acceptable in the public realm. This reading of the religious, as pointed out by Mahmood (2009), Danchin (2011) and others, is deeply influenced by a Christian understanding of religious freedom.[34] This will be discussed later in this book, yet it is relevant to mention it here inasmuch as one realises that this vision of religious freedom influences France as well as Turkey.

Notes

1 Kavakçı explains that there are actually two non-homogenous groups of women wearing headscarves. The first group, not considered to be threatening, is constituted of homemakers and women living in rural areas (2010: 22–23). These

women, she explains, wear traditional headscarves, which are 'tied under their chin with a knot' (ibid, 23). The second group of women is labelled by the state as *'türbanlı kadınlar'* (women with *türbans*). The *türban* is identified here as a head-covering that became predominant in the 1980s and that covers the shoulders and the head of its wearer. These women, who generally live in urban areas and seek to participate in the life of the polis with their headscarf on, have been considered as symbolising political Islam and as being a threat to the Republic by secular elites. Kavakçı notes that these women do not accept the label *'türbanlı kadınlar'*, and rather identify themselves as *'basörtülü kadınlar'* (women with headscarves). The usage of either expression is used to indicate where one stands with respect to the conflict around the headscarf in Turkey (ibid, 26–27).

2 Deutsche makes this argument with respect to homeless individuals, who are threatened with eviction from public spaces. She argues that their presence in these spaces 'embodies the fantasy of a unified urban space that can – must – be retrieved' (1996: 278).

3 As will be discussed later, these notions of neutrality and equality have been challenged. Danchin (2011), for instance, argues that this neutrality is based on a Christian inspired reading of religion, where modern religion is understood as being located in one's private conscience. Other scholars, informed by a feminist perspective, have argued that the baseline around which this neutrality has been articulated is a bourgeois male one (Salih, 2009: 421; Scott, 2007: 169), which explains why women, who have for a long time been depicted as being unable to abstract themselves from their sex and thus become neutral, have posed, and continue to pose, a deep challenge to this concept (see Scott, ibid; Hurd Shakman, 2013).

4 Some of the reasons behind this increased presence of visible Islam are explained in Chapter 4.

5 The Stasi report was released in 2003, and summarised the findings of the Stasi Commission, which was set up by the French President (Jacques Chirac at the time) to determine whether a law should be passed to prohibit visible religious symbols in public schools. One of the recommendations of the report was that the neutrality requirement affecting public servants be systematically included in their work contract (Stasi, 2003: 56).

6 The Rossinot report, focusing on *laïcité* in public services, was commissioned by the president of the political party *Union pour un Mouvement Populaire* (UMP) for the 100 years anniversary of the 1905 Law. One of the aims of this report was to reflect on how the rules underpinning the concept of *laïcité* could be better implemented in French public services. The Gerin report, released in January 2012, had as its mission the evaluation of whether the *burqa* and *niqab* should be banned in France. One of its conclusions was that they should be forbidden in public services.

7 It is noteworthy that the category of public servant has not only been expanding, but that policy reports have also suggested that the responsibilities of public servants be extended so that one of their duties is to explicitly protect, promote and foster *laïcité*. What this implies is discussed in the Rossinot report (2006) and in the High Council for Integration (HCI) opinion on *laïcité* in public services released in 2010.

8 The HCI was created in 1989 by the French Prime Minister. Its mission is to give opinions and make suggestions on issues related to the integration of foreigners or citizens of foreign origins. For more information see http://www.hci.gouv.fr (accessed 5 November 2013).

9 The HALDE was created in 2004 and had the aim of fighting discrimination in France. Its functions included identifying discriminative practices, providing mediation services between parties and producing non-binding opinions and decisions on discrimination. It was dissolved in May 2011, and its activities were integrated into the mandate of a broader organization – the *Défenseur des Droits*.

10 The 1997 'soft' coup and its consequences are discussed in Chapter 5.
11 Women have replaced headscarf with wigs to bypass regulations on the headscarf. Kavakçı discusses this point in her book (2010: 95–97).
12 Drawing on this logic, the Higher Education Council (YÖK), supervising all universities in Turkey, issued directives banning the wearing of wigs, berets, hats, etc. (YÖK, 2002).
13 The Turkish Council of State (Danıştay) is the highest administrative court in Turkey.
14 Many Muslims, for instance, do not consider the hand of Fatima to be a religious symbol, but rather a cultural one (see, for example, Bouissa, 2003).
15 These cases are ad hoc, touch a wide range of institutions and vary according to the individuals in charge of these institutions. For instance, cases have been recorded in hospitals where medical interns have been dismissed, in driving schools where students have been denied the possibility of taking exams, in night schools, and even in a few university courses. For a list of those exclusions see CCIF, 2005, 2009a and 2009b; CCIF and 15 March Committee, 2005, and Chouder *et al.* 2008a.
16 Unlike the French case there is no nationwide law banning headscarves in Turkey, but bans are inserted in the internal regulations of specific public services.
17 During Özal's time as a Prime Minister (1983–89), several attempts were made to lift restrictions on the wearing of the headscarf and promote a reading of *laiklik* that supported this position. For a discussion of Özal's position on religious freedom and the place of Islam in Turkish society see Kavakçı, 2010: 53.
18 For further discussion on the Turkish *türban* see Kavakçı, 2010: 53–54. It is interesting that similar attempts to 'modernize' the headscarf were tried out in France prior to the passing of the 2004 law. For instance, teachers invited students to wear bandana-type headscarves where their ears and necks were visible.
19 For more information on this see Aydin, 2005: 53.
20 The Turkish-Islamic Synthesis refers to a strategy put in place after the 1980s, where the military tried to encourage the promotion of a state-controlled Islam to counter leftist threats (see Yavuz, 2003: 69).
21 To ensure a systematic enforcement of these bans, in a similar vein to the French public schools, universities established 'persuasion rooms' that became widespread after 1997. For more information on these processes in the Turkish case see: Elver, 2012: 31 and in the French case see: Chouder *et al.* 2008a: 17–135.
22 For a non-exhaustive list of these exclusions see: CCIF, 2005, 2009a and b; CCIF and 15 March Committee, 2005, and Chouder *et al.* 2008a.
23 In a similar vein, the Rossinot report suggested reinforcing the reference to *laïcité* in welcoming and integration contracts signed by immigrants when they settle in France (2006: 41). Likewise, the Gerin report recommended reinforcing the civic training given to immigrants and requiring that the study of *laïcité* and of Republican values be systematically integrated into public schools' curriculums (2010: 132, 135–36).
24 For more information on these exclusions, see Bouzar and Kada, 2003; CCIF, 2005; CCIF and 15 March Committee, 2005; Chouder *et al.* 2008a.
25 In fact, Aydin notes that with the triumph of the AK Party in the 2002 elections the headscarf conflict expanded to new areas (2005: 53).
26 The Merve Kavakçı case is further discussed in Chapter 6.
27 This campaign and the reactions of politicians are further discussed in Chapter 5. Note also here how male politicians continue to 'speak' for women. This echoes Shively's comments on the Merve Kavakçı case and the gendered dimension of Turkish nationalism: 'the nation configured as a female is passively defended and represented by a nationalist political body, configured as male' (Shively, 2005: 58).
28 Kavakçı made this point in reference to the conciliatory position of the AK Party when wives of its members were excluded from attending official receptions (2010: 88).

29 This is a good example of how shifts in the meaning and scope of *laïcité* go hand in hand with a discourse on religious resurgence in the French case – that is, the importance of understanding both discourses as being deeply related to each other.

30 An interesting parallel can be made with the requirements put in place in the nineteenth century with respect to the Jewish faith, where Jews were asked to tame their faith ensuring that it did not infringe on their ability to be 'productive' citizens (see Chapter 2). This neo-liberal argument of creating 'un-biased' and productive individuals is, in fact, very much entrenched within secular tropes (see Gökariksel and Mitchell 2005 for a discussion of the connections between neo-liberalism and secularism).

31 This law has never been implemented. The project was never approved by the French National Assembly, and lost momentum with the change in government in 2012.

32 The report argues that women in blue-collar professions are not as visible as women in white-collar positions, and are not required to have as many interactions with other institutions (Cindoğlu, 2011: 72).

33 I am indebted to John Chalcraft for pointing this distinction out.

34 Note that it is important, as Beaman argues in her work to make a distinction between a dominant interpretation of Christianity ('"good" Christianity') and minority Christian beliefs that are subject to similar processes of transformation (2008: 153).

© Maman Toutes Egales

4 French Muslim activists

Promoting a *laïcité* ante

> Before 2004 the legal frame protecting *laïcité* was working […] But all of this was distorted with the 2004 Law and the recent interpretation of *laïcité* it conveys. The state is now actively intervening in religious affairs. The President of the Republic indicates what Muslims can or cannot wear […] This new *laïcité* should not be called *laïcité* because it does not correspond to what it was before.
>
> (activist, 15 March Committee, Lyon, 2008)

> We are for an interpretation of *laïcité* in accordance with the 1905 Law […] Muslims in fact have become experts on the 1905 Law […] We know all the stages from 1882 to 1905. This allows us to identify individuals who have truncated interpretations of *laïcité*.
>
> (activist, CFPE and MTE, Paris, 2012)

This chapter explores how religious Muslim activists in France have responded publically to changes in the dominant interpretations of *laïcité* over the last decade, and more precisely to the March 2004 Law and its attempts to extend into multiple spaces. These responses are particularly interesting inasmuch as they are located within the boundaries of *laïcité*. In fact, as we will see, the tensions and shifts within the dominant interpretations of *laïcité* explored in the two previous chapters have facilitated this task. More precisely, French Muslim activists have been referring to a discourse that grounds itself in national jurisprudence to challenge the fact that the laws and regulations passed since 2004 are representative of a 'real' *laïcité*. Although this may seem at first glance to be a simple question of definitions, what is interesting is that activists have been presenting themselves as citizens whose duty is to protect and ensure that *laïcité* prevails throughout France – a *laïcité* ante that fosters a public order based on respect for difference and religious pluralism.[1] To put it differently, they have based their argument in a narrative where the 2004 Law and the climate from that point onwards is constructed as marking a distinctive break with foundational laws and jurisprudence on *laïcité*. In so doing, they are presenting a story in which the multiple debates around the definition that should be given to *laïcité*, including those that preceded the passing of the 1905 Law and those that have been taking place from the late 1980s onwards (see below), are not mentioned. Evaluating to what extent their account reflects 'reality' is a difficult (if not impossible) task to embark on and not one I am interested in – rather, what seems relevant is to underline that they are producing their own narratives on *laïcité*. Through this bottom-up approach, this chapter continues to explore the hegemonic character of secularism that has the power to determine the parameters of claims and is at the same time in constant movement.

On a comparative note, this discussion offers elements of contrast and similarity with our Turkish case. Activists in Turkey, as explored in the next chapter, have also been attempting to refashion secularism, yet international human rights conventions and treaties have played a key role in their discourse. In France, while activists have referred in some instances to these treaties, they have principally grounded their claims in national jurisprudence. These diverging techniques are representative of the different resources available to activists, as well as of the political positions in which devout Muslims find themselves in both countries. Turkish activists are increasingly influential and are part of wider groups of societal activists who are fighting for less state interference in their subjectivities. In the French case, they are members of a fragmented minority with little political influence and they are involved in a defensive struggle. Despite these differences, the discourse of activists presents similarities, which are, at least partly, a consequence of the influence of strict secular regimes and secular laws on their subjectivities. First, by challenging the position assigned to devout women, these two struggles question the gendered geography of secularism. Moreover, in both cases religious activists are fighting for a vision of secularism where the religious self is less subject to state regulation – challenging, to a certain extent, key dichotomies at the heart of the dominant secular imaginaries, such as the ones between freedom of conscience and expression of religious beliefs, duty and choice, as well as self-emancipation and religious authority.

A short overview

Remembering the recent shift in the dominant understanding of laïcité

As discussed in chapter 3, the 15 March 2004 Law banning visible religious symbols in public schools represented a shift in the dominant understandings of *laïcité* and of visible religious symbols, in particular the headscarf. Prior to this date, headscarves worn by students were not considered by the *Conseil d'Etat* to be incompatible with *laïcité*, and while schools could exclude a student if her actions were considered disturbing to public order, they could not do so solely because she publicly expressed a religious conviction (Conseil d'Etat, 1989).[2] However, as of 2004, headscarves have been understood to be, in themselves, disturbing the values of collective life promoted in schools (as well as in other public spaces), and this regardless of the actions of the wearer. In fact, by targeting students this law has introduced another novel element, whereby not only providers, but also users of public services are now affected by the neutrality requirement.

This shift did not happen abruptly in 2004, but was the result of an evolution that started with the first big headscarf controversy in 1989. Kuru explains that between 1989 and 2004 there had been a division over the dominant meaning of *laïcité* between the *Conseil d'Etat* and other activists such as the League of Education,[3] a few intellectuals, members of the Catholic Church (who were in favour of a '*laïcité plurielle*' (a plural *laïcité*) that would not be incompatible with diversity and religious freedom in the public realm), and another group comprised of leftist MPs, members of organizations such as the Freemasons and Freethinkers and intellectuals (who were fighting for a '*laïcité combative*' that would require the public sphere to be neutral) (Kuru, 2008: 8–9, 11–12). Kuru stresses that the headscarf debate led to the creation of an unprecedented coalition between the French Right and Left. This coalition, which started in the 1990s, became quite powerful as of 2002. After the French 2002 presidential elections, which saw a significant rise in the Far Right, the mainstream Right, headed at the time by President Chirac, started to actively support headscarf bans to appeal to this Far Right electorate opposed to immigration and Islam. In so doing, they aligned their position with that of the Left, which has been traditionally in favour of a '*laïcité combative*' (Kuru, 2008: 14). This new alliance has not only resulted in the passing of the March 2004 Law and in shaping other French policies towards Muslims, but has also triggered a shift in the jurisprudence of the *Conseil d'Etat* and other courts.

A brief sociological portrait of French Muslim activists

General overview

Because the French state considers that ethnic and religious characteristics are private, it does not keep statistics on citizens of immigrant origin. In the absence of official numbers, there is a wide divergence in the estimated number of Muslims living in France, which varies between approximately four and six million (Laurence and Vaisse, 2006: 17).[4] The level of religiousness of these individuals is also vague and subject to debate. Laurence and Vaisse indicate that a poll on religion in France, carried out between September 2003 and December 2004, revealed that 38 per cent of individuals who considered themselves to be Muslims declared that they prayed every day, compared with 13 per cent of Catholics (2006: 76).[5] Yet the same authors also stressed that French authorities have estimated that less than five per cent of Muslims attend mosques each Friday. This contrast probably illustrates the difficulty of quantifying the level of religiousness in the particular context of France, where no official statistics on these issues are produced and, more generally, in a world where individuals' perceptions and relations with faith are expressed in increasingly diverse and subjective ways.

This significant presence of Muslims on French soil is quite recent. Laurence and Vaisse (2006: 16) note that the most substantial wave of immigration can be traced to the end of the colonial wars of independence (1962), when Muslims from former colonies were recruited to work in French factories and other workplaces. Until the 1970s, these individuals were considered to be temporary workers, who would not be staying in France, and they came without their families. However, with the oil and economic crisis in 1973–74, the French government decided both to put an end to large-scale immigration and to facilitate family reunification. In other words, these years marked a shift in the sociological profile of the migrant community from a male dominated population to one consisting of nuclear and extended families settling in France (Laurence and Vaisse, 2006: 17). As of the late 1980s, and even more in the 1990s, many Muslims started to feel dissatisfied with the French state, as they were experiencing high levels of unemployment, poverty, and discrimination. As a result, several of them – particularly members of the second and third generations – opted for an orthodox practice of their religion in their quest for identity, turning to a more abstract and global form of Islam than the one of their parents, who had generally followed Islamic traditions marked by the customs of their countries of origin (Laurence and Vaisse, 2006: 80). This can explain, in part, why, as of the late 1980s, one notices a growing number of young French Muslim women wearing headscarves in the public realm, a practice that their mothers had rarely adopted.[6]

Nevertheless, one has to note that the number of girls wearing a headscarf on school grounds has been quite small in comparison to the overall number of Muslims in France. In the late 1980s, when the first headscarf affair erupted, a report estimated that around 2000 girls out of 300,000 female students were wearing it (Salton, 2007: 131). This number actually decreased in the 1990s, and it was reckoned that approximately 1254 girls were wearing it prior to the passing of the March 2004 Law (Laurence and Vaisse, 2006: 80).[7] The overall number of girls who were expelled from schools as a consequence of the law on religious symbols, was estimated to be around 50, while 533 were re-integrated after a phase of dialogue, where they accepted taking off their headscarf. French Muslim activists have emphasized that some of the other girls removed their headscarves before they went back to school in September 2004, while others, who were over 16 years old, dropped out of schools and others decided to finish their education abroad or attend private schools.[8] It is important to note that these numbers are not representative of the total number of women in France wearing a headscarf – this has not been systematically recorded.

Overview of Muslim activism and its paradigm shift

As mentioned, prior to the 1980s, the majority of Muslims had only the status of workers in France. Thus, they did not plan to stay in France, and this affected their claims, which were more about their wages and living conditions in facilities hosting workers than related to religious demands (Crisis Group International, 2006: 3). However, family reunification policies, as well as the reform of the association law in 1981 giving foreigners the right to organize themselves in associations, slowly changed the nature of these claims leading to the formulation of concrete religious requests (ibid. 4). The first Muslim associations were created at that time, with the principal aim of asking for religious places of worship in the suburbs. At the same time, a younger generation of Muslims was engaged in non-religious activism, which focused on demands related to social and cultural concerns. This activism was known as the *beur movement* and had as its central goal the fight against racism affecting Arabs in France.[9] For Césari (1998: 10), these two types of activism complemented each other. The first one, headed by an older generation, dealt with demands linked to the management of religious affairs, while the other focused on formulating non-religious claims.

This reality had changed by the end of the 1980s, when some young Muslims started to increasingly ground their activism in Islam – blurring, in so doing, the boundaries between religious demands and social and cultural ones (Césari, 1998: 10; Crisis Group International, 2006: 9). This reliance on a religious paradigm evolved throughout the 1990s as activists, while remaining influenced by their religiosity, began to stress at the same time their commitment to French citizenship and secularism, in particular when asking for greater religious freedom. In fact, many young activists started to present themselves as French citizens of Muslim faith. In a sense, this identification located itself in between the 1980s *beur movement,* which made no reference to religion, and the discourse of the late 1980s, which was highly influenced by a religious perspective.[10]

The experience of Saida Kada, a second-generation Muslim activist based in Lyon and her association, created in the mid-1990s,[11] is a good illustration of the discursive shift that took place throughout the 1990s.

> […] If you take my association, for instance, Engaged French and Muslim Women (FFME), you can trace neatly this evolution. At first it was purely communitarian. It wasn't intentional, but it was a reality […] Just our name [indicated this]: Union of Muslim Sisters in Lyon … Initially, we simply wanted to help girls wearing a headscarf. We thought that this was a problem internal to Muslims, even if we never thought to reduce our inquiry or identity to the headscarf. Rapidly teachers from all backgrounds came to offer their services […] We started to work on the question related to the lack of positive image from which Muslim women suffer. At the same time, we also realised that there was within them an internalization of a certain idea of the veil that did not help their personal development. We began to put in place circles of reflection that moved away from traditional themes related to what is 'licit and illicit' and what are the 'rights and duties' of a woman in Islam … We wanted to encourage a general debate around societal problems: *laïcité*, politics, globalisation,

> Europe, etc. At the same time, we wanted to encourage Muslim women to create an associative space that they could use as a stepping stone to develop actions that reflected their image of new French women of Muslim faith […] so that they could participate to the construction of society. It is thus to be coherent with our evolution that we had to change our name, and move on to 'Engaged French and Muslim Women.'
>
> (Kada, in Bouzar and Kada, 2003: 135–36)

A similar shift is noticeable in the rhetoric around the headscarf. Devout Muslims, who expressed themselves publicly on the first attempts to ban headscarves in the late 1980s, described the headscarf as being a religious prescription, yet in the mid-1990s the issue started to be presented in their discourses as an individual right that could be compatible with *laïcité* in the public realm. One can trace this change, for instance, in the discourse of the Union of the Islamic Organizations of France (UOIF), who closely followed the different headscarf crises starting in the late 1980s.[12] This marks, in my view, the beginning of a discursive battle, where religious organizations and individuals label specific interpretations of *laïcité* as unlawful and appropriate the concept into their own struggle:

> For us, '*laïque*' [secular] originally meant 'against god'. Against the religious. Then we discovered that this was not the case, but that *laïcité* had been put in place to allow pluralism: it was a framework that enabled all religions to live together, without one dominating the other […] The understanding of *laïcité* finally gave us hope again and calmed us.
>
> (Akim, in Bouzar and Kada, 2003: 130)

> [We are for] a neutral *laïcité*, which protects rights and laws, and not a *laïcité* that persecutes religious beliefs and philosophy.
>
> (Brèze, 1996)

Thus it became a concept with a strong legal canvas that could be used to defend one's religious freedom against more restrictive interpretations of the term. One grasps here, quite clearly, how *laïcité* is best understood as a hegemonic process setting, in France from the mid-1990s onwards, the broad framework for any type of public challenges on issues related to religious freedom and whose meaning, at the same time, remains subject to alteration.

A description of French Muslim activists

The rest of this chapter explores the public discourse of French Muslim activists regarding the March 2004 Law and the climate of restriction that has followed this law. Several of these activists, as mentioned, are women and consider themselves to be French citizens of Muslim faith. To embark on this investigation, this chapter draws on the written material produced by these activists on this subject (e.g. press releases, reports, written testimonies, newsletters), as well as on loosely structured interviews conducted in Paris and Lyon during the course of several field visits from 2008 to 2012.[13]

This chapter draws on the public discourse produced by members of the 15 March Committee. This committee, closely linked to the UOIF, was created in July 2004 to help students who would be facing exclusion once the law was implemented in schools in September 2004.[14] According to one of its founders, it provided support to around 95 per cent of the girls who were excluded from schools.[15] Over time it extended its mandate to provide legal support to victims of the law's extensions, and other religious discriminations. Most of its members are second or third generation Muslims. I also conducted interviews and analysed the material produced by activists working with the Collective Against Islamophobia in France (CCIF) created in 2003 in response to an increase in Islamophobic acts in French society. Most of their activities have focused after the March 2004 Law on fighting 'illegal' extensions of the law and denouncing new regulations, as well as providing legal support to victims. As of 2012, they had approximately 700 members and three permanent lawyers, and had won several cases against 'illegal' extensions of the law in national courts.[16] The organization is based in Paris, but has eight nodes in cities across France.[17] I met and analysed the documents produced by members of the former A School For All Collective (CEPT). This collective was created spontaneously in December 2003. It organized protests as well as events to discuss and think about the law and *laïcité* throughout the months prior to the passing of the law and just after it was voted in. The interesting aspect of this collective is that it has brought together, for the first time on a national scale, secular activists[18] and French Muslim activists, including members of French Muslim organizations, such as the Muslims' Collective of France (CMF),[19] Muslim Spirituality and Participation (PSM),[20] Muslim Students of France (EMF), and Young Muslims of France (JMF).[21] Many of these Muslim organizations have been influenced, to varying degrees, by the thoughts of the intellectual, Tariq Ramadan, who also participated in the collective. This collective was dissolved after the heated period of 2004. For many this was because it focused only on the law and not on wider discrimination concerns, leading to a quick loss of momentum. However, it spearheaded the creation of another group in 2004 – the Collective Feminists For Equality (CFPE) – which brings together approximately 30 Muslim and non-Muslim women (including known French feminists). The impulse that led to the creation of this collective was the need to reflect on and articulate a response to the connections made in dominant discourses between feminism, gender equality and *laïcité*, recalling that the secular Republic had traditionally not been in favour of female emancipation. This pushed the group to develop a common position on headscarf bans and on *laïcité*. It became, with time, a space to discuss, organise activities and produce material (press releases, newsletters, and so on) on issues ranging from gender equality to abortion. In fact, former members of the CEPT, as well as members of the CFPE, came together in 2008 to publish a book bringing together testimonies from the students and women wearing headscarves excluded from schools and other spaces (Chouder *et al.* 2008a). In 2011, several members of the CEPT and of the CFPE joined with the Mothers All Equal Collective (MTE) to denounce the exclusion of mothers wearing headscarves from partaking in school activities, as well as the limits put on nannies and day care providers to exercise their profession if they wear a headscarf. Members of the MTE include mothers who are fighting exclusions in their schools, as well as members of other organizations such as the CCIF, CFPE, New Anti-Capitalist Party (NPA), Green Party and so on.[22]

It is important to note that although most of the aforementioned collectives are formally located in Paris, their actions are decentralised and activists come from different agglomerations in France. Moreover, participation in these groups is fluid, as activists are often members of different collectives and groups, both at the national and local levels.

The March 2004 Law and the extensions of exclusions: sketching an argument

While French Muslim activists had started to position their argument within the boundaries of *laïcité* before the passing of the March 2004 Law, the debates leading to the law and the period afterwards offer a particularly insightful terrain to study their discourse. Indeed, the threat of a law and then the extensions of restrictions have been an invitation to sketch out a clear argument positioning themselves for a *laïcité* that would not restrict the wearing of headscarf in the public realm. In doing so, they have also been outlining the contours of what ought to be religiously acceptable. To that effect, even if there has been divisions in respect of the overall strategy to adopt (where, for instance, members of the 15 March Committee or the CCIF have opted for a more legal route, while others, like members of the CEPT and CFPE, have expressed a preference for protests and creating coalitions) there seems to have been a consensus regarding the fact that the interpretation of *laïcité* articulated from March 2004 onwards failed to follow the spirit of the 1905 Law, the jurisprudence produced by legal bodies such as the *Conseil d'Etat* and the HALDE, and was a source of discrimination affecting the rights of specific groups of French citizens. Thus, the 2004 Law is identified as the event opening a Pandora's Box of exclusions – 'The problem is that we should never have let the 15 March 2004 Law pass, since then we have seen a real drift' (activist, CCIF, Paris, 2012).

The 1905 Law

> Since the March 2004 Law forbidding access to public schools to Muslim students wearing the headscarf, exclusions have multiplied, affecting not only students but also the mothers of students who want to partake in school

> outings or participate in school meetings […] These measures follow the same logic of stigmatisation and exclusion, in a total break with the 1905 Law and the Ferry-Goblet laws on education.[23] We refuse this misappropriation of *laïcité*.
>
> (MTE, 2011)

> For several years, for the Left like the Right, *the principle of laïcité has become a Trojan Horse* to facilitate the passing of measures that have for their only objective the disappearance of Muslims from public space. *A misleading and denatured laïcité, who is laïc [secular] by name only*, since it does not respect the founding principles of the 1905 Law: the separation of church and state, the non-interference of the state in religions, the protection of freedom of conscience and freedom of religion of everyone, and equality of all citizens without religious distinctions.
>
> (CCIF, 2013 (original emphasis))

Recall our discussion at the end of Chapter 2 on Algerian resistance movements, headed by independent Ulemas, who were already using in their petitions and speeches the 1905 Law to ask for full separation between state and religion. Today, again, French Muslim activists are using this law as the basis of their understanding of the separation between religion and state. They recall that the 1905 Law ensures that the state ought to guarantee freedom of conscience, as well as remain neutral towards all religions in the Republic – this neutrality requirement is considered to be what makes the separation between religion and state possible, and allows for pluralism in the public realm.[24] In other words, activists also make reference in their argument to the languages of secularism. However, their meaning is influenced by their positionality.

For instance, the language of neutrality is understood here as a prerequisite for the state but not for citizens. It is based on this interpretation that concerns regarding the March 2004 Law have been expressed. Indeed, by systematically restricting religious expressions in the public realm, this law has been considered to favour one moral ethic over another – a moral ethic that favours atheist, non-practising individuals or individuals whose religion remains confined to their conscience, over believers who wish to express their faith in public. This is understood to be problematic since a neutral state should not favour one ethic over another.

> [Today] *Laïcité* is therefore diverted from its initial meaning so that it has become a tool for excluding believers in general, and Muslims in particular as soon as an element of their practice is visible […] The neutrality and the inclusiveness, which the idea of *laïcité* itself should enable in the common space, are being unfortunately translated more and more by censorship, a silence of all expressions of identity, spirituality and, tomorrow, choice.
>
> (CCIF, 2012: 8)

Moreover, it is argued that these restrictions have been made possible precisely because the state authorities have passed judgement on religious expressions – that is, they have considered the wearing of the headscarf and other head coverings as expressions of proselytism and symbolising values that are in contradiction with Republican precepts.

> Indeed, the principle of *laïcité* is a principle of political organization that obliges the state to abstain itself from intervening in religious affairs. Consequently, it should not declare what is part of the religious and what is not, attribute a meaning or a message to a religious sign, or even less so judge the legitimacy of a religious practice. This is the core meaning of the rule of separation of Church and state that comes from the 1905 Law.
> (CCIF, 2010: 17–18)[25]

Thus, in attributing a meaning to the wearing of head coverings the state is violating its neutrality requirement. Arguably, it is meddling in theology, by making statements regarding which religious expressions are compatible with the Republic and which are not. This is particularly problematic as it has been understood as depriving French Muslim women, identified as being the first and principal target of this exclusive interpretation of *laïcité*, of their freedom to choose and express their religious convictions.

Here, also, the language of neutrality, as in the discourses produced by state officials and politicians, is connected to the notion of personal autonomy. However, in this case it is because this requirement is supposed to limit state interference in the religious self, rather than allowing it, that subjects are able to fully enjoy their individual sovereignty. In this understanding, the wearing of the headscarf is therefore described as an individual freedom pertaining to the 'private' self.

> Let me make my own choices: today my choice is to wear jeans, a sweat-shirt, and a headscarf on my head. If you take this freedom of choice away, you oppress me and imprison me in a unique model of emancipation that I respect but that does suit me anymore.
> (Malika in Chouder *et al.* 2008a: 300)

Building on this notion of individual autonomy, the importance of putting the French situation back in context is highlighted – 'we were asking to speak about what we were leaving as French interlocutors, here and now' (activist, CFPE, 2008). Indeed, activists have deplored the fact that during debates around headscarf restrictions, commentators (e.g. journalists, politicians, intellectuals, and so on) have made parallels between the wearing of head-scarves in Pakistan, Afghanistan or Iran, and its wearing in France.[26] In so doing, they have overlooked the fact that the main difference between these countries and France is the importance given in the latter to the enlight-enment principles of non-imposition, individual sovereignty and freedom of choice – 'to wear a hijab in France, is not the same thing as to wear it in Pakistan' (activist, 15 March Committee, 2008). Activists have argued that it is precisely because these values are dear to them that they feel it is their responsibility as French citizens to question any type of outside imposition, including being forced to wear or not wear head coverings:

> It is not the veil as an essence that has to be challenged but rather it is its imposition […] to fight against the compulsory veil and the compulsory de-veiling, for the right to go to school bare-headed and for the right to cover oneself, is one and the same fight: to fight for the freedom of choice […] The 15 March 2004 Law needs to be revoked, and we need to fight against discriminations towards women wearing headscarves and to implement real public policies for girls who are forced to wear it – it is one and the same challenge.
>
> (Chouder *et al.* 2008b)

One therefore sees that a distinction is drawn between an autonomous choice to follow religious authority and dogmas, and an imposed form of authority from outside forces (whether it be a state, a community, and so on). It is the latter that has to be subject to serious state scrutiny and limitation, and which is considered to be incompatible with collective life. In other words, these concerns are pointing to the similarities between projects that are imposing the wearing of headscarves and those that are imposing the reverse. In both cases, this affects women who are not permitted to make their own decisions. In a sense, their interpretation of autonomy also questions the entrenched colonial perceptions that have informed the dichotomy between individual autonomy and subjugation to a religious authority, hinting at the fact that 'secular' subjects may be less autonomous than they are invited to believe.

> The defence of equality, freedom and dignity of women can only be supported by all. But the argument becomes problematic and unconvincing when its main line of defence and the lens through which these principles are analysed are limited to a Manichean way of reasoning, *to a unique model of being a women,* to which we try today to give a republican colour […] This totalitarian concept of being a woman is so strong that its followers are ready to sacrifice the freedom of some women for the freedom of others […].
>
> (CCIF, 2010: 16 (author's emphasis))

To sum up, we can see how the 1905 Law serves as a canvas enabling activists to anchor their own interpretation of the languages of *laïcité*, as well as why they argue that it provides them with a unique frame to live their faith and develop their own practice of collective life. Through this investigation, the reader also comes to realise how religious freedom is being conceived. It is understood as being deeply related to individual autonomy – an autonomy that, in this case, allows the possibility of making the decision to follow a life of heteronomy. Needless to say, this interpretation of religious freedom is a way to respond to concerns that have depicted the headscarf as a public symbol of women's patriarchal oppression, as symbolising 'civilizational "others"' (Kandiyoti, 1997: 117). Yet it is, at the same time, an example of how a religious ethic can be associated with liberal notions, underlining that more than one model of self-emancipation is possible.

The jurisprudence of the Conseil d'Etat and other courts

> The *Conseil d'Etat* has stressed that the wearing of the headscarf was, in itself, not contrary to the precept of *laïcité* if it did not entail proselytism or disturb public order. Over 14 years, this dialogue was fruitful since the number of conflicting cases was greatly reduced.
>
> (Ramadan, 2004)

> The *Conseil d'Etat*, the supreme body arbitrating administrative disputes, repeatedly stressed the limits of this freedom [i.e. religious freedom] which students could enjoy so long as it did not interfere with public order, health and morals. Muslim religious practices had found some kind of balance […]
>
> (15 March Committee, 2005:9)

A 'dangerous' amalgam between the users and providers of public services

Activists have also grounded their argument against the March 2004 Law and its extensions in the pre-2004 jurisprudence of the *Conseil d'Etat*. Doing so has allowed them to provide a more detailed interpretation of their understanding of the language of neutrality, including whether and when limits can be put by the state on the right to religious freedom.

As explained in Chapter 3, the language of neutrality has often been interpreted by policy makers as affecting providers of public services. Concretely, this has meant that, over the last decade, public servants have been required to refrain from wearing visible religious symbols. Activists have, occasionally, over the last decade, questioned this interpretation of neutrality. For instance, they have underlined that although public servants are required to be neutral when they work for the state, this neutrality should affect their actions rather than their religious expressions.

> [The neutrality of public servants] is a fundamental principal of the law of public function, an intrinsic part of the republican precept of *laïcité*. The neutrality of the public servant allows him to guarantee equality between users of public services […]. However, it is also possible to remain neutral with all users of a service while showing one's ethnic or religious belonging. *The essential thing is that this visibility of difference is not used to advantage or disadvantage a user.* Thus, the difference of the public servant can simply be part of his individual right to religious freedom in private and public, in his professional life and in his daily private life.
>
> (CCIF, 2009a: 78 (author's emphasis))

However, most of their argument has not focused on challenging the restrictions put on providers of public services. Since the jurisprudence of the *Conseil d'Etat* has been quite categorical in this interpretation of neutrality over the past three decades, it has been difficult to do so. On the other hand, activists have built on the distinction in the *Conseil d'Etat* jurisprudence between users and providers to articulate their narrative. Starting in its 1989 Opinion, and in its rulings until 2004, the *Conseil* had argued that students and other users, in opposition to providers of public services, were allowed to express their religiosity by wearing religious symbols, provided that their actions did not disturb public order. Activists have therefore referred to this interpretation to highlight the inconsistencies of the March 2004 Law.

> It is therefore first as users of public services that Muslim victims are targeted. More precisely, this user status is denied by providers of public service who make reference to 'laws' or regulations linked to the principle of *laïcité* to justify discriminatory practices [...] In these cases, the provider of public services is not respecting the neutrality principle in which relations between the Republic and its users are grounded in, and breaks away radically from the principle of equality and freedom of conscience.
> (CCIF, 2012: 15).

The jurisprudence of the *Conseil d'Etat* and of other courts has also been used to denounce the extensions of the neutrality principle to other users of public services.[27] For instance, with regards to the extension of the law to university students, activists have drawn on rulings of the *Conseil d'Etat* addressing precisely this issue:

> Indeed, in this judgement 'Achouch, El Massi Kannouh/University of Lille II' of July 26 1996, the Conseil d'Etat judged that as long as a [religious] sign is not an obstacle to good functioning of teaching activities, its wearing is not illegal.
> (CCIF and 15 March Committee, 2005)

Likewise with respect to the exclusion of mothers from partaking in school outings, activists have recalled the HALDE decision (HALDE, 2007a) that based its recommendations on a ruling of the *Conseil d'Etat* arguing that the requirement of neutrality affecting providers of public services should not be extended to users who partake in public services on a temporary or volunteer basis, as long as they do not engage in proselytising activities (CCIF, 2011). In other words, through their reference to selected pieces of jurisprudence they have underlined the illegality of all these extensions.

In this narrative, activists are not making a distinction between freedom of conscience and the freedom to express a belief – a distinction that has been central to the March 2004 Law – but one between a personal belief (which includes the public expression of this belief) and the actions of a believer. This distinction broadens the boundaries of one's personal sphere, as it understands religious expressions to be part of the private self and not subject, therefore, to state interference and scrutiny. On the other hand, the actions of believers, whether these are users or providers of public services, are considered to be 'public' acts and are therefore subject to scrutiny. In other words, while the discourse of *laïcité* is also used to delimit the access to public services, what determines this access is not the 'physical appearance' of individuals but rather whether their actions disturb the freedom of others (including through being engaged in proselytising activities). This distinction comes out quite clearly in a press release denouncing a judgement from the appeal court of Versailles in 2011 that sided with the decision of a private day care facility to lay off one of its employees because she wore a headscarf – 'The decision of the appeal court of Versailles reinforces the systematic exclusion of those *who have chosen to follow a belief. Without, at the same time, disturbing public order, or being engaged in proselytism*' (CCIF, 2011 (author's emphasis)). Needless to say, this interpretation affects what is religiously acceptable in the polis. In effect, activists, by grounding their argument in French case law, are not challenging the distinction between religion as a private belief and religion as a public action, where the former is frequently understood in dominant interpretations of secularism as being the 'proper'/'modern' interpretation of religion (see Danchin, 2011; Mahmood, 2009). They are, however, questioning the boundaries of what is considered to be a public action in a post-2004 climate.

Potential consequences of a shift in the jurisprudence

> For us the jurisprudence of the *Conseil d'Etat* was pertinent because it protected children. Yet there was a political shift within the *Conseil d'Etat*, where its members started to feel social pressures. They felt they had to fight communitarian feelings […]. The *Conseil d'Etat*'s judges started to consider themselves as messiahs.
>
> (activist, 15 March Committee, Lyon, 2008)

Grounding one's argument in the jurisprudence of the *Conseil d'Etat* and other courts seems to have become harder over the last couple of years. In effect, the *Conseil* has been embracing a vision of *laïcité* closer to the spirit of the March 2004 Law. This, as Lepinard suggests, is partly linked to the fact that this body has no power of judicial review over the March 2004 Law (2012: 18). It is unable, therefore, to challenge it. It is, at the same time, indicative of the influence of policy makers on the *Conseil* and its interpretation of *laïcité* (ibid.). In other words, the *Conseil* in several of its recent decisions seems to have accepted the idea that a sign in itself, worn in schools, can be a threat to *laïcité* and therefore subject to the neutrality requirement – siding, probably, with a political attempt to fix the meaning of *laïcité* at least on school grounds. This is clearly illustrated by the case of Ms X, who was suspended from school in September 2004 after wearing a bandana in her hair.[28] The *Conseil d'Etat* (2004b), making little distinction between a bandana and headscarf, ruled on the basis of the March 2004 Law that this prohibition was not illegal. It argued that even if doubt existed as to the reasons why the student was wearing it, the school by temporarily suspending her, as well as initiating a dialogue with her parents (to assess whether the bandana was worn for religious reasons or not), had interpreted the March 2004 Law in a satisfactory manner.[29] This trend seems to be also extending to other cases beyond the March 2004 Law. For instance, in 2008 the *Conseil* confirmed the decision to refuse French nationality to the wife of a French citizen because of a 'radical' practice of religion.[30] One of the reasons behind this judgement was based on the fact that the woman was wearing a *niqab*, which did not allow her, in the eyes of judges, to integrate into French society.[31] Members of the CCIF released a press statement on the issue strongly criticizing this decision. They considered that the court was ill equipped to judge on the 'radicalism' of a religious practice.

> With this decision, the *Conseil d'Etat* is creating a dangerous precedent with regards to the fundamental right to express freedom of religion. Indeed, the tendencies noted by the CCIF in the administration against women and men of Muslim faith, aimed at limiting the right to express their faith, will, from now on, be more numerous, and their perpetrators, invigorated by this decision, will give themselves the arbitrary permission to judge on the opportunity to give or not a right to a citizen of Muslim faith [...]
> (CCIF, 2008)

Thus, while the *Conseil d'Etat* would have in the past refrained from judging a religious practice in itself, this position has been changing. Similar trends are noticeable in decisions produced by the HALDE,[32] which considered, in two cases, the *niqab* to be in itself disturbing the values of the Republic, and have restricted its wearing in different spaces.[33] Despite this climate, activists continue to position themselves as the guardians of a *laïcité* ante. However, national jurisprudence seems to be slowly losing parts of its appeal as a basis for arguments for less state interference in an individual's subjectivity. As discussed in Chapter 6, this, in my opinion, partially sheds light on why activists have begun to more frequently utilise human rights treaties in their public discourse and to send complaints to international human rights bodies.

Seeking equality of treatment as French citizens

Fighting against 'special treatment'

By positioning themselves as citizens, activists have underlined that they are not asking for special treatment as a religious minority, but rather they are asking for the same rights as other citizens. The stress put on equality is, for many, significant in the light of French history, where Muslims have been subject to 'special treatment' throughout colonial times. Arguably, by emphasising that they are fully-fledged citizens, activists are making the point that Islam ought to be separated, like other religions, from state affairs. Several of them have noted that their faith should not be subject to overt state regulation, denouncing the intervention of their government in the CFCM or in the training of Imams.[34] Likewise, they question the fact that a body such as the HCI, in charge of dealing with integration questions that affect French residents of foreign origin, has been assigned a '*mission laïcité*'. They ask whether this means that questions related to *laïcité* apply only to immigrants or the children of immigrants.

> The fact that a '*laïcité* mission' was given to the HCI raises a question in respect of the misuse of this term […] Are we to understand that *laïcité* is only of concern for immigrants or children of immigrants? That only citizens of Muslim faith ought to respect *laïcité*?
>
> (CCIF, 2013)

Similar arguments have been brought to the forefront in respect of their own subjectivity. They have stressed that they should not be subject to a discriminative and partial implementation of *laïcité,* where the state ends up producing a judgement on their personal beliefs and not on that of other citizens – 'I would like to be perceived first as a French woman, and that the detail of my veil be perceived in a similar way as the cross of my friend' (Kada in Bouzar and Kada, 2004: 69).

Building on this, and as hinted at earlier in this chapter, the March 2004 Law has been understood as unravelling discrimination against, and 'special treatment' towards, particular beliefs. Activists point to the fact that this law targets minority religions which have religious prescriptions encouraging their followers to wear visible religious symbols:

> The final aim of promoting equality, when conveyed through a law which prohibits the expression of religious belonging, can paradoxically create injustice among citizens. Indeed, some religions are not touched by the prohibition of religious symbols since their dogmas do not have any prescriptions with regards to religious signs. However, others like Islam and Judaism give a philosophical, spiritual, psychological and social meaning to the wearing of the veil or the kippa. *This is why particular religions and therefore particular citizens can be the target of a law even though in form it appears general and impersonal.*
>
> (CCIF, 2009a: 80 (author's emphasis))

This is understood as infringing upon the principle of equality between all citizens, as some citizens become subject to greater state intervention in their beliefs than others.

To further explain this discriminative tendency, a parallel has been drawn with the situation in Quebec (Canada), where the fact that a national law might favour the majority or dominant culture has been taken into consideration by policy makers. In other words, laws, in this context, are not taken as being de facto 'neutral or universal', and accommodations are devised to make up for potential inequalities. This model is thought to anticipate the possibility that citizens can have multiple identities, whereas the French model fails to do so.

> […] In France, legislative ethnocentrism is so strong that legal precepts are not subject to adaptation […]. However, in Quebec accommodations are considered to be necessary because it is recognized and agreed that all laws and norms currently in force in Quebec society do not necessarily originate from 'neutral or universal' principles but can, on the contrary, be at the service of the majority of citizens.
>
> (CCIF, 2009a: 80)

A similar argument is developed with regards to extensions of the 2004 Law which confirm the large-scale discriminations against a specific group of citizens, defined in terms of their religiosity and gender.

> It seems that civil and political rights, social, economic and cultural rights embedded in the rule of law are not accessible, in an equal manner, to all citizens […] *Within one same nation, this deprives Muslims, not only of the recognition of a secondary identity as 'user of public service, student, employee, consumer', but also disinherits them of a primordial identity, that is of being citizens of a state based on the rule of law.*
>
> (CCIF, 2009b: 86 (author's emphasis))

> We refuse this war and the exclusive logic that identifies women wearing a headscarf as plague victims, that tends to disqualify them in the eyes of their own children, and that sends them this implicit message: 'stay in your kitchens!' […] *Because it is once again Muslims, and once again women, who are discriminated against; we will, during the coming months, women and men, with or without a headscarf, stand together to defend an elementary right: the right for a woman wearing a headscarf to live, work, and be engaged as much as she wants in the schooling of her children, to the same extent as any other parent.*
>
> (MTE, 2011 (original emphasis))

The reader becomes aware, here, that a central demand of activists is that their expression of religious belief be considered like any other type of individual trait and not used to define their identity or their capacity or incapacity to be fully-fledged citizens. This argument is interesting in several respects. First, it points once again to the fact that the interpretation of *laïcité* conveyed by headscarf bans mediates access to 'universal' citizenship in function of affiliations (Yuval-Davis and Werbner, 1999). In so doing, activists are questioning the fact that the requirement of neutrality leads to equality for all in general, and gender equality in particular. They are highlighting that the ethnocentric dimension of this language favours individuals who belong to the 'dominant culture'. They are also showing how, in this process, the bodies of devout Muslim women are used to reinstate boundaries between public and domestic spheres. One could argue that they are, in a similar way to the French feminists at the beginning of the last century who were using inconsistencies in the notion of citizenship to ground their claims (Pateman 1989), (re)appropriating the 'universal' character of *laïcité* to ask for their full inclusion in the polis. In fact, one member of the CFPE underlined how their struggle has been inspired by the accounts of members who belonged to an older generation of French feminists.

> The fact that these historical feminists share with us parts of their lives is fantastic because they tell us that they have lived the same things […] and we arrive behind them, in our thirties, and we will go through similar events but because they shared things with us we are not starting from zero like they did.
>
> (activist, CFPE and MTE, Paris, 2008)

Protecting 'universal' values as citizens: attempts to put a vision into practice?

While French Muslim activists are asking for their full citizenship rights, they stress, at the same time, that they consider that it is part of their civic responsibility to denounce violations of Republican values. As discussed, this is noticeable in their criticisms of the March 2004 Law and its extensions. Some argue that their motivation to do so lies less in receiving gains for the Muslim 'community', and more in ensuring that the universal values of the Republic are protected and continue to flourish.

> The aim of the CCIF is not to promote the particular fight against Islamophobia to the rank of a national priority […]. Its emergence puts itself within the intransigent and undifferentiated fight against all forms of racism, contributing to reinforcing the values of Humanism.
>
> (CCIF, 2009b: 9)

In other words, they are suggesting that different personal ethics should not infringe on the ability to believe and ensure the protection of a common societal project. Attempts to put this vision into practice first unfolded through the creation of the CEPT and the CFPE in 2004, and then again in 2012 with the creation of the MTE, where, in all these instances, activists from different walks of life have come together to promote an inclusive understanding of *laïcité* based on the possibility of coexistence.[35] This was well spelled out by Tariq Ramadan, member of the CEPT, in his call for mobilisation against the March 2004 Law:

> The terms of the engagement have to be clear nevertheless. To oppose the law against the headscarf, for instance, does not have to mean that we adhere to the principle of this prescription. To acknowledge that the other has the right to live freely accordingly to his convictions does not mean to share these convictions. As such, many women and men, believers, agnostics, atheists, feminists strictly oppose the law against religious signs, the exclusion and racism, but do not share the choice of Muslim women who decide to veil [...]. The strength of the resistance movement will reside in the acceptance of these divergences, *while at the same time creating an awareness that a great number of values and principles are common and that these consolidate collaboration in the engagement.*
>
> (2004 (author's emphasis))

These attempts to bring together different types of individuals and create coalitions beyond one's community find some echo, as the reader will come to realise, in the Turkish context. However, contrary to the latter case where some of these have had limited success, in France similar calls seem to have failed to create standing and/or large coalitions,[36] or even greater societal awareness of the exclusive character of a post-2004 *laïcité*. This is partly due to the fact that, in France, Muslims are a minority who are very much divided and have limited economic power.[37] Moreover, the political climate of both countries is quite different. France has not gone through a recent process of political liberalisation like its Turkish counterpart, in which a variety of groups have been able to identify with a common project based around demands for greater individual freedom.

Notwithstanding the fact that collaborative work has been rather limited, what remains relevant is that the March 2004 Law and its exclusions have led activists to sketch out clearly their vision of *laïcité,* and how it is related to their understanding of citizenship. Similarly to the dominant interpretation of *laïcité,* they also imagine it as a space enabling collective life. Yet, what makes this space unique is that rather than requiring a certain uniformity between all subjectivities, one of its common values is respect for individual differences. They are pointing to the fact that in order for collective life to aspire to its 'universal' character, it needs to be grounded in a secular ethic where equality is not based on an arbitrary understanding of 'sameness', but on a respect for coexistence. This, consequently, challenges the distinction between 'private' and 'public' realms based on the exclusion of differences in the latter. Thus, through their discourse and activism, French devout activists are not only involved in a (re)conceptualisation and, perhaps, even a democratisation of *laïcité*, but are also pushing for a redefinition of the terms of access to full citizenship rights.[38]

> *Laïcité* has to guarantee the *vivre ensemble* [i.e. collective life] in the respect of differences, without exclusion, attack or discrimination, to ensure equality between human beings.
>
> (Nadjia in Chouder *et al.* 2008a: 149)

Conclusion

This chapter has captured aspects of the hegemonic character of *laïcité*. Not only has it become an important part of the discourse of activists, who to aspire to have a public voice need to refer to its languages, but it is also being altered. Activists have, in other words, used the tensions and shifts within dominant interpretations of these languages to challenge the 15 March 2004 Law and its extensions, and sketch out their understanding of *laïcité*. In this process, one realises that the space for challenges remains restricted. The struggle seems, indeed, to locate itself within the legal canvas already developed throughout French history. In grounding their argument in the founding laws of the Republic and in the jurisprudence produced by the courts, they not only stress their knowledge of French laws, but also that they consider that it is their responsibility as citizens to protect and defend these values. However, as argued, this reliance on national jurisprudence comes with its own sets of paradoxes and limits. This becomes particularly evident in a context where national laws and court decisions have started to embrace a post-2004 understanding of *laïcité*. It is possible that this shift is narrowing substantially the space available for challenges, leaving activists with no option other than to conform to the dominant rules in the public realm or to stay in a shrinking private realm.

Over the past decade, activists have developed a narrative in which the post-2004 climate is identified as marking a clear break with the 'true' and 'historical' meaning of *laïcité*. In doing so, they have emphasised that by imposing a neutrality requirement on both users and providers of public services, the March 2004 Law has strongly restrained the individual freedom to express one's faith, which was protected by the 1905 Law. For them, therefore, neutrality remains a core concept of *laïcité*, but this ought to affect the state and not individuals. The March 2004 Law and its extensions deny this understanding, since by imposing a neutrality requirement on users it invites state authorities to directly judge religious dogmas and their expressions. This leads the state to scrutinise the behaviour of a particular set of citizens and contradicts, in turn, the principle of equality. Accordingly, activists highlight how this interpretation of *laïcité* limits devout Muslim women's access to citizenship. In so doing, they not only underscore the particularities of 'universal' citizenship, but also the fact that the languages of *laïcité,* including gender equality, can be used to discipline women's bodies and practices – bearing similarities with the patriarchal discourses these languages often denounce.

As discussed, in a similar way to the dominant interpretations of the term, activists understand *laïcité* as not only providing a legal basis for the separation of religion and state, but also as producing a framework for collective life.

> To think of *laïcité* in terms of laws and structures, is to forget that it is also and mainly built on a particular idea of citizenship and on the organization of the social: equality, the non-acceptance of discrimination and racism, access to education, to employment, to housing, opposing an economic and social communitarianism are the many principles and values that give sense and orientation to the legal frame of *laïcité*.
>
> (Ramadan, 2004)

> One can be secular and Muslim. Of course, this blurs all the categories. But if we conceive of *laïcité* as a tool to manage diversity, a tool that does not favour one religion and that is not against religion, one can be both secular and Muslim.
>
> (activist, MTE and CFPE, 2012)

This collective life is imagined, here, as enabling the coexistence of multiple identities in the public realm. This understanding remains, as seen, very much influenced by liberal values. Although individual belief is considered to be one identity among many others, this identity along with its expressions are described as private and sovereign choices. The distinction made by activists between private expressions of faith and public behaviour is particularly noteworthy. Following the lines of the pre-2004 French jurisprudence, actions that impose an ethic or disturb the rights of others are condemned. In others words, while symbols of personal ethics can be allowed in the public realm, these should not preclude the ability of a believer to respect individual differences. The state is therefore not deprived in this interpretation of its intervening function – on the contrary, it is asked to exercise this function when citizens' actions effectively interfere with the principles of coexistence and respect for difference.

As one may have noticed, it is important to keep in mind that in this understanding the discursive power of *laïcité* continues to shape the boundaries of the religiously acceptable, as well as set the rules for citizenship. For instance, because beliefs are described as personal and sovereign choices, those that are imposed by outside forces are understood to be incompatible with *laïcité*. In a similar vein, although *laïcité* is not considered to be incompatible with individual expressions of faith, it condemns practices, such as proselytism, that are understood as not respecting coexistence and plurality in the public realm. Therefore, this interpretation also ends up interfering with and shaping religious dogmas. With regard to citizenship, by making respect for difference a core principle of *laïcité*, one could easily foresee that individuals who are identified as not respecting this precept would be excluded from being able to partake in public spaces.

Notes

1 The term *laïcité* ante is used to refer to the legal framework defining *laïcité* prior to the March 2004 Law.

2 The *Conseil d'Etat* expressed this view in its 1989 Opinion. It served as a guiding principle for judges and headmasters until 2004.

3 The league is a significant union of educators that has around 2,000,000 members. For more information see Kuru, 2008: 8.

4 Since there are no official figures on the total number of Muslims in France, approximate numbers are often used for political purposes to increase or decrease the potential growth and threat of Islam in France. Laurence and Vaisse estimate that there may be around five million Muslims (roughly 8 per cent) out of a total population of 61 million (these figures do not include France's overseas territories), and that half of these Muslims are French citizens while the other half are residents. For more information see Laurence and Vaisse, 2006: 1, 17.

5 This poll was conducted by the statistical French institute CSA. For a more detailed reading of these findings see Laurence and Vaisse, 2006: 76.

6 This factor is often explained in terms of identity politics. Several scholars have looked into these reasons and have also written more broadly on individuals of Muslim faith in contemporary France (e.g. Laurence and Vaisse, 2006; Bouzar, 2001; Césari, 1994; Kepel, 1987; Ternisien, 2002; Gaspard and Khosrokhavar, 1995).

7 Likewise, while the French state passed a law in 2010 to ban the *burqa* and *niqab*, the number of women wearing these remained quite low, estimated to be between 200 and 2000. Given these quite small figures, debates over the headscarf are perhaps best understood as being representative of a symbolic threat rather than a tangible one.

8 No official or definitive figures exist for these options. However, activists have estimated that around 100 girls dropped out of school because they were 16 years or more, 70 decided to study abroad or in private schools, 26 decided to pursue their studies by correspondence, and 12 students were accepted with a 'discrete' religious sign (for a detailed list of those figures see 15 March Committee, 2005; CCIF and 15 March Committee, 2005). Where girls had the means to opt for the private school option, some went to Catholic schools that had not implemented the ban and others to new Muslim schools.

9 It is important to note here that their focus was explicitly on Arabs and not Muslims. For more information on the *beur movement* see Césari, 1998: 55–67

10 For a discussion of this shift, see Crisis Group International, 2006: 11–12.

11 Her association, Engaged French and Muslim Women, was closed in 2004 and was replaced by the 15 March Committee.

12 The UOIF was founded in 1983 as a 'challenge to the monopoly of the Great Mosque of Paris' (Laurence and Vaisse, 2006: 104). Caiero describes the organization as the 'most dynamic organization at the grassroots level' (2005: 73) in France and it gathered around 200 associations. It has often been depicted in the French media as preaching an orthodox understanding of Islam and was considered to have links with the Muslim Brotherhood. The UOIF has tried over the last two decades to counter this perception, positioning itself as the sole group truly representing Islam of France. For more information see Laurence and Vaisse, 2006: 104–8. With respect to the headscarf issue, Darif (2004) discusses how the UOIF leadership considered its wearing to be a religious requirement in the 1980s. This changes as of the mid-1990s, when the issue starts to be framed as inconsistent with *laïcité*. This shift is visible in the annual speeches of the President of the UOIF (see, for instance, Brèze, 1996).

13 With regard to the selection of information for the analysis, it is important to note that I do not focus on members of the *Conseil Francais du Culte Musulman*

(CFCM), the body that was put in place to 'represent' French Muslims in France in 2003 (for more information on this body see Laurence and Vaisse, 2006: Chapter 5). This is because while members of the CFCM did publicly position themselves against the 2004 Law before its passing, since finding themselves in a dynamic of representativity with the French state they have refrained from participating in protests or condemning the law once it was passed. Even the UOIF, who had been the most vocal member of the CFCM on this issue and had been following headscarf affairs since their beginning, did not instigate protests or directly criticize the law. Rather, its leaders ended up supporting the creation of an offspring organization, the '15 March Committee', to which they delegated the task of managing schools and other types of exclusion (Brèze, 2007). Studying the public discourse of the leadership of the CFCM on the March 2004 Law and its extensions would therefore have limited substantially our analysis, and our understanding, of how *laïcité* is being conceived.

14 The 15 March Committee is partly funded by the UOIF, but has also been seeking other sources of funding (15 March Committee, 2005).

15 This support included legal, psychological and educational help (activist, 15 March Committee, 2008).

16 Some of those cases are discussed in Chapter 6.

17 For more information on its membership and nodes see: http://www.islamophobie.net/le-ccif-cest-quoi (accessed 5 November 2013).

18 Participants included, for instance, Monique Crinon and Christine Delphy, two well known French feminists.

19 The CMF was created in the late 1990s. It is a collective made up principally of second and third generation Muslims. Its aim is to serve as a national platform that regroups local Muslim groups, and fosters among French youth both spiritual and citizen engagement.

20 The organization PSM was created in late 2000. Some of its members whom I interviewed, argue that the frontiers between them and the CMF are permeable, but that they mainly focus on spirituality.

21 EMF and JMF are two youth organizations created by the UOIF. Both of these groups joined the CEPT at its beginning, but dropped out once the law was passed. My interviewees argued that one of the reasons for this was that their participation in the CEPT had gone against the guidelines of their leadership, and that they were subject to strong pressure to leave once the law was passed, as the UOIF wanted to send the message that even if it did not agree with the law it would respect it.

22 For a non-inclusive list of members of the collective see: https://sites.google.com/site/mamanstoutesegalestest/participez/signez-la-petition (accessed 5 November 2013).

23 The Ferry-Goblet laws are laws that were passed between 1881 and 1886 rendering French education free, compulsory and secular.

24 The 1905 Law is explained in greater detail in Chapter 2, note 1. For a full reading of the law see Conseil d'Etat, 2004c: 258–60 and 405–15.

25 This statement is a comment on the 2010 law banning the *niqab* and *burqa*, and the debates that preceded it, in which many government officials and politicians assigned a meaning to both of these head coverings.

26 It is interesting to note that the debates prior to the passing of the 2004 Law coincided with the launch of a book entitled *Bas les voiles* ('Taking off the veils') (Djavann, 2003) written by an Iranian woman, who emigrated to France and was sharing her experience of oppression in Iran. This testimony was referred to in many of the French public debates, as proof of the oppression conveyed by the headscarf – making, therefore, little distinction between the French and Iranian contexts.

27 For a discussion of these extensions see Chapter 3.

28 For more information see Conseil d'Etat, 2004b.

29 Two other court rulings confirmed this shift of position by legal bodies. The case *Union Francaise Pour la Cohésion Nationale v. Ministère de l'Education* (2004a) looked into the legality of the *Circulaire Fillon* (Ministry of National Education, 2004) put in place to implement the March 2004 Law. The *Conseil d'Etat* concluded, in the autumn of 2004, that the directive was not illegal since it simply confirmed the 2004 Law, and gave explicit details on how to apply it to head-teachers and teachers. Moreover, it highlighted that in light of preserving the particular secular context of French schools, it was not in violation of article 9 of the ECHR or of article 18 of the ICCPR (articles protecting religious freedom). Another case concerning a ruling of the Paris Administrative Appeal Court is also relevant. Indeed this court, in the Ranjit Singh decision (Cour Administrative de Paris, 2005), confirmed the expulsion from school of a Sikh boy wearing a turban. What is important is that the court stressed that although the turban worn by the student was smaller than a traditional one, and that it was of a sobre colour, it could not be considered to be a discreet sign. It also underlined that although the intentions of the boy were not of a proselytizing nature, by wearing it conspicuously and refusing to take it off he violated the March 2004 Law. Therefore, although his actions were not aimed at disturbing public order, his physical appearance did.

30 For more information see Conseil d'Etat, 2008.

31 It is important to note that it is the first time that such a judgement was given in France. As Le Bars emphasizes (2008), French citizenship had until then been refused to people who had spoken publicly in favour of a 'radical' vision of Islam, but not because someone was considered to 'radically' practise a religion.

32 Despite these trends, the HALDE still produced important decisions which activists have used, including the aforementioned 2007 one supporting the participation of mothers in school outings (2007a). Yet, these were not legally binding. Moreover, this body lost most of its power when it was absorbed, in 2011, by the *Defenseur des Droits.*

33 The HALDE considered that the fact of asking a mother to take off her *niqab* in a hospital when accompanying her child for surgery (HALDE, 2007b), and a student to do the same to attend language classes for immigrants (HALDE, 2008) was not a violation of the right to religious freedom. The *Conseil Constitutionel* is another legal body that has started to give legal weight to a post-2004 reading of *laïcité*. Indeed, this body that gives advice on pieces of legislations when consulted by the head of state, was seized before the passing of the 2010 law banning the *niqab* and *burqa*. In its opinion it 'adhered to the rationale put forth by the legislature that the wearing of the full veil "ignored the minimal requirements of life in a shared society"' (Lepinard, 2012: 19).

34 Activists are referring to attempts by the French state, as discussed in Chapter 2, to interfere, to different extents, in the organization of Islam. This discourse is predominant amongst second and third generation activists, who question different aspects of the institutionalisation process of Islam in France and the concessions made by leaders of big federations, such as the UOIF, in that process.

35 It is important to stress that while prior to 2004 some individuals were defending a vision of *laïcité* consistent with French diversity, alliances around this topic between religious and non-religious activists were not frequent.

36 As mentioned in the first part of the chapter, the CEPT was dissolved soon after the passing of the March 2004 Law. Moreover, although the CFPE is an interesting initiative, it has a quite limited number of members and confines its membership to women. Finally, there are also divisions among French activists with regard to how claims are made, as some prefer a legal approach while others favour a coalition/protest based one.

37 Economic power plays an important role, as it limits, for instance, the access to mainstream media, who can relay concerns beyond a particular circle (in contrast, the Turkish devout bourgeoisie owns newspapers (e.g. Zaman) and TV channels, offering a platform to a variety of intellectuals to intervene in public debates). This consequently puts significant constraints on the ability of French Muslim activists to be heard publicly.

38 Salih notes that Italian Muslim activists are likewise involved in a reconceptualization of citizenship (2009).

5 Turkish devout activists

Reconfiguring *laiklik* with human rights

> I don't need to tell people why I cover my head – the secular law says that my body is private. The state should not discuss whether the headscarf is in the Koran or not – because the state is secular it should not make religious judgements.
>
> (activist, AKDER, Istanbul, 2008)

In this chapter I explore how Turkish *laiklik* has been refashioned by Muslim religious activists.[1] In this endeavour, I discuss how they have been using, over the last decade, a rights-based discourse to propose an alternative understanding of *laiklik* to the one implemented by the Turkish state and Kemalist elites – an understanding that seeks to offer space for the subjective expressions of their faith. As in other chapters, headscarf bans are used as a window to investigate this understanding.

This refashioning, in a similar fashion to the one undertaken by French activists, allows the reader to understand that claims for greater religious freedom are not necessarily based outside the frame of *laiklik*, but can be located within its hegemonic frame. To do so, activists, here again, (re) appropriate concepts that are often thought to be the product of the Enlightenment and of a liberal secular era in explaining the terms of their relationship to their creed. Unlike their French counterparts, however, Turkish religious rights activists have not based their public claims on national jurisprudence, but rather on international human rights law. The use of this discourse allows them to use, nevertheless, the same languages of secularism, and to propose an understanding of *laiklik* and religion dominated by notions of individual choice, equality and autonomy.

Because activists have been using a human rights discourse, this chapter explores aspects of the relationship between Islam and human rights. Rather than embarking on the normative task of assessing the compatibility of these two paradigms, my aim, in line with other studies (e.g. Osanloo, 2009), is to draw attention to the importance of analysing, on the ground (re)appropriations of human rights. This is done, in this case, by studying how religious rights activists have been using a rights-based discourse to frame their claims to wear the headscarf, and how this endeavour has enabled them to create bonds with, in some cases, improbable actors. Studying this practical use of human rights allows an analysis of why and how this discourse is used by religious activists. It also sheds some light on how rights can be invested with context-specific meanings – in other words, how 'universal' rights can carry particular meanings.

This chapter starts by analysing the discursive shift that has been happening in Turkey among devout Muslims. This first part allows me to write about the current discourse of religious rights activists in a broader context, affecting Turkish society as a whole. Indeed, because of the economic and political liberalisation undergone by Turkey over the last decades, individuals have been challenging the terms of the secular settlement established by Kemalists, as well as the place of religion in that settlement. Yet, to do so, many have been locating their claims within discourses of liberalism, democracy and individual freedom. In other words, unlike France, this refashioning of the secular settlement has been part of a wider societal struggle. The second part of this chapter explores in detail why and how activists have been using a rights-based discourse to challenge state secular scripts. This is done by analysing their discourse with regard to three key rights that are perceived as being infringed by bans on the headscarf – religious freedom, gender equality and non-discrimination.

Setting the context: a discursive shift

The pre-1997 period: the growth of Islamic elites and political parties

Since the 1980s, Islamic idioms, elites and intellectuals have become more prominent in the Turkish public scene. This is, in part, a consequence of the Turkish-Islamic Synthesis programme adopted by the Turkish state after the 1980 military coup. During this period, the state tried to reinforce the role of Islam in society, hoping that it would serve as a kind of societal glue. Although this was heavily controlled by the state, as it coincided with a time of greater democratisation, economic liberalisation and rural migration to cities (1983–93),[2] it had a significant impact on the development of Islamic thinking, politics, culture, and economy. Yavuz (2003: 122) argues that the printed word played a particularly important role in this process, not only in facilitating the spread of Islamic ideas, but also in allowing for the expression of different views on Islam, challenging both the discursive authority of the state and the Ulemas.

This climate led to the development of an important support base for the Islamic party of the time: the Welfare Party (Yavuz, 2003: 238).[3] Although Islamist parties had existed in Turkey since the 1970s, the Welfare Party received the greatest popular support, coming out first in the 1995 general elections with 21 per cent of the votes. This political party was led by

Necmettin Erbakan who had led the previous Islamic parties, and who was also the head of the 'National View' movement created in the 1970s, bringing together Islamic intellectuals and serving as an ideological anchor to those parties, including the Welfare Party (Dağı, 2004: 136). These intellectuals were, at that time, critical of Turkey's relationship with the West and its 'westernization' reforms, arguing that they had excluded Islam from having any political, social or intellectual role in society.

> The Islamists of the 1980s believed in the possibility of re-forming an Islamic way of life and thought that would eliminate the ills of modernity. The writings of the young Islamists conceived of Islam as an ahistorical social theory with a claim for reordering life in modern times, rather than merely a religion derived from the revelation of God […] Their rejection of modern concepts and ideas was total; the latter had to be criticized, falsified and rejected in favour of an Islamic alternative.
>
> (Dağı, 2004: 138)

They believed that Islam had to play a crucial role in organizing all aspects of life, including politics, culture, economics and even knowledge, and argued that 'western' concepts such as modernity, democracy or human rights had to be replaced by an alternative terminology grounded in Islam.

The Welfare Party based its discourse and policies on several of these ideas. For instance, it voiced a clear antagonism against the West, and the westernizing secular state, which was described as undermining Turkey's 'true identity' (Çınar, 2005: 12). In this vein, it positioned itself clearly against Turkey's accession to the EU – calling the EU a 'Christian Club' (Daği, 2005: 31). The Welfare Party attempted, also, to rewrite modern Turkish history emphasising the importance of the Ottoman Empire, which had been undermined in the accounts of Turkish history by the Kemalist regime (Çınar, 2005: 127). Thus, this political party exemplified the fact that Islam was no longer fully under state control, and rather was used as an ideological and political contender to the Kemalist project.

The 1997 'soft' coup: a turning point

Secular elites tried to stop these attempts to Islamize state institutions and establish an alternative societal ethic. One of their responses came with the soft coup of 28 February 1997. As discussed, this coup was supported by the military, part of civil society, the judiciary and the bureaucracy and led to an intense repression of Islam in the public realm. Among other things, the coup was an opportunity to reinforce and extend strict state management of religious subjectivities, in particular devout women's subjectivities. This campaign led, finally, to the closure of the Welfare Party which was accused of having become the centre of anti-secularist activities. The Constitutional Court considered that statements by the Party – such as 'the headscarf must be free in universities' or promoting 'the right to choose your own legal system, including sharia' – were proofs of its anti-secular aims (Yavuz, 2003: 247).

The 1997 soft coup has often been considered to be the central turning point in explaining the change of discursive paradigm that took place among Islamic elites. It seemed that through this harsh repression many Islamists became aware of the need to adopt a broader language, hoping that this would enable them to create wider coalitions in Turkey and abroad. Commenting on this shift, Dağı (2004: 140) makes a useful distinction between social and political Islam arguing that Islamists had realised that their political use of Islam had exposed Islam's social bases, such as its educational, commercial and civil society networks, to threats and repressions – undermining not only the political, but also the social expression of Islam. From then onwards, many decided to prioritize the social role of Islam over its political one.

This shift in strategy was first exemplified by the creation of the Virtue Party in 1998, the successor to the Welfare Party, led by Recai Kutan, who replaced Erbakan who was banned from politics for five years. This new political party did not position itself against the West, rather it began to use a discourse promoting values such as democracy, pluralism, and human rights. In a similar line, it is noteworthy that members of this party brought the closure case against the Welfare Party to the ECtHR, a move which showed a certain trust in the western justice system or at least an acknowledgement of that system (Dağı, 2004: 28). Yet, for Çınar (2005: 21) the nuances of these changes need to be recognised. Although they allowed the Virtue Party to adapt to a new political climate, they did not mark a decisive shift in its ideology, as it kept the same structure, cadres, and ideological tenets as the Welfare Party.

This discursive change became more strident when the Virtue Party divided into two after its closure by the Constitutional Court in June 2001.[4] The more conservative constituency regrouped around the leadership of Erbakan, who created the Felicity Party, while the more reform-minded found a leader in Tayyip Erdoğan, a former member of the Welfare Party and mayor of Istanbul from 1994–98, who created the AK Party. This party quickly became popular and won the November 2002 election with 34 per cent of the votes. According to Dağı (2008) and others (Gümüşçü, 2010; Yavuz, 2003), one of the reasons for its success and 'moderation' could be found in the support it received from a growing Anatolian conservative bourgeoisie. Because this bourgeoisie relied on a liberal and pro-western, market-oriented economy, it could not afford to be at the same time anti-western and anti-liberal. In other words, they found in the AK Party a middle way, where the Party still had conservative values but at the same time supported capitalism and economic liberalism.[5]

The AK party and many Islamist intellectuals have therefore been embracing a different language than the one used throughout the 1980s and 1990s. During its first mandate, the AK Party became, for instance, a strong defender of the EU integration process using notions of pluralism, democracy, freedom, rule of law, and human rights to position itself against Kemalist elites (Dağı, 2004: 139).[6] Thus, the AK Party renounced using a religious discourse publicly, replacing it with one that resonates with audiences beyond religious circles. This discursive shift also led the AK Party to frame its claims for greater religious freedom within a wider redefinition of *laiklik*. As Kuru (2006) and Grigoriadis (2009) have emphasised, some of its MPs have cautiously attempted to propose an alternative definition siding with a more Anglo-Saxon understanding of the term. 'Banning is a method the French use. We, the Turks, prefer the Anglo-Saxon interpretation of secularism' (Erdoğan cited in Today Zaman, 2008). Yet, as discussed in Chapter 3, their ability (and willingness) to openly reshape *laiklik*, and address concerns around headscarf bans, has remained limited. Rather, doing so has been narrated as a potential threat the AK Party's survival.

Religious rights activists: a window into understanding how *laiklik* can be refashioned

The main focus of this chapter is not on AK Party parliamentarians. Indeed, this discursive shift has touched many devout Muslims and to understand all of its facets it is important to go beyond the AK Party, especially given its reluctance to tackle concerns around headscarf bans. Thus, this chapter looks at the religious activists who have been actively using a human rights discourse and human rights international mechanisms to challenge state secular scripts and ask for greater religious freedom. To conduct this analysis, I interviewed and analysed the written works (e.g. reports, press releases, and so on) of religious rights activists who have been working or collaborating with religious rights groups,[7] or who have brought individual cases to the ECtHR.[8]

Some of these activists are members of the Organization of Human Rights and Solidarity of the Oppressed People (MAZLUMDER), which was founded in 1991 with the aim of protecting and improving human rights inside and outside Turkey, and has branches throughout Turkey. It was created by a group of primarily Sunni conservative elites, who wanted to cater to the human rights needs of the conservative/religious part of society (until then most human rights organizations were of a leftist tendency). Although this religious facet has brought them to work on issues of religious freedom (e.g. headscarf bans), they have also been working on a variety of other issues, such as the fight against torture, freedom of expression, the right to life, violations of Kurdish rights and so on.[9] Other activists have been collaborating with the Women Rights Organization Against Discrimination (AKDER) based in Istanbul and the Capital Women's Platform based in Ankara. AKDER was created in 1999 in reaction to the February 1997 coup by students and professional women who were unable to continue studying or working after the coup. It considers itself to be a human rights association, independent of any political party, and stresses that its main purpose is to fight against discriminations against women and to strengthen awareness of human rights. Although the ban on the headscarf is one of its central focuses, it is also interested in other facets of women rights such as the reform of the civil and penal code, violence against women and honour killings.[10] The Capital Women's Platform was created earlier, in 1995, by a group of women theologians. It is the first umbrella grouping for religious women organizations throughout Turkey. One of its principal aims has been to try to act as a bridge between secular and religious women groups, which it has been doing by, for instance, participating in the Turkish CEDAW working group. Following the 1997 coup, the organization started to work with students wearing headscarves, as well as with women graduates who had been unable to enter the workforce. They have taken cases to court, and have been involved in lobbying work at the international level.[11] Finally, some activists have also been working with the Free Thought and Education Rights Association (Özgür-der) created in 1999 in Istanbul. One of its aims has been to address headscarf violations, but it has also been working on other human rights concerns, both at national and international levels, such as on the Kurdish issue, the war in Iraq and the Palestinian conflict.[12] It is important to note that these organizations often collaborate with each other and that membership remains fluid between these groups.

Most activists actively engaged in this struggle are women who have themselves been affected in a way or another by the ban on headscarves. They are active in different sectors such as academia, think tanks, theology, the media and so on. Some are also engaged in the reinterpretation of Islamic texts, fighting patriarchal interpretations of Islam, and are involved in women's rights training activities with smaller organizations throughout Turkey. They often appear on television, radio shows or in newspapers and participate in seminars, lectures and protests. Most of them are members of the new devout Muslim bourgeoisie, which explains why they are well educated and often fluent in English,[13] as well as having the time and financial means to be involved in national and international networking.

Choosing to embrace a rights-based perspective

For many religious rights activists, the 1997 coup played a crucial role in pushing them to embrace a rights-based discourse in expressing themselves publicly, and in framing their concerns in respect of headscarf bans. For instance, the coup led to the creation of religious rights organizations such as AKDER and Özgür-der, and to the shift in some of the policies of already existing religious NGOs, such as Mazlumder and the Capital Women's Platform that had to cater to the needs of individuals affected by the purge of Islam from the public realm.

Notwithstanding that this use of a human rights discourse has allowed activists to have a voice in the public realm – at a time when a religious idiom was heavily controlled or banned – they also argued that it was a way for them to engage and touch audiences beyond their circles. Indeed, they stressed that framing one's concerns in terms of human rights claims was a way for non-religious or non-Muslims to grasp and relate with their situation, as well as, when possible, extend their base of support inside and outside Turkey. This was well expressed by a member of Mazlumder in Ankara who explained that:

> In our press releases we refer to universal human rights because otherwise you cannot be understood by everyone. Universal human rights represent a common point of view … *In order to reach out to other parts of the community we must use universal terms.*
>
> (Ankara, April 18 2008 (author's emphasis))

Concretely, at the national level, this has led to attempts to create coalitions or collaborate with other non-religious human rights organizations, leftist groups, or minority groups on a variety of issues going beyond religious freedom, including torture, freedom of expression, the right to life and so on.[14] At the international level, as explored in the next chapter, using a human rights discourse has been described as an important way for their claims to be understood by representatives of other states, and transnational activists.

In relation more specifically to headscarf bans, these have gradually ceased to be described as a breach of religious duty, but rather as an infringement of a series of individual rights. For instance, for members of the Capital Women's Platform, speaking in terms of rights rather than duty has been more representative of the approach they have adopted towards religion over the past decade. They argue that for them the wearing of the headscarf is a personal choice. Framing it as a question of individual rights can, thus, be understood as a way to position oneself against any type of regulation, whether by the state or by a religious community:

> We don't think there is much to argue when it comes to religion. How you live your religion depends on your interpretation of your religion. As far as we are concerned there is no black or white in religion […]. It just depends on how much you can and you want to practise […]. It is not really right to put certain boundaries – this is Islam and nothing else. You cannot say that. I cannot say that a woman, who doesn't wear a headscarf is not a Muslim. This is why we are not arguing the religious point of view. Besides, religious arguments have been on-going from 1983 up until the 28 February coup […] but they haven't achieved anything. For us this is clearly a human rights issue because it is a question of freedom of belief.
>
> (activist, Capital Women's Platform, Ankara, 2008)

This idea of putting an end to the regulation of the religious self is central to the claims of activists, and their attempts to refashion secular scripts. Indeed, as it will be argued below, through an analysis of three key rights used to challenge headscarf bans, their understanding of *laiklik* is one in which the state ceases to regulate individuals, and where different ethoses are allowed to coexist in the public realm. In the same way as with their French counterparts, what is particularly noteworthy about this narrative is that their religiosity is increasingly depicted as a personal choice that belongs to the sphere of the private self and in which the state has no right of interference.

The headscarf: a right to religious freedom

Headscarf bans have, from the first, been depicted as an infringement of the right to religious freedom. Activists have supported their claims by drawing on articles in international human rights conventions that protect the right to religious freedom, such as article 18 of the UN International Covenant on Civil and Political Rights (ICCPR) and the general comment adopted by the UN Human Rights Committee to clarify this article, Article 9 of the European Convention on Human Rights (ECHR) and/or Article 2 of the United Nations Declaration on the Elimination of All Forms of Intolerance and Discrimination Based on Religion or Belief (1981).[15] In citing these articles, particular emphasis is put on the fact that these do not only protect the right to believe, but also the right to express one's religion publicly.

> The United Nations Human Rights Committee interprets the freedom to express religious beliefs *in a manner that may include being able to wear special clothing and head covering.*
>
> (CEDAW Shadow Report, 2010:9 (author's emphasis))

In their argument, developed in different reports including in the 2010 CEDAW Shadow Report,[16] my interviewees stress that these articles do mention restrictions that can be put on the right to freedom of religion and conscience in order to protect public safety, or the fundamental rights and freedoms of others. While these restrictions are frequently evoked by individuals in favour of headscarf bans, activists attempt to demonstrate why these should not affect the headscarf in the Turkish context. They first emphasize that Turkish officials' fears of public disorder have not been confirmed by empirical facts. Indeed, grounding their narrative in shifts in dominant secular tropes, they emphasize that prior to 1997 women were allowed to wear headscarves in universities and this was not the source of any particular tension. To reinforce this point, they draw on a TESEV survey indicating that the majority of the Turkish public had not been disturbed by the fact that women were wearing or not wearing a headscarf, and that the idea of a Sharia based state had received little support in Turkey (2010: 12).[17]

To address worries that the headscarf would violate the rights of others, especially those of women being pressured to wear the headscarf, it is important to remember that prior to 1997 no such tensions were reported (AKDER, 2005: 8). To support this point, my interviewees point to the importance of taking into consideration the class dimension behind this phenomenon. While they argue that it is indeed possible that poor or uneducated women could be subject to pressures, they emphasize that the ban has been specifically affecting women working in the third sector and students in universities – that is, the population of educated women for whom it would have been easier to resign to pressures pushing them to take the headscarf off rather than keeping it on (CEDAW Shadow Report, 2010: 11). In so doing, they highlight that the wearing of a headscarf is often the result of a personal and autonomous choice.

> […] it is seriously insulting to women to assume that if a *woman cannot wear a headscarf by her own free choice*, but must be doing so at the behest of someone else. This assumes that women do not have the will to make a personal decision, yet choice *of attire is part of women's freedom and that choice will be conditioned by her personal ideas and beliefs.*
>
> (Benli, 2006: 8 (author's emphasis))[18]

To displace further the fear that wearing the headscarf infringes on the rights of others, the headscarf is compared to the length of one's hair. This analogy allows activists to argue that it would be unreasonable to think that hair length would restrain the rights of others.

> Would it be reasonable to claim that persons wearing long hair negatively affect those who keep their hair short, or that people who wear long hair want to restrict the rights of short haired, and must therefore be forced to cut their hair short too?
>
> (Benli, 2006: 7)

By making a parallel between the headscarf and hair length, or one's choice of clothing, activists stress the personal and private dimension of wearing a headscarf. One could suggest that in so doing they are, like their French counterparts, challenging the boundaries of what is considered to be public and private. Wearing or not wearing the headscarf is about one's private relationship with God – a relationship that does not concern the state – and that should not affect participation in the polis. Thus, this attempt to relegate religion to the sphere of the private self seems to correspond to a quite secular interpretation of the term. However, in this account as well, the limits of the private self do not only include one's conscience, but are also expanded to the expression of one's religion on one's body. Building on this understanding, my interviewees argue that by regulating personal expressions of religion, the state is determining the terms of a woman's personal relationship with God. They point to the fact that a secular state is ill-equipped to make such a call, as by its nature it is not considered to be an 'expert' in religion and is therefore not competent to have a theological opinion. It would be like 'a foot doctor making a diagnosis on the teeth' (Benli, Lawyer and member of AKDER in Tavernise, 2008a).

Understanding the expression of one's faith as a personal freedom pertaining to the private self seems to weaken substantially claims that consider the headscarf to be a political symbol of fundamentalism. If the headscarf is narrated as being about one's private relationship to God, and if it becomes the symbol for asking the state to respect coexistence between different types of beliefs, its threatening character withers – 'For many Muslim women wearing the headscarf is a deeply personal choice and a sign of their religious conviction and has nothing to do with Islamic fundamentalism' (CEDAW Shadow Report, 2010: 26). Following this line of thought, activists suggest that providers of public services (e.g. judges, MPs, teachers, and so on) should be free to represent the state while wearing a headscarf. Since the headscarf is considered to be part of the private self, it should not in itself be a reason to think that the public actions of a wearer would favour one belief over another. In other words, women can choose to be religious and, at the same time, promote an ethic of coexistence in their public functions. Consequently, a public agent should be judged by her actions and not by her appearance.[19] While Turkish activists, like their French counterparts, believe that the neutrality requirement should affect the state and not individuals, the distinction between users and providers of public services is however not central to their argument. Arguably, one of the reasons that could explain this difference is the fact that their claims are less restricted by national jurisprudence than the ones of French activists.

Thus, this investigation already highlights a few things about how *laiklik* is being refashioned. As with the understanding of French activists, *laiklik* seems to be about the coexistence of beliefs in a society. One could argue that it is precisely this stress on plurality that distinguishes their approach from one in which activists would be proposing an alternative *nomos* based on a religious ethic. Building on this, my interviewees emphasize that in order to protect the right to religious freedom, the state and its representatives should adopt a neutral position towards all faiths, and refrain from judging or restricting particular beliefs. In other words, secular languages (i.e. neutrality and autonomy) are in this case also used to redefine the role of the state vis-à-vis religion, and religion per se that becomes mainly a question of choice. This process reveals once again the power of secular languages that end up defining the boundaries of the religious

> We are for a secularism that does not ignore the religious, that is consistent in the same way with all beliefs and that allows *freedom of choice* in society.
>
> (activist, Capital Women's Platform, Ankara, 2008 (author's emphasis))

Religious freedom and its paradoxes

It is relevant to note that religious rights activists rarely speak about headscarf bans as being solely a breach of religious freedom, but combine it with other rights violations. This is perhaps best understood as a consequence of some of the paradoxes carried by the right to religious freedom, paradoxes which remain difficult to untangle.

As has been seen, activists have been using a language of choice to speak about religious freedom. This can be linked, as Wendy Brown has emphasized in her work (2000: 238), to the fact that ideas of individual sovereignty and autonomy are deeply ingrained in the contemporary human rights discourse. In other words, rights give the individual the possibility to 'choose' her or his own life.[20] In our case, this means that religious rights activists have to stress that they are choosing if and how they want to be religious. In doing so, it would seem that the importance given to religious duty and other ways of being religious are superseded by an understanding of religious freedom governed by individual will. Moreover, by not highlighting the role of religious duty one can wonder what distinguishes the right to religious freedom from other personal preferences. In effect, Sandel argues that what originally made the right to religious freedom an inalienable right is precisely the fact that faith was not considered a matter of choice but rather a duty that a person, even if forced to, could not give up (1998: 86, 91). In other words, when one speaks of religious freedom as a personal and voluntary choice, making a distinction between these claims of conscience and individual desire seem to become a more arduous task.

Thus, religious duty might play an important role in distinguishing freedom of religion from other personal preferences, such as wearing high heels, or wearing a pink shirt – preferences that could under particular circumstances be easier to give up.[21] One is therefore left wondering if defining religious freedom mainly through the prism of choice might not end up weakening the power of this right, and cast a shadow over the nuances and complexities of being religious.[22] Alternatively, it may, perhaps, be a sign indicating that efforts are being made to define religious freedom so that it conveys the idea that there can be a strong element of individual agency and self-discovery behind the decision to be pious – that is, proposing a hybrid meaning of the term that allows the possibility of combining notions of agency and religiousness. What this investigation certainly does, in my view, is to reveal that this right is marked by a tension between the notion of duty and the one of choice – a tension, which is, partially at least, a product of the different meanings given to this right, and which might explain why activists feel the need to find the basis for their claims in other rights.

The headscarf: a women's rights and the gender equality question

> It is a women's rights issue, because the bans triggered by the 1997 coup have targeted first and foremost women.
>
> (activist, AKDER, Istanbul, 2008)

Religious rights activists have also been describing the headscarf ban as a direct discrimination against women. Not surprisingly, my interviewees did not endorse the idea that a ban was the appropriate way to address fears around the headscarf being a symbol of submission to a patriarchal order. Rather they argued that the ban was a violation of the 1995 Beijing Declaration,[23] as well as many of the articles of the United Nations Human Rights Convention on the Elimination of All Forms of Discrimination against Women (CEDAW Shadow Report, 2005 and 2010).

In this argument, four key claims are noteworthy. First of all, they argue that the headscarf ban is restricting women's educational, employment, healthcare, and political possibilities.[24] This is particularly problematic since there is an inequality of treatment vis-à-vis religious men, who face less discrimination in all of these sectors.

> In Turkey, the religious man is able to take his place at even the highest levels of career, politics and status, while the religious woman is condemned to her home because of these bans.
>
> (Capital Women's Platform, 2005)

In a similar vein, it is emphasized that Turkey lags behind in terms of gender-based equality, and therefore that women are in general already disadvantaged. Women wearing headscarves are targets of additional discriminations, reinforcing gender discrimination as a whole in society.

> Surveys indicate that 62% of women in Turkey cover their heads. Consequently, the exclusion and discrimination to which women with headscarves are subjected to will inevitably be reflected at the very least to this extent in the indexes for gender discrimination in the country as a whole.
>
> (CEDAW Shadow Report, 2010: 27)

Thus, headscarf bans are considered to deprive women wearing the headscarf from having the same access to public life as women not wearing it.[25]

In detailing the consequences of these bans for women, my interviewees emphasized that rather than liberating them from customs and family, they have reinforced patriarchy by pushing them back into their household and rendering them fully dependent on a male. In other words, women have no other option than to embrace their housewife status. In this process, they are denied the right to be intellectually and financially independent and, therefore, the right to choose the life style they want to adhere to.

> The ban by depriving young people of their economic and *intellectual independence*, exposes them to a much greater extent to the pressure of their families and society.
>
> (CEDAW Shadow Report, 2010:11(author's emphasis))

> Last weekend my cousin got married – she couldn't go to university. I felt very sorry for her. She is not educated now, and I see that her husband is

> behaving differently with her. She got a traditional wedding and she will live a traditional life. If she had a chance to go to university her life would have been different. She was not able to work because her father did not allow it, but she could have gotten an education […]. Her only option to leave her family was to get married because she didn't want to take off her headscarf. Her life would have been different if she could have had an education.
>
> (activist, AKDER, Istanbul, 2008)

To shed light on the deeply restrictive character of bans, activists compare them to the imposition of head coverings in Saudi Arabia or Iran. In these countries states are controlling the woman's self, not trusting that she is autonomous enough to make her own decisions – a statement which makes reference to the ambivalent position of women, who because of their status as communities' 'border-guards' are subject to special scrutiny (Yuval-Davis, 1997a). This, consequently, impedes the possibility of her full emancipation:

> As in the case of Saudi Arabia and Iran, while describing how women should dress (the obligation to wear the 'hicab'), the religious and political authorities prohibit women from deciding what they want to wear; they see them as incapable of being individual or independent. *For us, however, such enforcements which deprive woman of the right of being an individual and making basic decisions about herself, cannot be accepted* […] The religious women reject all means of oppression related to forcing women to either wear or take off the head-scarf.
>
> (Capital Women's Platform, 2005 (author's emphasis))

> To force women to cover their head or to uncover it restricts fundamental principles of women's rights to individual autonomy and to make personal decisions.
>
> (AKDER, 2005: 11)

Thus, once again, activists express a strong commitment to ideas of individual freedom and autonomy. They are arguing that choosing to be faithful is a well-thought-out choice – one that might not follow the understanding of autonomy promoted by the state, but which is a mark in itself of independent agency as it breaks from the norms dominating the public square. In other words, bans on the headscarf are understood as setting limits on one's right to choose to evolve outside traditional patriarchal structures – to 'emancipate' oneself intellectually from the state and/or one's traditional/religious community. This argument reflects the history of *laiklik* in Turkey discussed in previous chapters, in which women came to occupy an important position but have nevertheless been subject to strict regulations and discipline (Kandiyoti, 1991a). The state has had, and continues to take, a patriarchal role defining the norms that citizens, and particularly women, need to follow in order to partake in the life of the polis (Arat, 2000). In so doing, terms such as emancipation, autonomy and neutrality have been used to advance a normative project that leaves little possibility for individual sovereignty – possibilities that devout activists through their (re)appropriation of these same concepts are reclaiming.

The headscarf: part of a culture of non-discrimination

As emphasized above, one of the reasons put forward regarding the usefulness of using a rights-based discourse is that it is understood as a way to go beyond one's struggle. In other words, it opens the door to go beyond concerns around headscarf restrictions and focus on other individuals and groups facing discrimination. Working on other human rights issues, such as providing support to Kurds, as well as fighting illegal detentions or preventing honour killings, has been on the agenda of religious rights-based groups since the mid/late 1990s. This has triggered collaboration, or at least attempts at collaboration, with other human rights organizations that do not necessarily describe themselves as faith-based.[26] What is particularly interesting is that over the past decade there seem to have been more frequent efforts to directly link the violations or restrictions of rights faced by different minorities in Turkey to those faced by women wearing headscarves. To be specific, activists have been emphasising that bans on headscarves are part of a wider culture of prohibition – 'One day prohibition is imposed on us. The next day, it could be someone else. If we work together, we can fight it' (Yilmaz, activist in Tavernise, 2008b).

In this vein, religious rights activists have almost systematically been linking headscarf restrictions to the limits placed on the religious freedom of other religious communities in Turkey, such as Alevis, Armenians, Christian minorities and so on. To illustrate these claims, some have questioned the legitimacy of the Directorate of Religious Affairs. For instance, they have deplored the fact that because the Directorate has failed to recognize Alevis as being members of a distinctive religious community they have not been able to be represented or funded by the Directorate, and their places of worship have been considered to be culture houses rather than religious establishments. 'We will not be happy unless it is acknowledged that the worship of Alevis is not just a cultural activity and their houses of worship are not only cultural centres' (Akbulut *et al.* 2008).[27] On a similar note, the fact that the state has been requiring that religion be indicated on nationality cards has been criticised. This has consequences for those individuals who are not members of a recognized religious minority,[28] including atheists who have been identified as Muslims (Ensaroğlu, 2004). Others have also stressed that the state should cease to force students in schools to attend compulsory Sunni religious classes – 'Sunni propaganda imposed on non-Sunni Muslims? Strange secularism' (Kaplan, activist in Birch, 2008).

The fact that religious minorities have not been able to freely practise their religion has also been challenged. Because these communities are not represented in the Directorate – which only represents Sunni Muslims – they face difficulties with regards to the ownership of religious estates or the education of their clergy. Moreover, several activists have objected to the fact that minorities not mentioned in the Lausanne Treaty (1923), such as Protestants or Assyrians, were not legally recognized as religious communities, and were deprived of most of their rights to worship and practise their religion (e.g. Akbulut *et al.* 2008).

In this argument, some of my interviewees suggested that, in the long run, the Directorate should be restructured, so that it could represent all religious communities equally, and not solely a specific form of Sunni Islam. 'In Turkey the state controls the religion through the *Diyanet*, this is a real irony. The *Diyanet* only serves one religious community whereas it should serve everyone' (activist, Istanbul, 2008). This was emphasized as being of crucial importance in establishing a 'true' type of *laiklik*, in which the state embraces an impartial position towards all beliefs.

> […] although Turkey is supposedly a secular state, it has a Religious Affairs Directorate under the Office of the Prime Minister, which controls and manipulates certain sects in Islam. By giving priority to a particular interpretation of religion the Directorate infringes the principle of impartiality between religions […]. The principle of secularism in a democratic society, where different religions or beliefs coexist, requires the state to be neutral towards religions or beliefs […].
>
> (Benli, 2006: 5)

My interlocutors also made wider parallels between their own struggles and those of other groups, such as Kurds or homosexuals. In this argument it is important to stress that what has been denounced is the state's will to define the boundaries of who is and who is not a righteous citizen in Turkey. This is particularly well illustrated by religious rights activists' position towards homosexuals. Indeed, while they expressed reluctance towards supporting homosexuality per se, as for many of them this practice enters into direct conflict with their religious beliefs, they have started to defend homosexuals' rights not to be discriminated against or to face pressures and interference from the state in their way of being.

> We defend human rights to the extent to which it does not violate our religious principles. It is difficult for us, for instance, to defend homosexual rights, but we defend their basic rights not to be tortured, mistreated, etc.
>
> (activist, Istanbul, 2008)

> In Turkey our problem is the same [i.e. headscarved women and homosexuals]. The state claims it is secular and therefore it should ensure that

> religious and non-religious groups have the same rights, but it does not do so.
>
> (activist, Istanbul, 2008)

It is particularly interesting to note that what is deplored again here is the attitude of the state, which fails, in their view, to be secular. Indeed, if one understands *laiklik* as being based on the fact that the state should be impartial towards personal beliefs and practices, it should therefore refrain from judging them. This is why the fact that the Turkish state has been attempting to close LGBT NGOs in the name of public morality is criticised, as in so doing it is precisely favouring one moral ethic over another. 'If the state was truly secular it should not be closing down NGOs by saying that they are against general morality' (activist, Istanbul, 2008, referring to LGBT organizations).[29]

As we can see from the above, what is criticised is the fact that the state is setting the terms of who can and who cannot have full access to citizenship rights – differentiating therefore access to citizenship as a consequence of affiliations. This can explain why, over the last couple of years, religious rights activists have been linking their demands to wider civic projects in Turkish society. Two concrete examples illustrate this quite well. The first one is a petition released in February 2008 by three young women religious activists – Hilal Kaplan, Havva Yilmaz and Neslihan Akbulut – a move that received substantial coverage in the Turkish media.[30] This petition was launched in the midst of an attempt by the AK Party in February 2008 to change the Constitution in order for headscarves to be allowed in universities. In this petition, the authors stressed that lifting the ban in itself would not suffice, but that it should come with much broader extensions of civil rights that would foster a 'legal and psychological environment, which is required for the Kurds and the others to feel themselves as an essential component of this country' (Akbulut *et al.* 2008). For them it is, therefore, not sufficient to modify one article in the Constitution, but rather the 1982 Constitution should be abolished all together, replaced by a new one protecting civil liberties in the public domain for all individuals.[31] 'We will not be happy unless the Constitution of September 12 is abolished to its slightest part and a new, civil constitution is realized.'(ibid.).

It could be argued that this petition is a micro example of wider ad hoc actions that have been taking place in Turkey, in which individuals have been coming together to denounce violations of personal freedoms and asking for a new civic constitution. This type of action has become possible over the last decade because of Turkey's growing economic liberalization and democratization triggered, in part, by the EU process: 'The coalitions existing today are much stronger – this is rare, as until now people feared the pressure of the army' (activist, Mazlumder, Istanbul, 2008). This means that the military has been perceived as less of a threat, and that a growing number of individuals have felt that they have the right to ask for changes. For instance, religious rights activists have been participating in coalitions with very different types of groups, including leftists, Kurdish organizations and LGBT groups. This trend started to materialize with the creation of a coalition against the war in Iraq in 2002, which held more than 100 protests throughout Turkey:[32]

> In Turkey there was no culture of coalition – this was the first time. Before that, Mazlumder had come together with other leftist groups but these were small initiatives […] With the Iraqi war, we realised that we could all work together […] On both sides [i.e. religious and secular] extremists did not participate to the coalition. This coalition was a way to learn to work with each other, and to respect the rights of each other […] We decided to organize protests in front of Mosques on Fridays because we wanted to rally the most people possible […] Of course this coalition created hopes that people with different interests could come together.
>
> (activist, Mazlumder, Istanbul, 2008)

For its participants, this anti-war coalition has been an experience enabling them to forge other coalitions on internal political issues. For instance, in June 2008, approximately 10,000 people came together to participate in a march called '70 Million steps against Coups' protesting against the attempt by the Constitutional Court and military elites to close the AK Party.

> Building on our coalition experience, we had homosexuals, Islamists, leftists, Kurdish coming together to protest against the closure case […]. This 6 years of coalition history has allowed us to develop a general coalition, if it becomes as big as the Iraq coalition it could be an influential force for democratisation.
>
> (leftist activist, anti-war coalition, Istanbul, 2008)[33]

Although the success of these coalitions has, until now, been limited, the diversity of the groups participating in them is noteworthy. One could see this as a practical example of the discourse put forth by activists, in which they stress that the ability to coexist should be the basis of a secular society. Indeed, the fact that their personal beliefs may differ from other members of the same coalition does not impede them from coexisting and working together for a societal project that would respect this plurality.

> My thoughts and beliefs are different from many people who are rallying beside me today. But, despite all our differences, our common wish is to live freely in this country.
>
> (participant in the march against the closure case,
> Zeynep AK in Çelen, 2008).

Postscript – 2011 and beyond: a struggle marked by old and new complexities

Fieldwork for this chapter was conducted mainly between 2008 and 2009. When I went back to Istanbul in 2011, the situation of several of my respondents had become more complex in the sense that they were not only denouncing headscarf bans enforced by secular elites, but also the (in)actions of the AK Party and its bureaucrats. In effect, as discussed in Chapter 3, while the AK Party has acquired an unprecedented amount of power, especially since 2008, it has made little effort to lift the bans. Yet, despite this greater complexity, activists have continued to use a similar argumentative script.

This is well illustrated by devout activists' reactions to the harsh criticisms their 'no headscarf, no vote campaign' was subjected to. As mentioned earlier in the book, the 'no headscarf, no vote' campaign was launched prior to the June 2011 election and was a platform through which activists asked that all Turkish political parties, including the AK Party, consider putting women wearing headscarves on their electoral lists. This campaign was heavily criticized by members of the AK Party and devout elites, who accused devout women behind the campaign as being at best 'naïve' and at worst a 'fifth column' of Kemalists aiming to destroy the AK Party from within (Akyol, 2011). Reacting to these comments, the spokeswoman for the campaign, Hilal Kaplan, asked:

> Is it possible that what Bulaç [an Islamic intellectual who criticized the campaign] cannot stand is the veiled [women] who work and make money, rather than just staying at home and looking after children? Or is it that these women can step up in society with intellectual and civil initiatives, creating public spaces for themselves, without looking at what the male intellectuals say?
>
> (Kaplan, cited in Akyol, ibid. (author's emphasis))

This question is illustrative of the fact that devout women are once again asking for the right to be autonomous individuals and to make their own choices. This is visible also in the concerns some of these women have expressed vis-à-vis Erdogan's comments on abortion in 2012, in which, after having labelled the practice 'murder' he positioned himself in favour of limiting it (Cengiz O., 2012). While activists argued that they were personally against abortion, they stated that they were also against the position embraced by the Prime Minister and the intrusive role he gave to the secular state in the lives of women. In so doing, they recalled the role of the secular state that should, in their opinion, refrain from promoting one ethic over another:

> I am against abortion, but Erdoğan's statement that abortion is 'murder' disturbed me […] In this country not everyone is Muslim, nor do they

> all share the same opinion […] The Religious Affairs Directorate could issue a fatwa about anything but a *secular state* cannot ban anything on the basis of a fatwa.
>
> (Tuksal, cited in Cengiz O., 2012 (author's emphasis))

> Some issues rush into the political agenda like a totalistic, essentialist, and bold storm […] Religious groups are unable to discuss these issues in a way that ensures the participation of women. Women are ignored to the highest extent in a so-called untouchable, sacred sphere […] When women assert dissident ideas or sensitivities, they are labelled and written off as 'feminists'. I am against abortion. *But I am also against the state's telling women what (or what not) to do* […]
>
> (Atlas, cited in Cengiz O., 2012 (author's emphasis))

Needless to say, while the struggle of devout activists is surely becoming more complicated, it continues to be of great importance, as it now openly highlights the patriarchal structures that underpin understandings of citizenship in both religious and secular circles. It is, thus, becoming a concrete example of the fact that religious and secular worldviews can be deeply interrelated.

Conclusion

What one may first retain from these attempts to refashion *laiklik* are the many similarities with our French case. Not only do religious activists in both countries ground their refashioning within the framework of secularism, but they also make reference to, and alter the meanings of, its languages – a process which, in turn, affects the boundaries of what is religiously acceptable in the Republics. In fact, they both refer to shifts in the dominant understandings of secularism (e.g. the 1997 coup and the March 2004 Law) to reinforce their claims. In both of these, refashioning secularism is not defined as being against religion, but rather as a concept that ensures the possibility of having a plurality of beliefs in a society.

The differences between French and Turkish activists lie not so much in their discourse as in the choice of means available for this refashioning – differences that seem to give more freedom and discursive space to Turkish activists. In effect, their inability to draw on national jurisprudence to the same extent as their French counterparts might give them more leeway to challenge dominant understandings of the term. For instance, this is illustrated by the fact that they do not make a distinction between users and providers of public services, arguing that state interference, in both cases, is a violation of the right to religious freedom. On another note, while both French and Turkish activists have tried to locate their struggle beyond their community, the ability of Turkish activists to link theirs with a wider process of political liberalisation has facilitated their capacity to forge unexpected alliances with individuals whose freedoms have also been restricted by the state. Finally, although this aspect has only been briefly mentioned, the fact that many Turkish activists are members of a new devout bourgeoisie plays a role, at least to a certain degree, with respect to their ability to be heard. Indeed, they do not only have, as further explored in the next chapter, the means to engage in international lobbying, but also have access to different discursive spaces, including in the media and intellectual circles.

The fact that the refashioning of *laiklik* has been triggered in large part to address the exclusion of devout women, and that devout women themselves are actively participating in this process, reflects the history of *laiklik* and the important place it has given to women. As we have seen, *laiklik* has been used to delimit the terms of access to citizenship. In that process, women's bodies have been used as barometers indicating the morality of different spaces, delimiting the boundaries between private and public realms. In a sense, therefore, emancipation and equality have had little to do with individual autonomy and more to do with the ability of women to (re)produce new secular moral codes in the public realm (Kandiyoti, 1997; Arat, 1997). Interestingly, devout women, by (re)appropriating the languages of *laiklik* and building on shifts and inconsistencies present within this discourse, are not only revealing its disciplinary tendencies, but are also using its hegemonic character to propose an alternative meaning that seems to be more consistent with the respect of their individual sovereignties. In other words, while the portrait that they offer of *laiklik* also delimits the contours of Turkish citizenship, the possibility for Turkish citizens to participate in the public domain even if they have different subjectivities and ethics is anticipated. This view also challenges the traditional boundaries between private and public realms, as the latter are not dominated by one ethic, but rather by an ethos of coexistence. Not unlike what has been conceived by French activists, the state still remains responsible for regulating and ultimately excluding beliefs and practices that do not respect this notion of coexistence.

I find it insightful here to recall Charles Taylor's definition of the secular, which he understands as being characterized by the coexistence of beliefs and un-beliefs (1998; 2003; 2007). Following this understanding, it could be argued that what makes the ethic proposed by my interviewees a secular one is precisely the fact that it is based on the idea of coexistence and plurality. It refrains from imposing a unique, exclusive set of morals on the public domain, and fosters an environment where individuals can freely choose their personal ethics. In my view, one could trace parallels between this understanding of *laiklik* and what Taylor has identified as his third secular ethic, the 'overlapping consensus model', which clearly stresses this possibility of coexistence. What is distinctive in this model is that different citizens gather around a set of convergent principles (e.g. like a charter of rights or a constitution) but with a different set of reasons for following them.

> […] there is more than one set of valid reasons for signing on to it […] [The overlapping consensus] will require a change of our mindset, away from the highly charged moralism which will only settle for the single right answer generated from unchallenged foundational principles […] but it is the only form of secularism available to us in the diverse societies today.
>
> (Taylor, 1998: 49, 52–53).

However, it is important to recall that this refashioning of *laiklik* and, by correlation, religion, is the fruit of a reflection of pious activists, who are urban, highly educated individuals and economically well off. Moreover, this refashioning remains very much at a theoretical level. In practice it is possible that in a Muslim majoritarian society, in which the state would limit its interference in religious subjectivities, the ethic dominating public life would end up being quite exclusive, reflecting the beliefs of the majority – reproducing a model in a Muslim context close to Shakman Hurd's Judeo-Christian secularism (2008) or Taylor's common ground strategy (1998: 33).[34] Yet, it is equally possible to imagine that in a context in which individuals are realising that they are not the only ones whose subjectivities have been repressed, and where they are working with individuals from different backgrounds, a terrain is being set out for an alternative type of secular ethic – a secular ethic that ensures the possibility of coexistence.

Notes

1 The terms 'religious rights activists' and 'faith-based rights activists' are used to convey the idea that these activists are using a human rights discourse, while remaining at the same time religious. The expression 'Islamist rights activists' is deliberately not used, as some of my interviewees openly disliked this label. They understood it as conveying the idea that they were challenging the structure of the state through their actions, which was not their objective.

2 This period is marked by the rule of Özal (Prime Minister and then President) who was known for having promoted an atmosphere of greater liberalisation and democratization in Turkey.

3 Yavuz notes that the Welfare Party received an increase in support because its platform was in line with both the people's conception of Islamic identity, and also with their understanding of politics. The Party's ability to articulate socioeconomic issues through a language graspable by the masses, as well as to oppose the Kemalist regime, were important factors explaining its success (2003: 222, 223).

4 The Virtue Party was closed down in 2001 by the Constitutional Court that argued, as in 1998, that it was a hotbed for Islamists, and therefore had to be outlawed.

5 Dağı considers the AK Party and its supporters to be 'post-Islamists' in the sense that they still give importance to Islam in the social realm, but have abandoned it as a political programme (2005: 30).

6 Accession talks with the EU were officially opened in 2005, but progress has been quite slow, partly because of the reluctance of some member states and because of the battle over the status of Cyprus. Due to this stalemate, commentators have argued that the AK Party, starting from its second mandate (2007) onwards, has put substantial efforts into developing its relations with the Middle-East and Central Asia (Cengiz A., 2012, Fisher Onar, 2011).

7 The four organizations mentioned in this chapter are, to my knowledge, the main ones in Turkey combining a human rights agenda, openly considering themselves to be inspired by their Muslim faith and working on headscarf discriminations.

8 The interview process is also discussed in the introductory chapter.

9 For more information on Mazlumder see www.mazlumder.org (accessed 5 November 2013).

10 For more information on AKDER see http://www.ak-der.org/?p=about_us&lang=eng& m = 508c75c8507a2ae5223dfd2faeb98122 (accessed 5 November 2013).

11 For more on the Capital Women's Platform see www.baskentkadin.org/ (accessed 5 November 2013).

12 For more on Özgür-der see http://www.ozgurder.org (accessed 5 November 2013).

13 The majority of my interviewees had at least an undergraduate university degree. Many of them also had a Masters degree or a PhD.

14 For instance, Mazlumder has been collaborating since the mid-90s with the Human Rights Association (IHD), which was created in 1986 to address cases of detention, torture and the disappearances of mostly leftists' individuals that occurred after the 1980 coup. They have worked jointly on campaigns around Kurdish discrimination, torture and freedom of expression. As of 2002, the Capital Women's Platform has also been working with secular women's organizations through its participation in the national CEDAW working group.

15 CEDAW Shadow Report, 2010: 9.

16 The CEDAW Shadow Report is a report on discrimination against women in a specific country prepared by NGOs and transmitted to the UN CEDAW committee. Its aim is to complement the periodic report that has to be provided by the state, signatory to the CEDAW Convention, to the CEDAW committee. Turkish religious NGOs have started to work on CEDAW reporting in 2001 contributing a short report, drafted by the Capital Women's Platform, on the headscarf ban to the 2005 review. For the 2010 process, 203 representatives of religious organizations came together in May 2008 in Konya (Turkey) to discuss the content of the report. The report was then drafted by AKDER and signed by more than 71 religious associations, including trade unions from 15 provinces across Turkey. For more information on the CEDAW process see Chapter 6. Other reports that develop a similar argument include AKDER, 2007, 2005 and 2004; Capital Women's Platform, 2005.

17 The CEDAW Shadow Report 2010, as well as most of AKDER reports refer to TESEV studies carried out in 1999 and 2006 that have shown that the majority of Turkish public does not believe that *laiklik* is under threat, and that the support for a religious state has decreased between 1999 and 2006 from 21 per cent to 9 per cent (Çarkoğlu and Toprak, 2007: 101).

18 Fatma Benli is a lawyer who has been working closely with AKDER on headscarf issues.

19 For several of my interviewees, this was particularly important in the context of Turkey, where society is deeply divided and where a judge who does not wear the headscarf might not necessarily be objective in her actions – 'When you look at a person you always see something – everyone is un-neutral. Take the example of a court, for instance a judge might not wear a headscarf but she might have bias inside' (activist, Istanbul, 2008).

20 Wendy Brown provides a critical discussion of the idea of individual choice (2000).

21 Limits can, for instance, be put on peoples' personal preferences when they are asked to wear uniforms (e.g. school uniforms, police uniforms).

22 This echoes Winnifred Sullivan's questioning of the ability of the right to religious freedom to capture the complexities of being religious, including the fact that religious practices are in constant flux (2005).

23 The Beijing Declaration was signed at the United Nations Fourth World Conference on Women in September 4–15, 1995 in Beijing (United Nations Beijing Declaration, 1995).

24 For instance, it is argued that women wearing headscarves do not have access to political positions such as being MPs, city councillors, and so on, stopping them from taking part in the decision-making process that directly affects their lives. This, it is argued, violates Article 7 of the CEDAW Convention that requires states to take all appropriate measures to eliminate discrimination against women in the political and public life of a country. Likewise, women face restrictions with respect to their access to healthcare, as some state's university clinics and hospitals have been refusing them treatment. This is understood to be a violation of Article 12 of the CEDAW Convention that requires equal access to healthcare for women (CEDAW Shadow Report, 2010: 4).

25 As discussed at the end of this chapter, these arguments continue to play a central role today in their struggle vis-à-vis a devout bourgeoisie and political elite, who remain reluctant to lifting the ban in many spaces.

26 For further information on those attempts of collaboration see note 14.

27 This statement was made as part of a broader petition launched by young Muslim women activists arguing that lifting the headscarf ban in universities was not enough, and that society needed to go through wider civic changes. More information on this is provided in the discussion that follows and in note 30. Similar concerns were echoed in my conversations with other activists.

28 Non-Muslim religious minorities recognized in Turkey are those that have been mentioned by the Lausanne Treaty (1923): Armenians Orthodox, Greek Orthodox, and Jews. For more information see chapter 2.

29 For instance a lower court in Istanbul along with municipal authorities considered that the LGBT organization *Lambda* was immoral and against family values, and demanded that it be dissolved. The organization filed an appeal with the Supreme Court of Turkey, which ruled in November 2008 against its closure

30 The petition – titled 'We Are Not Free Yet' – was endorsed by more than 1,300 women wearing headscarves. The writers were invited on TV and radio stations to explain their initiative. Two of the writers (Akbulut and Kaplan) have argued that this petition was implicitly critical of the AK Party, which had been putting a stop to its earlier reformist zeal, in particular with regard to religious minorities (Birch, 2008).

31 The 1982 Constitution was drafted by the military junta after a political coup in 1980, and contains many articles that limit citizens' freedom. As of 2011, the Turkish Parliament has started to work on a new constitution. Yet, this has sparked heated debates and consensus has yet to be found on key controversial questions. This stalemate has tamed initial enthusiasm for a new constitution. For more information see Amani, 2013.

32 The aim of the coalition was to stop both US intervention in Iraq and Turkey's participation to the war.

33 Members of AKDER suggested that I meet with this activist, as she had been involved in the coalition process since its beginning. For this activist, one of the most important aspects of this coalition has been the possibility it offers to understand each other. 'We start to understand each other – until that time I never knew the time of prayer, but if you are working with Islamic people you need to. It was a

good way to understand the others, their ethics, and values […] When you work with people you see them as individuals and not enemies' (activist, Istanbul, 2008).

34 Both Shakman Hurd's and Taylor's models are based on the fact that one ethic, which takes its roots in religions that are dominant in a society, sets the norms for collective life.

6 A rights-based discourse

A door to multiple sites of challenges

This chapter explores the means and sites used by religious rights activists in France and Turkey to challenge state secularism. While the two previous chapters analysed their discourse, this chapter focuses on how these activists have been bringing cases to existing national and transnational legal institutions. In so doing, I make three interrelated arguments. First, by exploring the impact of restrictive national laws on the strategy of rights-based activists, I highlight, along the lines of other works (e.g. Keck and Sikkink, 1998; Soysal, 1994), how the use of a human rights discourse has facilitated access to different international platforms to seek redress beyond the boundaries of nation-states. Second, I suggest that a rights-based discourse offers access to an empowering vocabulary, increasing the authority of complainants and allowing them to lobby and network with transnational activists (e.g. NGOs, policy makers, etc.). Finally, this chapter emphasizes that the possibility of bringing local issues to international platforms creates a dynamic, where key debates around the definition of secularism and the modern 'acceptable' religious subject are now also located in transnational spaces. This gives a particular authority to transnational activists and bodies in defining and regulating the boundaries of the right to freedom of religion. Not surprisingly, because women have been occupying an important place in national debates over secularism, their status is again subject to special scrutiny in these international forums. Overall, I argue, along with others (e.g. Shakman Hurd, 2012), that to be able to grasp all the facets of the contemporary discursive power of secularism, studies of secularism at the national level ought to be complemented by an analysis of how the 'ideal' secular settlement is being negotiated in international forums.

Through this exploration, this chapter participates in the scholarly efforts that seek to investigate how national human rights concerns are brought and presented to international platforms, and how supra-national bodies respond to these concerns, as well as deal with cases of the (re)appropriation of human rights that they might not have foreseen (e.g. Wilson, 2007; Merry, 2006). As Wilson says, although some studies have started to focus on this phenomenon,[1] more needs to be done to fully grasp the epistemologies and discourses of international human rights law (2007: 306). Following on these lines, this chapter examines comparatively the rulings of international human rights bodies (i.e. ECtHR and UN Human Rights bodies) on headscarf bans. While a number of scholars have analysed the rulings of the ECtHR on religious symbols (in particular rulings concerning headscarf bans in Turkey and Switzerland (see, for example, McGoldrick 2006; Marshall 2006; Gibson 2007; Gökariksel and Mitchell 2005; Lewis 2007; Vakulenko 2007; Danchin 2011)), those that have compared the rulings of UN bodies and the ECtHR on this topic are not numerous. The few who have done so have focused on revealing the differences in opinions between these bodies with respect to headscarf bans (e.g. McGoldrick 2006; Ssenyonjo 2007) but have not looked at how these rulings are the result of different approaches to secularism, and are therefore exercising dissimilar authority on the religious – that is, how interpretations of secularism regulate and enable different types of religious sensibilities, and the implications this has for the (in)ability of plaintiffs to get their religious freedom claims acknowledged and redressed. Capturing this relationship is important insofar as it continues to contribute to our understanding of secularism as a hegemonic process, as well as giving us further insights into how secularism is related to defining the boundaries of the religiously acceptable, and consequently of the right to religious freedom.

The following discussion is divided into three parts. The first part examines how French activists have started to specialise in litigation at the national level to protect their religious freedom. In the second part, the chapter explores why and how Turkish activists have, for their part, focussed more on lobbying activities in international forums. Finally, the last section compares the rulings of UN bodies and the ECtHR on secularism and the right to religious freedom. This section is insightful as it is a way to highlight that while secularism has become the de facto mode of religious governance in a democratic nation-state, there is no international consensus on its meaning.

Litigation at the national level: the work of French activists

For Turkish activists, using national courts has proven to be a particularly arduous task, especially after the 1997 coup and how the Constitutional court defined secularism at the time.[2] Partly because of these difficulties, the usage of international human rights mechanisms, such as the ECtHR or different United Nations' human rights mechanisms (e.g. UN Special Rapporteurs, CEDAW committee, etc.) has become a viable and interesting strategy. The situation in France has been slightly different. Indeed, individuals could use the national courts to challenge the exclusions of students from public schools before 2004. Some did, and the *Conseil d'Etat* positioned itself generally against these exclusions provided that wearers were not disturbing public order. McGoldrick notes that out of 49 school exclusions, the *Conseil* actually reversed 41 between 1989 and 2004 (2006: 70). This situation changed in 2004 with regard to the exclusion of students in public schools, yet complaints concerning exclusions from other types of spaces can still be brought to national courts.

As discussed in Chapter 4, French Muslim activists have been using a rhetoric that bases itself in national jurisprudence to challenge the March 2004 Law and its extensions. The CCIF and the 15 March Committee have actually chosen to specialise in litigation – providing legal support to victims (especially victims of the 2004 Law spill-over effect) and bringing cases to court when necessary. This is quite novel, as until the late 1990s Muslim associations were engaged in political lobbying but no group specialized in legal work.

The CCIF: seeking to foster a greater level of legal consciousness

Over the past decade, the CCIF has been thoroughly developing this legal angle.[3] Accordingly, as of 2013, the organization has had three full-time lawyers tasked with providing guidance to victims of Islamophobia – that is, to help complainants contact relevant authorities to report discrimination, to inform them of steps to take to file a complaint, and to provide them, in some instances, with legal help in courts. The CCIF has, for example, been actively involved in providing legal support to mothers wearing headscarves prohibited from participating in school outings with their children.[4]

The CCIF has also made a series of legal fact-sheets available online, where it provides legal advice for most common violations, including mothers excluded from partaking in school activities, higher education students excluded from schools, or discrimination, based on religious belief, in the workplace or in sport-centres. These fact-sheets are aimed at helping and encouraging victims not familiar with the details of French law to report and challenge discrimination. For instance, the fact-sheet looking at discrimination in sport-centres is divided into three parts. It starts by providing a short example of a case in which a women who has joined a sport-centre is asked to remove her headscarf to conform with internal regulations that prohibit visible religious signs. It then goes through what is said in the law, including the fact that the principle of *laïcité* cannot be applied to private spaces that welcome members of the public. It finally outlines the different steps that should be followed by a claimant.[5] These fact-sheets are part of a wider strategy, in which the CCIF seeks to create a greater awareness of rights and encourage French Muslims to systematically report and challenge discrimination. They see this as a way to substantially reduce endemic discrimination.

> The CCIF believes that only the vigilance of every citizen will put an end to discrimination. This is why it asks all parents of students to contact immediately the CCIF in all cases of discrimination linked to an affiliation to a particular religion, of which they could be a victim or witness.
>
> (CCIF, 2007)

Rights: an ambivalent tool set?

The CCIF has, over the years, participated in making rights more accessible and fostering a greater level of legal-consciousness among the victims of violations. Yet one could wonder, along with the worries expressed by other scholars (e.g. Vakulenko, 2007; Sullivan, 2005), if this legalization of religious concerns does not lead, at the same time, to a greater regulation of the religious – limiting, paradoxically, religious freedom. Indeed, this approach invites legal authorities to decide which behaviour and dress are considered to be religious and which of these are acceptable in the public domain. This implies increased scrutiny into the life of the believer, her body and her reasons for wearing certain types of clothing. It also invites, in some cases, legal authorities to produce a judgement on the nature of beliefs and practices. For instance, inquiries are conducted into whether one is considered to be a 'user' or a 'provider' of public services, whether a student's choice to wear a bandana, a hat or even a long skirt is motivated by fashion or by religious reasons, whether one is wearing a religious sign out of 'free' choice, whether certain attires are considered to be 'too' religiously radical to be worn in certain public spaces, whether a space is considered to be 'too' public for allowing particular religious symbols, and so on. Ironically, this scrutiny seems to participate in defining what is a 'suitable' religious behaviour and who is an 'acceptable' modern religious subject in the Republic. In other words, rights seem to be somewhat ambivalent. They appear, as Wendy Brown rightly argues, to be 'politically essential', as they allow an individual to defend her/his right to religious freedom. Yet, they are at the same time 'politically regressive' as their usage gives a particular authority to courts and policy makers in defining and judging the boundaries of religiosity in a modern state (2000: 239).

Needless to say, these concerns are not only valid with respect to the usage of national courts, but are equally relevant when activists choose to send complaints to transnational human rights sites. In fact, as discussed in Chapter 4, while the climate in France was more favourable for legal actions at the national level until 2004, it has become less so over the last few years. This shift partly explains why French Muslim activists, like their Turkish counterparts, have started to send complaints to the relevant international rights mechanisms.

> We just filed our first case with the ECtHR ... this is a historical moment [...] The injustice [i.e. headscarf bans] is now brought in front of the highest European Court.
>
> (Lawyer, 15 March Committee, oral intervention at the Annual Bourget meeting, Paris, May 17 2008)

Thus, in so doing, they are conferring a particular authority to transnational human rights sites, sanctioning their power as arbitrators of what is 'religiously' acceptable and what is not.

Access to international sites

Three reasons, in my opinion, best explain why complaints are presented to international human rights bodies. First, scholars have argued that the whole process of bringing a complaint to a human rights body and voicing one's concern, in terms of one's 'universal' human rights, empowers subjects, allowing them to gain a certain political recognition (Le Fort cited in Smith, 1998: 8; Wilson, 1997; Brown, 2000; Douzinas, 2007). This seems quite sensible, especially for complaints regarding the right to wear the headscarf, where women have often been considered to be 'objects' of their own culture in need of saving, rather than agents in control of their actions (Gökariksel and Mitchell, 2005). In fact, as emphasized in previous chapters, a human rights language invites devout Muslims to present themselves as autonomous individuals making sovereign and well-thought-out choices with regards to their faith. In international platforms, this discourse allows them to explain through a 'comprehensible' narrative, making reference to international human rights treaties and norms, the different human rights violations of which they have been victims. Consequently, one could argue that, regardless of the result, going through this process can provide a cathartic effect with victims creating a legitimate space, until then often unavailable, to recount or to acquire a certain authority over their story.

Second, building on this first idea, international platforms are also spaces that facilitate lobbying activities with other activists. For instance, these platforms allow plaintiffs and religious rights activists to interact, network and forge alliances with a variety of activists such as INGOs, UN member states, EU parliamentarians, and so on. Here again, apart from the rulings of international bodies, this work is a way to put concerns with regard to national secular policies on the international agenda. The Merve Kavakçı case and the Turkish CEDAW process, discussed below, illustrate the importance given to these lobbying efforts.

Third, and finally, these platforms are described as a way to seek 'worldly justice'.[6] While UN bodies' decisions are not legally binding, they may still put political pressures on the concerned nation-state and create public debates in society. On the other hand, ECtHR judgements are binding for states party to the ECHR, which explains why resorting to this body might be perceived as an efficient way to reverse national trends and regulations.

Lobbying for greater religious freedom: Turkish examples

> […] Appreciation of the success of these transnational legal campaigns begins not with an accounting of victory or defeat in the court, or on the floor of the legislature, nor merely with an assessment of their direct role in transforming existing international law or global norms, *but rather with the capacity of their participants to create an alternative discursive space in the legal records of the transnational struggles* […]
>
> (Dale, 2007: 316 (author's emphasis))

Because Turkish religious rights activists have longer experience in resorting to international bodies than their French counterparts, it has been easier to document their lobbying strategies. This is why this section focuses on two Turkish examples to illustrate this process. It is important to recall that this increased use of international human rights bodies has been possible, in part, because of the rising socio-economic status of urban devout Muslims in Turkey who have acquired the financial means to engage in these types of activities. Indeed, these are quite costly, as they imply frequent trips to UN offices (Geneva or New York), where human rights experts meet, as well as to Strasbourg and Brussels, cities hosting EU mechanisms. Moreover, these activities also require a certain fluency in English, as it is the lingua franca of these international forums. As mentioned, due to headscarf restrictions, a number of rights-based activists have been educated in foreign English-speaking universities (e.g. England, Sweden, Malaysia and so on).

INGOs and the Merve Kavakçı case

The Merve Kavakçı case at the ECtHR, in which the court ruled in favour of the complainant in April 2007 (Kavakçı vs Turkey, 2007), is interesting inasmuch as it is illustrative of how filing a complaint with the ECtHR can be used to network with different international activists, and gain access to other sites than the ECtHR.[7]

Merve Kavakçı, whose story was discussed earlier, was the first woman elected in Turkey while running for the former Virtue Party and wearing a headscarf in 1999. She was, subsequently, banned from parliament and saw her Turkish citizenship revoked because she had entered parliament to take her oath wearing a headscarf.[8] She and two of her former colleagues were also banned from politics for five years, and the Virtue Party was closed by the Constitutional Court. Subsequently, Kavakçı filed a complaint with the ECtHR. On 5 April 2007, the court ruled that Turkey was in violation of Article 3, Protocol 1 of the ECHR, requiring that states 'ensure the free expression of the opinion of the people in the choice of the legislature' (Kavakçı vs Turkey, 2007).

Throughout the preparation for her case, Kavakçı received support from a number of INGOs, providing her with legal counsel and testifying in her favour during hearings. For instance, the Inter-Parliamentary Union (IPU) adopted a resolution during its 171st annual session highlighting the illegality of the Turkish Constitutional Court decision in the Kavakçı case.[9]

> [The IPU] fears, in view of the information on file, that Ms. Kavakçi was not only arbitrarily prevented from assuming her mandate and duties as an elected representative of the Turkish people, but may also have been deprived of her membership without valid legal basis and according to a procedure not provided under Turkish law.
>
> (IPU, 2002)

The IPU, also, testified in her favour at the ECtHR – a testimony that was included in the ECtHR final decision (Kavakçı vs Turkey, 2007: 37 to 39).

Likewise, she received support from the Becket Fund for Religious Liberty,[10] a US based firm providing international legal aid to individuals who feel their religious freedoms have been breached. They offered her legal counsel for her case at the ECtHR, and released a press statement stating that 'Religious expression in public and in public institutions is a natural part of religious faith, and its peaceful exercise is expressly protected by the ECHR' (Becket Fund, 2007). They also provided her with an accreditation to the UN. She was thus able to testify in front of the former Commission for Human Rights (known today as the Human Rights Council) arguing that the headscarf ban:

> contravenes the Turkish Constitution as well as the international conventions that Turkey is signatory to, including the Universal Declaration of Human Rights (UDHR), International Covenant on Civil and Political Rights (ICCPR), and the Convention of Elimination of Discrimination Against Women (CEDAW) [...] This is a blatant manifestation of staunch secularism i.e. secular fundamentalism. Via this unique construct of secularism, the State systematically stifles and ostracizes women with headscarves.
>
> (Kavakçı, speech at the UN Commission for Human Rights, 2005)

More broadly, this case is indicative of the influence of US non-governmental rights organizations, such as the Becket Fund or Human Rights Watch, in participating in shaping authoritative interpretations of secularism and religious freedom.[11] Not only have both organizations provided support to a few women affected by headscarf bans, but they have also publicly positioned themselves in favour of an interpretation of secularism compatible with the expression of religion in the public realm (e.g. Human Rights Watch, 2004a, 2004b). Related to this last point, it is interesting to note that Merve Kavakçı, in an interview that I conducted in September 2007, stressed that Turkish *laiklik* ought not to be confused with American secularism, as in the Turkish case the state exercises a total monopoly over religion, obstructing a true separation between religion and the state. She suggested that Turkey consider embracing a model closer to the American one, where the state poses neither as a religious nor as a non-religious entity.

CEDAW: a transnational lobbying site

UN meetings have also been providing an engaging platform for Turkish religious rights activists to lobby and network. CEDAW meetings are one of these sites. The CEDAW committee, a UN expert body, is responsible for monitoring if states party to the CEDAW Convention respect, implement and make efforts to improve the status of women in their country. To do so, states are responsible for submitting a report every four years to the committee, who then calls for a formal dialogue during one of its session, in which reports are examined and commented upon. As is the case with many UN bodies, NGOs can follow the work of the committee and submit shadow reports to the CEDAW pre-session working group and the committee containing country-specific information on the state under review,[12] as well as make oral statements during the pre-session meetings and formal reviews.

Activists in Turkey started to use this mechanism in 2005 to highlight why they considered headscarf bans to be a violation of women's rights. This work was initiated mainly by members of the Capital Women's Platform. They have, in fact, been the only faith-based group to participate in the national CEDAW working group organized by non-religious women NGOs in Turkey in 2004 and 2005 to draft a common shadow report. However, they felt that this report did not do justice to the discrimination affecting women wearing headscarves, since it included only one sentence referring to the issue.[13] They therefore decided to submit their own shadow report focusing on the ban directly to the Committee during the 2005 review session. In this report, as explained in Chapter 5, they argued that because headscarf bans affect only women it should be considered as a women's rights concern not compatible with secularism that should ensure an impartiality of the state towards all subjectivities (Capital Women's Platform, 2005).[14] In other words, they linked headscarf bans with secularism, pointing to its gendered dimension in the Turkish context, and asked the committee to redress this issue.

Members of the platform also participated in the Committee session, where they distributed briefing notes to its members with additional information on the ban. Through this process, they became aware that Committee members had almost no knowledge of the ban and its consequences. The issue had, in fact, not been raised by the Turkish state or by Turkish NGO representatives of a non-religious background who had been working with the Committee during previous review sessions.[15] As a result of lobbying efforts by devout activists, the committee asked several questions to the Turkish state on this issue and included a reference on this point in its final report.[16] Activists considered this to be a real breakthrough, as it meant that the Committee had taken their concerns seriously. Not only had they asked questions to the Turkish state representatives and made a written comment on the situation but, more importantly, they had requested that the Turkish state report on this issue in its next national report.

The latest Turkish state review took place in New York from 12–30 July 2010. This time, to prepare for this review, more than 70 Muslim religious NGOs throughout Turkey participated in the drafting of a thematic shadow report focusing entirely on the headscarf ban. This was coordinated by AKDER. 'We decided to do a focus shadow report for CEDAW on the headscarf because it is not covered by the other reports' (activist, AKDER, Istanbul, 2008).[17] In addition to the coordination of the report, AKDER members took an active role in preparing for the review session. They participated in the CEDAW pre-session working group in New York in July 2008[18] and attended the review session in July 2010 to present their report.[19]

Thus, lobbying in international forums seems to be of significant importance as it puts issues of religious freedom and of the limits of Turkish secularism on the international agenda. In so doing, activists are able to highlight the exclusive and gendered dimensions of secularism, and to ask these international bodies to position themselves vis-à-vis their struggle. These activities seem to have been perceived as particularly useful in countering the influences of 'secularist' networks. Indeed, several of my interviewees argued that a decade ago devout women did not have the education or the funds to engage in such lobbying activities and build their own networks. This is, for them, one important reason why international policy makers have not been aware of, or have not grasped, the extent of the discrimination.

> When I went to the CEDAW meeting in 2005 my prerogative was lobbying. It was interesting that the CEDAW committee had no idea that there was a headscarf ban in Turkey, and this was so because the Turkish representative was a 'secularist/Kemalist' woman and it wasn't her issue so she didn't speak about it […] In the EU, we have been doing specific lobbying with the EU MP Emine Bozkürt. When she first came to Turkey, she had a totally Kemalist perspective. We have been doing lobbying with her, and now she sees the headscarf as a women's rights issue. This is very important for us. She is an MP with a Turkish background and how she will reflect the issue with the EU is central …
>
> (activist, Capital Women Platform, 2008)

One therefore becomes aware of how the possibilities of creating an 'alternative discursive space'[20] and acquire a certain level of authority in transnational sites remains deeply conditioned by one's ability to have the financial and educational means to access and speak the languages of these forums.

Decisions of international bodies: an illustration of the hegemony of secularism

Through these lobbying and networking activities, activists are triggering transnational discussions around the 'ideal' type of secular settlement among a variety of activists (e.g. INGOs, members states). They are also asking transnational bodies to develop an opinion on the concept of secularism and the limits it should put on religious freedom. Interestingly, while secularism is understood in both UN and ECtHR opinions/rulings as a quasi-unquestionable model of religious governance in a democratic polity 'respectful' of human rights, the meaning and shape it should take remains open to different interpretations. Thus, the limits put on the right to religious freedom are not stable and differ from one human rights site to another. In other words, transnational sites also seem to be deeply influenced by the hegemony of secularism.

UN experts' positions on secularism and religious freedom: exercising a supervising capacity

While the UN's opinions on the Turkish bans are yet to be detailed,[21] various UN bodies have given quite comprehensive opinions on the 2004 French law banning conspicuous religious symbols in public schools (see, for example, Diène 2004; Jahangir, 2006a, 2006b, 2009a, 2009b; McDougall, 2008; United Nations Committee on the Rights of the Child 2004; United Nations Human Rights Committee 2008).[22] To be specific, UN experts have been vested with the authority to evaluate if this law should be considered an acceptable interference in the right to religious freedom – they have, therefore, produced a discourse on secularism and the form of religious freedom it should protect and foster.

While these bodies have not questioned secularism as a model of religious governance in a democratic polity 'respectful' of human rights, they consider nevertheless that they have a responsibility to supervise and evaluate whether national models of religious governance are compatible with international human rights law or not. They foresee the possibility that there can be different types of secularism, including interpretations that may not always be in tune with human rights and lead to unjustifiable intrusion into the right to religious freedom. For them, this seems to be the case with the French 2004 Law and the vision of secularism it conveys.

> [The Special Rapporteur] is concerned that, in some circumstances, the selective interpretation and rigid application of the principle [secularism] has operated at the expense of the right to freedom of religion or belief [speaking on the French 2004 Law].
>
> (Jahangir, 2006b: 19)

> The [Human Rights] Committee notes that respect for a public culture of *laïcité* would not seem to require forbidding wearing such common religious symbols [conspicuous religious symbols] (article 18 and 26). *The state party should re-examine Act No. 2004/228 of 15 March 2004 in light of the guarantee of Article 18 of the Covenant concerning freedom of conscience and religion, including the right to manifest one's religion in public as well as in private, as well as the guarantee of equality under Article 26.*
>
> (United Nations Human Rights Committee, 2008: 7 (original emphasis))

One of the main concerns of these bodies is that secularism should ensure both the neutrality and impartiality of the state vis-à-vis religion. This implies first and foremost that states should take into account whether a particular prohibition affects disproportionately one religious belief more than another, ensuring that all beliefs are treated equally and that no distinction is made between the beliefs of majorities and those of minorities. It also means that states, courts, and policy makers should avoid judging or conferring a meaning on religious beliefs – a function that should be left to believers. This is clearly illustrated by the position of the Special Rapporteur on religious freedom or belief, who recalled that it is not the role of a state or a court to determine whether wearing religious attire (including headscarves) is a religious 'observance' (i.e. compulsory) or a 'practice' (i.e. an authorized but not prescribed religious expression).[23]

> A certain appearance or exhibition of a symbol may or may not be linked to any religious sentiment or belief. It would therefore be most inappropriate for the State to determine whether the symbol in question was indeed a manifestation of religious belief.
>
> (Jahangir, 2006a: 13)

This understanding of the role of the state affects experts' interpretation of the limits that should be put on the right to religious freedom. While they agree that restrictions can be put on the right to manifest one's religion in compliance with the limitation foreseen by articles on religious freedom in international human rights law,[24] these limitations ought not to be based on 'speculation or presumption' nor on an interpretation of a religious belief but rather on 'demonstrable' facts (Jahangir 2006a: 16). Not unlike the approach promoted by the French *Conseil d'Etat*, this interpretation favours a case-by-case strategy in which states and courts are asked to evaluate each time if the actions of an individual manifesting his or her religion are disruptive, and to review whether tangible proofs of this disruption are available.

In the light of this approach to secularism, experts evaluate the French 2004 Law as trespassing on their understanding of state neutrality, which requires states to adopt the same attitude towards all beliefs. Indeed, even if the law is conceived as affecting equally all conspicuous religious symbols, it has been disproportionately targeting Muslim women as they represent the largest religious minority touched by this ban and a minority that has also become the focus of increased acts of intolerance beyond public schools. By not taking into account the 'specific features' of religions (e.g. whether the wearing of visible religious symbols is more frequent in one religion than in another) (Jahangir, 2006a: 17), the law ends up introducing an indirect bias in favour of members of the dominant religion and puts an extra burden on religious minorities.

> This ideological climate [belief in the theory that conflict is inevitable between different cultures and civilizations combined with the refusal to

> recognize their interaction and cross-fertilization] has coloured the debate on secularity currently taking place in France, through its negative connotations with regard to discrimination; whatever the intentions were behind the bill forbidding the wearing of ostensible religious signs in schools, it has been seen as essentially aimed at the Islamic headscarf, and therefore as a form of stigmatization of Islam.
>
> (Diène, 2004: 6)

> The concerns of the Special Rapporteur are more serious with regard to the indirect consequences of Law 2004–2228 in the longer term. […] the stigmatisation of the headscarf has provoked instances of religious intolerance when women wear it outside school, at university or in the workplace.
>
> (Jahangir, 2006b: 19)

Moreover, by considering secularism to be a sufficient reason in and of itself to systematically regulate religious practices and, as a result, failing to embrace a case-by-case approach, experts consider that the 2004 Law represents a disproportionate interference in the right to manifest one's religion as it invites the state to confer a meaning to a religious belief regardless of whether the actions of a believer disturb public order or not.

In this interpretation, the principle of neutrality is applied, therefore, first and foremost to the state and not to citizens in the public domain, as it is understood that the latter interpretation could lead to certain groups being treated differently from others. This interpretation is, however, not devoid of its own authority. In practice, attempts to avoid judging religious beliefs are not entirely successful, and this seems to be due to the importance given by experts to protecting individual sovereignty. For instance, the Special Rapporteur on freedom of religion or belief in her review of the French 2004 Law considered that it could be appropriate to limit the right to express ones religion by wearing a specific attire if it was forced upon someone, yet if the believer chose to wear it 'freely' then it had to be respected.

> The law is appropriate insofar as it is intended, in accordance with the principle of the best interests of the child, to protect the autonomy of minors, who may be pressured or forced to wear a headscarf or other religious symbols. However, the law denies the rights of these minors, who have freely chosen to wear a religious symbol to school as part of their religious belief.
>
> (Jahangir, 2006b: 19)

In other words, the ability to make an 'autonomous' choice is, in this interpretation, set as a prerequisite for one's beliefs to be protected by the right to religious freedom. One could argue that this understanding resembles a theological statement inasmuch as the notion of 'free choice' is considered, here again, to be an intrinsic component of a 'rightful'/ 'proper' faith and religious subjectivity. To put it differently, this statement reveals how international human rights opinions end up authorizing specific interpretations of religious freedom, while disabling others. Indeed, along similar lines to what was discussed in Chapter 5, this process carries the risk of undermining the possible complexity behind the decision to manifest one's religion. For instance, as Mahmood has argued in her work, the headscarf is considered in these types of interpretation as a sign or symbol (2009: 73) – an arbitrary representation of the sacred – located outside the subject and her sovereign conscience and that can therefore be interpreted, judged, examined, and ultimately whose pros and cons can be weighed in order to make a free and rational decision on wearing it or not. Yet, this interpretation fails to take into consideration the fact that it could be considered a divine duty, a religious prescription that is part and parcel of one's ethical practice and subjectivity. That is, it leaves little space for nuances and in so doing fails to consider the point of view of women for whom the headscarf may not be considered an object located outside of the self but 'a means and an end to realizing the "will of god"' (Mahmood, 2006: 343).

ECtHR judgements on secularism and religious freedom: validating national models of religious governance

Among the reasons mentioned by activists to explain why they have been sending complaints to international bodies is their quest for 'worldly justice'. While UN human rights bodies' opinions and comments are not legally binding, the judgements of the ECtHR are. This could be where the added value of resorting to the ECtHR lies, as it has the power to ask a state to change its laws, and therefore modify national models of religious governance.

The court has, however, adopted quite a different approach to secularism to the UN experts. It views its supervising capacity to be limited when it comes to models of religious governance as it considers that these differ substantially from one national context to another. This argument is used as a justification to give a wide margin of appreciation to national states in cases dealing with the presence of religious symbols in the public realm. As a result, the court, in contrast to UN experts, does not make a distinction between models of secularism and avoids exploring whether the ways they are being implemented in specific cases are compatible with the ECHR. Secularism, which is understood as being in accordance with the values of the Convention (Sahin vs Turkey, 2005: para. 115; Dogru vs France, 2008: paras 17–22), is thus considered to be in and of itself a valid justification for limiting the right to religious freedom and more particularly the right to publically manifesting one's faith. This trend is visible in recent rulings related to the right of specific states to put, or abstain from putting, restrictions on religious symbols in the public realm.

Most of the cases reviewed by the court are related to bans on visible religious symbols – predominantly bans on headscarves – in public spaces (see, for example, Dahlab vs Switzerland, 2001; Sahin vs Turkey, 2005; El Morsli vs France, 2008; Dogru vs France, 2008; Aktas vs France, 2009; Bayrak vs France, 2009; Gamaleddyn vs France, 2009; Ghazal vs France, 2009; J. Singh vs France, 2009, and R. Singh vs France, 2009), including bans foreseen by the French 2004 Law.[25] The Leyla Sahin ruling is perhaps the case that has received the most scholarly attention and is one of the first judgements that clearly outlines the position of the court vis-à-vis secularism – a position almost mimicked in the French cases in 2008 and 2009. In the Sahin case, which was about a Turkish medical student who was unable to pursue her medical studies because she wore a headscarf that was understood as threatening the secular character of Turkish universities, the court sided with the state. It gave a wide margin of appreciation to the state and, while it admitted that restraining the headscarf was an intrusion into the right to manifest one's belief, it argued that this was not unreasonable to protect secularism. Consequently, it agreed with the interpretation of secularism of the Turkish state, who considered that the state could interfere in the subjectivities of citizens in certain public institutions (e.g., schools and universities) to ensure that they do not demark themselves from others, and therefore are all 'equal' in the public realm. This was understood as important, in a country with a majority of Muslim citizens, to ensure that pluralism and public order prevail in state public institutions (Sahin vs Turkey, 2005: para. 115). To put it differently, similarly to UN bodies, the majority of judges considered that the right to manifest one's religious freedom could be limited in accordance with Article 9 (2) of the Convention. Yet, for the ECtHR the 'special' socio-political context of Turkey was understood to be a valid justification in itself for allowing interference in the right to religious freedom. By validating this interpretation of secularism, the court authorized the meaning conferred on the headscarf by the Turkish state as being a religious symbol that carried a proselytizing project undermining the values of democracy regardless here of the actions of the believer (Sahin vs Turkey, 2005: paras. 114–16).[26]

The fact that the court adopted a similar approach to secularism in the French cases, including the Dogru and Kervanci cases (2008) and more recent French cases on the 2004 Law (see, for example, Aktas vs France, 2009; Bayrak vs France, 2009, or J. Singh vs France, 2009), allows for an even better evaluation of the politics enabled by this approach and the limits it puts on presenting claims regarding the public expression of one's religion. Indeed, even if these judgments draw extensively on the Leyla Sahin case and are grounded in a similar respect for national models of secularism, the political and sociological makeup of France is quite different to the Turkish one. While in the Turkish case bans on headscarves were justified to protect state secularism and plurality in a country with a majority of Muslims, in the French case similar arguments are brought to the forefront to regulate the practice of a religious minority.

> The Court also reiterates that the State may limit the freedom to manifest a religion, for example by wearing an Islamic headscarf, if the exercise of that freedom clashes with the aim of protecting the rights and freedoms of others, public order and public safety.
>
> (Dogru vs France, 2008: para. 64)

In other words, the wearing of the headscarf in public schools is considered to be a threat to the French public order protected by secularism and its concept of neutrality; however, in this case, public order is not conceived in terms of the 'eventual' threat a majority can pose to minorities like in the Turkish case but rather as favouring and protecting the dominant culture and its interpretation of acceptable religious sensibilities. 'In this approach religious diversity is indeed to be respected, but only on terms that conform to the majority's conception of the good' (Danchin, 2011: 702). While in the Sahin case the court approach ends up protecting a secular state from a possibly threatening Islamic 'majority' culture,[27] in the French case the court sides with a state that proposes an interpretation of secularism protecting the majority. Inasmuch as protecting secularism is justified by arguments of state neutrality and impartiality, one realizes in these cases how the concept of neutrality ends up favouring and protecting the majority's understanding of acceptable religious sensibilities. Consequently, unlike UN experts that saw themselves as invested with a supervising responsibility, where they had to evaluate whether models of secularisms were implemented in a way that could discriminate against a minority or favour a dominant culture, ECtHR judges rely entirely on the interpretations of states and the limits they put on Article 9 (2) in the name of public order.

In this process, the court reinforces the power of national states and their interpretations of the right to religious freedom, offering almost no possibility for critically assessing this interpretation and/or challenging it. This is quite visible in the attitude adopted by the court regarding the concessions made by French plaintiffs to best conform with national regulations – concessions that ranged from replacing headscarves by hats or bandanas when entering school grounds or participating in sports classes (see, for example, Dogru vs France, 2008 and Kervanci vs France, 2008 and Gamaleddyn vs France, 2009; Bayrak vs France, 2009; Aktas vs France, 2009; Ghaza vs France, 2009; J. Singh vs France, 2009; R. Singh vs. France, 2009), removing one's head covering altogether when entering school classrooms (Aktas vs France, 2009) to agreeing to remove headscarves for identity checks if conducted by a woman (El Morsli vs France, 2008). In all these cases, the judges argued that they felt incapable of determining whether these compromises were sufficient or still represented a threat to secularism and should be limited in accordance with Article 9 (2). As a result, relying on the opinion of the French state that did not consider these concessions to be appropriate, they failed to seriously review the arguments of the applicants.[28] In so doing, they also gave their opinion on the 'religiosity' of the symbols (i.e. the hats or bandanas), as they agreed with the French state that such attire could be considered a conspicuous manifestation of religion, contravening secularism. It is particularly interesting to note that, in this approach, hats and bandanas have been considered signs allowing the court and the state to examine, to scrutinize, and ultimately to justify their exclusion.[29]

> With regard to the applicant's proposal to take off her headscarf when entering classrooms or to replace it by a hat or a bandana that would have, in her opinion, no religious connotations or at least would not be a conspicuous sign exercising pressure, the Court reiterates that such an understanding falls squarely within the margin of appreciation of the State […]. Internal authorities have been able to evaluate, that in this specific case, the wearing of such an accessory inside high school premises constituted as well a conspicuous manifestation of religion, and that the applicant had therefore trespassed the regulation. The court subscribes to this analysis and stresses that with respect to the terms of the current legislation, that expects that the law can address the emergence of new signs as well as eventual attempts to bypass the law (notice of May 18 2004 above), the reasoning of the internal authorities is not unreasonable.
>
> (Aktas vs France, 2009: para. 2)

To sum up, this approach confirms that the court embraces an interpretation of secularism that considers certain religious beliefs to be incompatible with secularism, regardless of the actions of believers or whether they have freely chosen to embrace a belief. For Danchin, this standpoint cannot be understood without taking into consideration the deep historical connection between Christianity and how the courts (and European states) interpret religious freedom, a connection that becomes more visible through the claims of non-Christian plaintiffs. In this view, Christianity is understood as a religion in which beliefs remain in the private conscience – an interpretation that has been shaped and is intrinsically linked to narratives of secularism that make a clear distinction between the private self that remains out of the purview of the state and the public realm. In other words, it is precisely harm rendered upon this private belief that needs to be protected by the right to religious freedom (a belief that is located in one's own conscience), while personal manifestations of religion in the public realm are considered to deviate from this dominant interpretation of the religious.

> Any non-Christian or non-Western religion such as Islam which deviates from this notion of religion as a private belief and subjective experience thus faces a double charge: not only is it a threat to the secular political order, but it is also not religion in its true, modern form.
>
> (Danchin, 2011: 689)

This is quite enlightening, as one first sees how the right to religious freedom as conceived by the ECtHR has been shaped by the dominant form that Christianity has taken in Europe over the last century and has been developed to protect this 'modern' belief. One also realizes how, in these cases, the discourse of secularism whether referred to by states or by the court ends up protecting a type of neutrality that favours this interpretation of religion. Religious plurality is, thus, undermined since religious beliefs and subjectivities of religious minorities or non-Christian groups are being regulated and reshaped in order to fit the shape and form religion ought to have in modern times (e.g. Danchin, 2011). This process is clearly illustrated in the Sahin case where, as pointed out by Gibson (2007: 9), judges have underlined that, even if the wearing of the headscarf is banned, practicing Muslims still remain able ' … to manifest their religion in accordance with habitual forms of Muslims observance' (Sahin vs Turkey, 2005: para. 118). In other words, in this statement, the wearing of the headscarf – the individual public manifestation of one's religion – is not judged as being an 'observance' of Islam, but rather a non-prescribed 'practice', not essential for the private observance of religion.[30]

> The majority [of judges] thus consider that wearing the headscarf contravenes the principle of secularism. In so doing, they take up a position on an issue that has been the subject of much debate …
>
> (Sahin vs Turkey, 2005: Dissenting Opinion, para. 7)

To sum up, in the cases reviewed above, the court was asked to position itself by plaintiffs vis-à-vis secularism and its principle of neutrality. In order to determine whether neutrality is threatened or not, it has been invited to produce theological-like statements with respect to the religiosity of attire (e.g. hats) – that is, conveying a symbolic religious meaning to attires that might not have been considered as such elsewhere (e.g., hats and bandanas), to the power of these attires, and to whether they should be considered religious prescriptions. It would seem, therefore, that framing claims under Article 9 of the Convention explicitly encourages the regulation of the religious. Unlike UN experts who have put a particular emphasis on evaluating whether the actions of a believer on a case-by-case basis threaten neutrality and public order, in the case of the ECtHR the 'symbol' and value system it conveys is thought to be sufficient to determine if it is a threat to state neutrality. One also realizes through this comparative analysis that the fact that ECtHR and UN experts approach secularism in a different manner greatly influences their interpretation of the right to religious freedom, and as a result what is considered to be religiously acceptable in a 'modern' nation-state. This does point to the fact that the 'universal' right to religious freedom is not easily defined and is interpreted in a different manner not only by states, but also by transnational human rights bodies.

Overall, while differences between UN opinions and ECtHR ones can be partly explained because the latter are legally binding while the former are not, one should also realize that these are representative of two quite different political projects and understandings of the ethos of the public realm in a secular nation-state. The ECtHR anticipates a public realm where the neutrality of individual citizens can be a prerequisite for equality and societal cohesion – a neutrality that seems to be coloured by a dominant interpretation of religion as a private belief and that justifies active intervention in the faith of subjects ensuring that their faith conforms to this homogenous conception of religion. To put it differently, religious minorities and/or non-mainstream Christians are asked to conform to this dominant interpretation of religion, which is a move that is thought to ensure stability and order in the public realm. As we have seen, this public realm is not necessarily a-religious. Rather religion can have a place in it as long as it is not perceived as disturbing public order. It seems, therefore, that the discourse of secularism inscribes itself within a wider political project that contributes to setting the boundaries and norms of a cohesive Europe – a project that has become more tangible in a post 9/11 climate.

On the other hand, UN experts embrace a different secular ethic that seems more open to plurality or at least, by focusing on protecting the right to individual differences, takes into consideration the fact that secular models can in some instances favour the dominant culture. In other words, they acknowledge the possibility that, in some cases, imposing a neutrality requirement on individuals can burden some specific groups more than others. Comparing the opinions of the UN experts with those of the ECtHR on the French 2004 Law is particularly revealing in that respect, as it allows us to see how the rulings of the ECtHR fail to even take that possibility into consideration. However, as seen by putting individual autonomy at the centre of their interpretation of secularism, this usage of secularism is not devoid of its own authority.

Conclusion

This chapter has explored the means used by religious rights activists to challenge headscarf bans in France and Turkey. As seen, one of the main differences between these two contexts is that in France religious rights activists have been, to a certain extent, able to use national courts to challenge exclusions, whereas this has been more difficult in Turkey. However, the French climate is changing, and, as a result, it seems that activists are starting to use international forums more actively.

In my view, the cases brought to international forums highlight quite interesting trends. First, it is a good example of the growing authority of transnational bodies in shaping 'religious and political lives' (Shakman Hurd, 2012: 955). In a sense, therefore, it points to the fact that one cannot examine debates on secularism and the boundaries of religious freedom just at the national level, but that it is essential to also consider this transnational dimension. Second, it provides further evidence of the usefulness of looking at secularism as a hegemonic process, since it is understood in transnational human rights spaces as the sole model of religious governance, but a model whose terms are not fixed. This reality is noteworthy, if only because it can influence the strategies of faith-based activists. Indeed, it is possible that the approach embraced by the ECtHR, favouring a particular interpretation of secularism and consequently of religious freedom, pushes devout activists who do not adhere to this reading to increase their involvement with UN mechanisms and embrace the understanding of secularism favoured by these bodies.

> We are also going to send complaints to the UN [regarding mothers who are excluded from partaking in school outings]. We participate in sessions of the UN Human Rights Council, and members of the CCIF, CFPE as well as excluded mothers are going to be heard [...]. We are going more to the UN than the ECtHR, as it [the ECtHR] is heavily influenced by France. For us it is especially important that people become aware of the situation. It is generally difficult to do that beyond our circle.
>
> (Member of CFPE and MTE, Paris, 14 April 2012)

In so doing, they position themselves in favour of an interpretation of secularism that gives particular importance to individual differences and sovereignty. As discussed, while this approach recognizes the importance of protecting the beliefs and practices of minorities, and therefore sets out an interpretation of neutrality that affects the state rather than citizens, it also ends up shaping, in its own way, the boundaries of what is religiously acceptable in a modern nation-state. It is worth considering, therefore, to what extent this process participates in the reshaping of their religious creed for it to be compatible with a liberal modern project. In other words, while this understanding of secularism, and the right of religious freedom it conveys, does recognize the freedom to express one's religion, it also carries the (dangerous) possibility of homogenizing religious practices and beliefs to questions of autonomy and choice. Being aware of this reality is, in my opinion, important insofar as it might open a space for both scholars and activists to think of novel and creative societal models that take seriously into consideration the question of religious plurality.

Notes

1 For a list of some of those researchers see: Wilson, 2007: 306, as well as the different contributions to Goodale and Merry, 2007.

2 Interviews with activists, AKDER, Istanbul, 2008.
3 The 15 March Committee has also been active on the legal front. During the implementation of the March 2004 Law, they set up a legal clinic for students. They also put in place a 1–800 number, where they were providing legal advice to students. 'We simply intended to keep them [the students] informed about the framework of the new law: what the text allowed and what it banned, the more general background of human rights and individual freedom defence laws, the addresses of institutions such as education authorities, administrative courts, human rights defence bodies, and possible sources of support available in their area such as mutual support, psychological help or tutoring organizations'(15 March Committee, 2005: 16).
4 Members of the CCIF follow a number of steps when they take on a case. They first try to initiate a dialogue and send a written letter stating the presumed illegality of a situation to the institution under scrutiny to resolve the matter informally. If this is not successful, they issue a press release on the situation, and finally file a complaint with the relevant judicial authority to resolve the matter formally (interview with activist and plaintiff, CCIF, Paris, 2007).
5 For a reading of different fact-sheets see http://www.islamophobie.net/vos-droits-fiches-pratiques (accessed 5 November 2013).
6 This quote is taken from an interview with Kavakçı, former Turkish MP, Washington DC, USA, 2007. Similar arguments were provided by members of the 15 March Committee.
7 While the ECtHR ruled that Turkey was in violation of Article 3, Protocol 1 of the ECHR, and asked the Turkish state to pay 4,000 Euros in compensation to Kavakçı, its judgement remained somewhat ambivalent. Not unlike other judgements discussed later in this chapter, the court was keen to be seen to uphold the 'secular' character of Turkey. Accordingly, in this judgement the court first emphasized that the measures taken by Turkey were appropriate in the context of attempts by a state to preserve secularism and public order, and then stipulated that the sanctions given to Kavakçı were still disproportionate.
8 The official reason given for revoking her citizenship was that Kavakçı had acquired US citizenship prior to her election without obtaining permission from the Turkish authorities. Generally, authorities have never been strict about citizens informing them prior to acquiring double nationality (Çemrek, 2004: 57).
9 The Inter-Parliamentary Union is an organization that aims to foster collaboration between parliamentarians across different countries, as well as contribute to the promotion of human rights. It is funded by MPs who are members of the IPU. Turkey is a member of the organization. For more information see http://www.ipu.org/english/whatipu.htm (accessed 5 November 2013)
10 The Becket Fund is a US public interest law firm, founded in 1994, whose mission is to protect the free expression of religious traditions. They provide legal support to religious freedom cases in the US and internationally. For further information see http://www.becketfund.org/ (accessed 5 November 2013).
11 Several scholars have discussed the influence of US governmental and non-governmental organizations in shaping the boundaries of religious freedom beyond US borders, including Shakman Hurd, 2012; Mahmood, 2006 and Cozad, 2005.
12 The CEDAW pre-session working group is responsible for preparing the list of issues and questions on a specific country for its formal review in front of the committee. For more information on the CEDAW process see Merry, 2006: 72–102 and CEDAW, NGO information note.
13 Interviews with activists, Capital Women's Platform, Ankara, 2008. The sentence reads as follow: 'Disability, sexual orientation, and dressing according to religious beliefs, lead to particular difficulties in being recruited and establishing

a business' (The Executive Committee for NGO Forum on CEDAW – Turkey, 2004).

14 For further information on the argument in this report see Chapter 5.

15 Interviews with activists, Capital Women's Platform, Ankara, 2008.

16 The reference included in comment 41 reads as follow: 'The Committee requests the State party to provide in its next report information, sex-disaggregated statistics and data relating to women in the judiciary, trafficked women and girls, as well as Kurdish women and other groups of women subject to multiple forms of discrimination and their access to health, employment and education, as well as various forms of violence committed against them' (CEDAW, 2005: comment 41).

17 A list of those NGOs is available at the end of the shadow report (CEDAW Shadow Report, 2010).

18 Following their meeting, the pre-session working group, in a list of questions to the Turkish state in preparation for the 2010 review session, included a specific question on headscarf bans: '[…] Please indicate whether any study has been carried out on the impact on girls' right to education following the Government's decision to ban the wearing of headscarves in school settings' (CEDAW, 2009 (comment 21)).

19 It is relevant to note that the drafting of this report has been the subject of media attention in Turkey, and articles on the issues were published in the Turkish newspaper Zaman and Today Zaman (Özdemir, 2008). Subsequent to their publications, AKDER was put under investigation by the Governorship of Istanbul, which asked that the organization submit some of its publications for examination. This in itself is quite noteworthy, as it shows that this international networking triggers reactions inside Turkey.

20 This expression is making reference to Dale's quote previously mentioned in this chapter (2007: 316).

21 Most of the aforementioned reports and opinions have been developed in reaction to the French 2004 Law. One reason that can explain this is that unlike France there is no specific law banning religious symbols in Turkey on which experts can base their opinions.

22 It is noteworthy that members of the CCIF and of the 15 March Committee have sent complaints and met with some of these experts, including with the UN Special Rapporteur on freedom of religion or belief, Asma Jahangir, during her visit to France in September 2005.

23 Her statement makes reference to a remark made by a committee member during the drafting of General Comment 22 on Article 18 of the ICCPR.

24 Limitations on the right to religious freedom are found in Articles 29 (2) of the UDHR, Article 18 (3) of the ICCPR and Article 9 (2) of the ECHR. These articles foresee limitations on the ground of public safety, order, health, moral, fundamental rights and the freedom of others.

25 Except for the El Morsli case that pertains to the requirement of removing one's headscarf for an identity check in a French Consulate, the other cases concern bans on headscarves or Sikh turbans affecting students or teachers (e.g. the Dahlab case) in public schools or universities (e.g. the Sahin case). Rulings for which decisions were given in 2009 are cases where plaintiffs contested the validity of the French 2004 Law.

26 For a detailed analysis of the Sahin case see, for example, Gibson (2007), Lewis (2007), Marshall (2006), McGoldrick (2006) and Ssenyonjo (2007).

27 The dissenting judge, Tulkens, in the Sahin ruling pointed to the fact that the majority of judges failed to review whether the Turkish state provided proof that the wearing of the headscarf was in fact disturbing public order or pluralism (Sahin vs Turkey 2005: Dissenting Opinion, para 8).

28 The court failed to review the arguments of the plaintiff in the Sahin case as well. For a detail discussion of this see Judge Tulkens' dissenting opinion.
29 This point makes reference to the previously mentioned implications, set out by Mahmood (2009), of considering religious dresses as signs or symbols.
30 The terms 'practice' and 'observance' are used in reference to the aforementioned distinction by the Special Rapporteur on freedom of religion or belief.

Conclusion

An invitation to transcend the secular/religious divide

> Perhaps the conversation we should be having, in this 'post-feminist' era, is about the resilience of patriarchy, about the global oppression of women in all of the forms that it takes. Although we would like to imagine that our 'culture' does not support this 'sort of thing', the statistical data as well as the stories of women, should we choose to hear them, offer another version of the truth about the equality of women.
>
> (Beaman, 2012: 244)

I am writing this conclusion in the midst of a heated summer. Turkey with its Gezi Park chapter and Egypt and Tunisia with their unfinished revolutions and counter-revolutions are making the headlines. Once again the religious/secular card is too often used as the most 'evident' and perhaps the easiest way to comprehend these events, at least in western media. And yet, once again, I am startled at how this either/or dichotomy fails to capture the complexity of what is happening. Take the Gezi Park event for instance – if one looks at the different activists who have taken part in it, as well as their actions and claims, one realizes that it brings together a rainbow of individuals with multiple identities (one of which might be religiosity but not necessarily), who are coming together to denounce a legacy of exclusions that is being repeated by the AK Party, and to ask for a different, more equalitarian polity. In fact, Yildiz argues that their demands 'stand prior to the question of religion and politics' (2013). Whether this is the case or not might be difficult to assess when events are still on-going, yet one thing that seems evident is that understanding these demands with a dichotomic lens creates an 'analytical myopia' that leads to a 'disregard for stories […] [that] do not neatly fit into the banally familiar and mutually exclusive positions …' (Yildiz, 2013).

In this book, I have argued for the importance of completing a top-down analysis of secularism with a micro-approach. In my view, doing so provides another example of the limits of dominant institutional discourses that try to (re)produce and sustain clear boundaries between the 'secular' and 'religious' – boundaries that fail to capture the complexity and blurriness of what is happening on the ground. In effect, by looking at the discourse of devout activists challenging headscarf bans in Turkey and France, the reader becomes aware that these individuals draw on dominant secular narratives to ground their claims. Not far from the demands of Gezi activists, they are involved in sketching a secularism that is compatible with an inclusive and more equalitarian interpretation of citizenship.

This micro-approach is interesting on several levels. First, it points to the hegemonic character of secularism – a hegemonic character marked by shifts that facilitate (re)appropriations and (re)articulations. As discussed in Chapter 6, this hegemonic character has a global dimension but, nonetheless, the contemporary Turkish and French contexts lend themselves particularly well to the study of this process. Indeed, both of these countries are marked by a tradition of 'assertive secularism' (Kuru, 2007) in which religious activists, to have a voice and be heard outside their circles, have been inclined to draw on the hegemonic character of secularism to formulate their claims. In other words, both cases have proven to be unique fields for exploring hybrid (re)articulations and better understanding how this process shapes the boundaries of religious freedom. Second, this approach highlights how gender is intrinsically linked to the spatial workings of secularism. One comes to realize that devout women, because they have been among the first to be affected by secular shifts, are at the forefront of the production of secular tropes, tropes in which gender equality occupies a central place. Finally, similarly to the Gezi events, in both cases this refashioning of secularism from below is also, and perhaps mainly, about promoting an inclusive and equal vision of citizenship in which respect for religion is one element among others rather than the central element. Whether this vision can be brought to life has not been the central subject of our discussion, yet the conscious efforts to create small and bigger coalitions, especially in the Turkish case, might be the first step towards achieving this goal.

Unwinding the argument

In order to capture the hegemonic workings of secularism, all of the chapters were constructed around unravelling and exploring the shifting character of this process and its impact on what is considered to be religiously acceptable. In the first part of the book, I investigated how dominant understandings of the term evolved over time and in response to different political climates. This allowed me to set the stage for the second part of the book, which focused on how devout activists have been challenging contemporary understandings of secularism in France and Turkey. By looking into their discourse, one realizes that the shifting character of secularism, explored in the first chapters, has facilitated the ability of activists to challenge the boundaries of their state secularism and (re)appropriate its languages, opting for a content that is more compatible with their piety.

Chapters 2 and 3 explored how the place of religion in the public realm, who can participate in that space and the level of state interference in religious affairs have shifted over time, in function of religions and political climates. The central aim of Chapter 2 was to highlight the importance of taking into consideration the historical legacies of secular discourses. Doing so allows us to situate and shed light on the different layers of meaning given to secular languages in Turkey and France. It also underlines how both Republics have a tradition of heavy state interference in the organization of faiths, in the content of their dogmas, and in the life of individuals identified as believers – a process which has been facilitated by defining and controlling religious family law. In excavating historical legacies, Chapter 2 explored the workings of the languages of neutrality and separation. In discussing the latter, the comparative analysis highlighted one important difference between our two cases. In the French case, the dominant interpretation of this language and the level of state interference it conveys have been, and continue to be, the source of vivid debates. For some, the 1905 Law lays out a clear separation between religion and state – a separation that requires a certain level of impartiality from the state and that therefore has difficulty coinciding with heavy state intervention in religious affairs. For others, reaching this separation actually requires the state to intervene in religion. Recent attempts by state elites to create a training programme for Imams illustrate these tensions. While they first tried, in 2005, to organize this training in the public University of Marseille, faculty members considered this to be incompatible with the impartiality requirement of public institutions. State elites who remained convinced that training Imams was 'one of the big challenges of Islam *of* France', and that the state had to pursue its endeavour of 'building and mastering an Islam *of* France' (office of Ms Alliot-Marie, Minister of Interior, cited in Le Bars, 2007a (author's emphasis)), sought alternative solutions and launched a similar programme with the private Catholic Institute in Paris (a private university). This exemplifies the difficulty of reaching a consensus over the interpretation of this separation principle, and the role religions should play in the public realm. Identifying and exploring these tensions and contradictions have proven to be important, especially since religious activists have drawn, and continue to draw, on these to ground their claims. The lack of such a legal framework in Turkey makes these contradictions less explicit, and sheds partial light on why religious activists have used alternative resources at their disposal to frame their claims. This first contextual chapter, therefore, emphasized the importance of unravelling the different layers of meanings given to secularism – meanings that are the product of specific histories, and that influence both the content and form taken by attempts to (re)articulate secularism.

Chapter 3 continued the exploration of the multi-vocal and shifting character of secular languages. It did so by offering a detailed comparative analysis of the evolution of headscarf bans in both countries. By analysing how exclusions unfold in multiple sites, it invited the reader to become acutely aware of the intimate relationship that exists between secular tropes, the production of space and gender. This discussion captured how the boundaries of what is considered public space extend or retract in accordance with different times and political climates, and points to the consequences of these shifts on the lives of devout women. In effect, by documenting these movements, one is able to clearly realise their vulnerable position as they find themselves at the margin of spaces – their ability to enjoy their citizenship rights varies therefore as a consequence of these shifts.

The systematic comparison offered in this chapter plays a triple purpose. First, it is an invitation to put in perspective a discussion that otherwise stays focused on one country. In so doing, one realizes how secular tropes are deeply related to modern constructions of space (e.g. private vs public, political vs familial, secular vs religious) that have a global dimension. Moreover, positioning the French case next to the Turkish one renders evident the fact that the (re)production of the gendered spatial workings of secularism is not only the concern of secular elites – it is also being (re)produced, at least to a certain degree, by religious elites. This is interesting inasmuch as it, yet again, shows how these workings are ingrained in conceptions of modernity and citizenship that transcend the religious/secular divide. Finally, the reader is invited to see how shifts in the languages of secularism shape the boundaries of what is religiously acceptable. A recurrent trend that flows throughout the discussion is that it is embodied practices that travel between the acceptable and the non-acceptable. On the other hand, beliefs that stay in one's conscience are not challenged; they remain within the boundaries of what is acceptable in the public realm.

This exploration of the shifting character of secular tropes sets the stage for understanding, in the rest of the book, how devout Muslims have been (re)appropriating secular languages to challenge headscarf bans. As discussed in Chapter 4, while some French devout activists were already sending complaints to courts in the late 1990s regarding ad hoc school exclusions, they were encouraged to formulate their claims in a clear and systematic manner after the passing of the March 2004 Law. The overall sense that comes out of this chapter is that the space to challenge bans has been quite limited, as it has located itself within the legal canvas already developed throughout French history. For instance, this has substantially restricted the possibility of activists to challenge bans affecting providers of public services, as there have been few openings in the jurisprudence to do so. Nonetheless, over the past decade, activists have developed a narrative in which the post-2004 climate is identified as marking a clear break with the 'true' and 'historical' meaning of *laïcité*. They have anchored their interpretation of *laïcité* in the 1905 Law and the pre-2004 jurisprudence of the *Conseil d'Etat*. In this process, they have argued that while neutrality remains a core concept of *laïcité*, it ought to affect the state and not individuals. The March 2004 Law and its extensions gainsay this understanding, since by imposing a neutrality requirement on users it invites state authorities to directly judge religious dogmas and their expressions. This leads the state to scrutinise the behaviour of a particular set of citizens and contradicts in turn the principle of equality. Activists highlight how this interpretation of *laïcité* limits devout Muslim women's access to citizenship. In so doing, they do not only emphasize the particularities of 'universal' citizenship, but also the fact that the languages of *laïcité*, including gender equality, can be used to discipline women's bodies and practices – bearing similarities with the patriarchal discourses these languages often denounce.

It is relevant to note that because this interpretation of *laïcité* is being sketched out by devout Muslims, it also challenges tropes inherited from the colonial past that stress the need for Islam and Muslim subjects to be brought into the frame of *laïcité*. Accordingly, my interviewees highlight that they are fully-fledged citizens who embrace and believe in *laïcité*, and that they are able to do so while choosing a life of heteronomy. In so doing, their interpretation of *laïcité* lays out the conditions for an understanding of collective life that does not prioritize one identity over others, but rather enables the coexistence of identities. '*Laïcité* has to guarantee the *vivre ensemble* [i.e. collective life] in the respect of differences, without exclusion, attack, discrimination, to ensure equality between human beings … ' (Nadjia, 43 years old, testimony in Chouder *et al.* 2008a: 149).

The main difference between Turkish and French activists seems to lie more in the resources used to challenge bans rather than in their discourse. Because Turkish courts have had a tradition of producing rulings confirming the exclusion of headscarf wearers from the public realm, activists have relied less on national jurisprudence. They have preferred to anchor their claims in a national process of political liberalisation, as well as in international human rights conventions ratified by the Turkish state. However, despite these differences, the content of their discourse presents noteworthy similarities that seem to be partly the result of the influence of strict secular regimes and secular laws on their subjectivity and how they frame their claims. Indeed, the argument of Turkish activists has centred on the fact that *laiklik* should protect their right to freedom of choice. This is one of the central reasons that has pushed them to argue that systematic headscarf bans are a direct infringement of their 'universal' right to religious freedom. While they are aware that international human rights law anticipates that restrictions can be put on the right to express one's religious freedom, they argue, like their French counterparts, that a distinction needs to be drawn between actions in the public realm of a believer and how she chooses to express her religion. In this argument, activists have been expanding their understanding of their personal space. It is precisely because the wearing of the headscarf belongs to that space that it should not be a basis, in itself, for restricting users, and even providers of public services, from participating in collective life. Rather the ability to participate or not should be evaluated by the actions of an individual, and whether these are disrespectful of the rights of others. To sum up, in this interpretation of religious freedom the distinction that is essential to evaluate whether limits should be put on this right is not between freedom of conscience and freedom of expression of one's piety, but rather between one's personal ethic (including how one chooses to express it) and one's actions in the public realm.

This notion of choice has also been central to the argument that headscarf bans infringe on women's rights, as it prevents them from being able to become fully autonomous. Activists stress that these bans have pushed women back into their household, denying them the possibility of being intellectually and financially independent, and therefore from the right to choose the lifestyle they want to adhere to – a right that, as they emphasize, is clearly spelled out in international human rights conventions (e.g. CEDAW, Article 11). Headscarf bans are compared with headscarf enforcements in Iran or Saudi Arabia, where in both cases states attempt to control women's subjectivity, not trusting that they can be autonomous enough to make their own decisions and judgements – depriving them, in so doing, of their sense of self. 'To force women to cover their head or to uncover it restricts fundamental principles of *women's right to individual autonomy*, and to make personal decisions' (AKDER, 2005:11 (author's emphasis)). In their interpretation therefore, *laiklik* also conveys the idea of individual autonomy. Yet, here as well, rather than requiring individuals to transcend their particularities to reach this state – inciting the state to embrace a patriarchal attitude to regulate subjectivities – it is understood as a principle that puts in place the conditions in collective life for subjects to have the possibility of 'freely' choosing their personal ethic. One understands, therefore, how *laiklik* can serve as a common imaginary that facilitates coalitions between unexpected activists.

While Chapter 6's central focus was to complement Chapters 4 and 5 by investigating some of the means used by activists to challenge bans (e.g. national and international legal mechanisms), it has made, in my view, a strong contribution to the book's overall argument. By exploring how restrictive national legal contexts have pushed activists to seek justice in international forums, the chapter unravelled how these forums have been producing their own discourse on secularism. Yet here, as well, these bodies have not been able to come up with a consensual interpretation of the term – it has remained a source of deep debate among international human rights experts. In effect, because the ECtHR has been giving a wide margin of appreciation to national states, it has been endorsing Turkey's and France's understandings of secularism and the limits they have put on the right to express religious freedom. UN experts, on the other hand, have favoured an understanding of secularism that can be, under specific circumstances, compatible with the display of religious symbols in the public realm. By doing so, they have embraced an interpretation of the term that differs substantially from the one being enforced by the states under scrutiny. Gender equality and women's rights have come to occupy an important place in both these articulations of secularism. This is not surprising since these bodies were asked to rule on headscarf bans and, therefore, to determine whether or not their understanding of secularism would allow devout women to participate in the activities of the polis. However, in my opinion, it is also indicative of the fact that women continue to be identified as markers of the ethics of modern polities. In the case of the ECtHR, the court sided with the states, which see the 'transformation' of devout women as a necessary step for equality and social cohesion in the public realm. For UN experts, by contrast, respecting individual 'free' choice has been considered to be of utmost importance for a secular polity. Paradoxically, while these are two very different models of public life, one should be attentive to the fact that in both cases devout women seem to remain subject to particular scrutiny, whether it is related to their ability to transcend their differences or to the fact that they have 'freely' chosen their faith. Finally, aside from possibly influencing the strategies of faith-based activists, these divergences are representative, yet again, of the shifting character of secularism and therefore of what is considered to be religiously acceptable in a modern nation-state. This character could, in fact, explain changes or wider discrepancies between rulings in the future, resulting from successful lobbying efforts, and/or of the need to delimit clearly the boundaries of a European identity and an Islam *of* Europe, as opposed to an Islam *in* Europe.

Evaluating the success of this (re)articulation

Throughout the years of researching and writing *Refashioning Secularisms*, I have been confronted, when presenting my work, with two different types of assumptions that vary according to the background of my audience, and these have, unsurprisingly, articulated themselves roughly along the secular/religious dichotomy. The first one was based on the idea that the mere fact that religious activists were (re)appropriating a secular paradigm meant that they had been co-opted into the secular hegemony, and that it would end up governing their ways of being. The second, quite different, was that these activists were actually using a language of secularism in an instrumental way, and that their attempts to modify this paradigm was simply the first step toward imposing a religious ethic on the public realm. I found it particularly difficult to react or respond to these statements. Part of the reason has been that this requires making assumptions about the inner motives of my interviewees, and predictions about the future, which I felt deeply uncomfortable and ill-placed to do. These were also, in many cases, an invitation to frame my responses in an either/or framework, which again was far from the initial objective of the book. However, in my view these recurrent statements still point to the need to discuss, at least partially, some of the results of this activism, including to what extent they are located beyond this either/or framework.

With regard to the first assumption, one realises that devout activists, through their reference to the discourse of secularism, do end up shaping the boundaries of what is religiously acceptable in a polity. By making a clear distinction between personal piety, including its expressions, and the actions of believers, they argue that while the state should not put limits on the former it should do so on the latter. In other words, an ethic that leads a believer to act against other values impeding peaceful coexistence in the public realm is considered to be incompatible with a secular imaginary – 'users [users of public services] manifest their respect for the right to difference' (CCIF, 2009a: 79). This also has implications for citizenship. By making respect for difference a core principle of this imaginary, one can easily foresee that individuals who fail to respect it would be excluded from being able to fully participate in the activities of the polis – setting, in so doing, the terms of inclusion and exclusion. However, even if here the discourse of secularism continues to shape the boundaries of the religiously acceptable, religious activists have been attempting to widen them to accept individuals with a variety of personal ethics.

This interpretation of religion is also influenced by the language of autonomy, which requires an individual to be fully sovereign to participate in collective life. In effect, activists are stressing the importance of being able to make an intellectually independent choice. However, they also suggest that this intellectual reflection can lead one to choose a life of heteronomy.

> Let me make my own choices: today my choice is to wear a jean, a sweat-shirt and a headscarf on my head. If you take this freedom of choice away, you oppress me and imprison me in a unique model of emancipation that I respect but that does not suit me anymore.
>
> (Malika in Chouder *et al.* 2008a: 300)

In a sense, therefore, they are proposing a hybrid understanding of autonomy, combining notions of agency and religiousness. It is relevant here to recall that religious duty has been barely mentioned in their public discourse (e.g. reports, press release, etc.). In my view, this is partly because activists consider that they are speaking to the secular state, and feel that they do not need to share details about their personal lives. Concretely, whether a believer considers the wearing of a headscarf to be a religious obligation or not remains a personal concern, as long as is not imposed by outside authorities. They are making a distinction between their well-thought-out choice to follow religious authority and an imposed form of authority, the latter being subject to scrutiny and limitations.[1] Despite this distinction and their attempt to show that piety and choice are not mutually exclusive, their focus on choice comes with its own share of conundrums. Indeed, it carries, among other things, the possibility of homogenizing religious practices, and therefore of failing to capture or provide space for the plurality of religious experiences. However, this process of exclusion is perhaps inevitable when tackling questions around the boundaries of religious freedom.

To sum up, while the (re)articulations of activists do end up clearly delimiting religious freedom, they do also in this process question the boundaries of the key dichotomies around which the dominant secular discourses in

Turkey and France have been articulated, including distinctions between freedom of conscience and the expression of religious beliefs, between duty and choice, and between self-emancipation and religious authority. A central question that remains to be answered is the extent to which this (re)articulation can succeed in modifying the dominant understandings of secularism, or at least pluralise them. In some ways, the success of activists seems to depend on their ability to find spaces for their claims to be heard and understood. The Turkish and French settings offer, in that respect, different possibilities. These differences are not only due to the fact that Muslims are a minority in one case and a majority in the other, but are also a consequence, as hinted throughout the book, of different political and economic climates.

In the French context, the possibilities of finding such spaces have become quite rare. First, due to the quite restrictive legal and political climate, challenging bans is becoming a more arduous task. On a more conceptual level, one can wonder if there is space in the dominant French imaginary to understand the nuances of the activists' (re)articulations, in particular when it comes to combining personal choice and piety. For instance, while they have referred to the concept of choice in response to the idea that they were forced to wear a headscarf, Fernando notes (2010: 26–27) that the usage of this concept provided further justification for French policy makers to put limits on that choice. They perceived it to be an indication that the wearing of a headscarf does not demarcate itself from other personal preferences, and is therefore voided of its inalienable character. Along similar lines, Fernando (2010) and Bowen (2007a: 176) highlight that individuals who have been arguing in their community that they understand the wearing of a headscarf to be a divine prescription, while stressing outside their community that it is their choice to opt for that practice, have been criticized for being inconsistent and having a double discourse, 'representative of either an incoherent subjectivity or an insidious plot to mask a "fundamentalist" agenda with liberal-republican language' (Fernando, 2010: 30).

In my opinion, these observations are illustrative of the limited prospects for challenging bans. As stressed, France seems to be going toward a general consensus around a secular imaginary where rigid binaries are being reinforced – where women's bodies are thus increasingly identified as the 'border-guards' of spaces in which collective life ought to be enacted. In practice, therefore, women who fail to accept the terms of this imaginary but still aspire to be active in society are increasingly confronted with two options, well summarized by Le Bars (2010):

> With her large black bandana, which covers her hair, Hayette, a student in business law, hopes to work in Islamic banking – 'to avoid having to expatriate myself'. Speaking about the situation of veiled graduates, she expresses her regrets, saying, 'France is wasting its potential, it still pays for our studies' […] Zoubeir also wonders, 'Is it a solution that the

> most qualified leave, while leaving the terrain open for those who are harming us?'

The first remedy, which is rather limited because of the quite grim financial situation of French Muslims, has been to create communitarian spaces, such as private Muslim schools or Islamic businesses, in which bans are harder to enforce.[2] Yet, as seen with the attempts to enforce bans in private day cares, this solution remains at best precarious. Moreover, the creation of such spaces in reaction to a new political arrangement that had as its aim the promotion of unity and assimilation seems to be a bit ironic, since it may well end up fostering greater segregation and divisions along religious lines. Another route for those who have the financial means and are qualified enough has been to seek employment in other countries, including in the UK or Canada, where the dichotomies haunting the French imaginary are not, or at least not for the moment, considered to be incommensurable.

> [...] since 2004, a number of French Muslim women leave our country. I met one of them when I was doing a survey. She had a PhD in philosophy and was explaining Levinas to Quebecers 'pure laine' [native-born] an expression used over there: she left after the adoption of this 2004 law, despite the fact that it did not affect her. We [the French] have been depriving ourselves therefore of Muslim feminists – because they do exist, even under a scarf for that matter ...
>
> (Baubérot, cited in Gerin, 2010: 429)[3]

Although both options are viable alternatives, they are indicative of France's success in slowly rendering expressions of piety, or rather selected visible expressions, an anomaly in collective life – locating them, in other words, outside the boundaries of the right to religious freedom.

The situation is different in Turkey. With the considerable growth of a pious Muslim bourgeoisie one could be inclined to think, in line with the aforementioned second assumption, that devout Muslims have been instrumentally (re)appropriating a secular discourse in order to impose an exclusive ethic that reflects the beliefs of the 'majority' of society. And, in fact, some of the recent policies and proposals of the current government might be indicative of such a trend.[4] One could also foresee that this economic power is enabling devout Muslims to create their own Islamic spaces, in opposition to secular ones, dividing society and rendering (re)articulations of secularism obsolete. Again, there is probably some truth to this vision as well. However, in my view, even if this book has focused on educated and urban activists, it has highlighted that in some cases, at least, the situation is more complex than the two options outlined above. One realises that repeated state restrictions, limiting considerably one's ability to participate in collective life, have influenced how devout and urban Muslims conceive of their subjectivity, and has incited some of them to find innovative solutions to combine piety and secular languages. Moreover, this restricted climate has also rendered them aware that they have not been the only ones affected by heavy state interference in their ways of being, pushing them to link their own struggles with wider demands for societal reforms and forge alliances with individuals with different personal ethics – making their struggle less about replacing a dominant secular ethic by a religious one, and more about developing an ethic of coexistence. Finally, the Turkish economic and political liberalization seem to be factors that, at least until recently, have given a greater discursive power to devout activists in comparison to their French counterparts. Indeed, it has facilitated their access to a plurality of discursive spaces, including transnational spaces, in which the terms of the secular imaginary can be debated and (re)articulated.

Yet, as discussed in Chapters 3 and 5, the position of Turkish activists is not without its share of conundrums. In effect, one realises that the role played by devout women in enacting divisions between the private and public realms, central to the spatial workings of secularism, is at best partly challenged by conservative elites. These elites seem to embrace, in several instances, a similar patriarchal attitude to their secular counterparts, where they assign, and ask pious women to (re)produce, an identity defined in terms of their familial bonds, and often fail to consider the possibility that these women might have multiple identities. While this double exclusion has rendered the struggle of devout activists more complicated in many ways, it seems to have, at the same time, allowed them to refine their discourse so that it explicitly points to the deep parallels that exist between the worldviews of conservative and secular elites. This last point is quite important as it renders explicit trends that would, if one were to focus only on the French case, be less visible. Again, this points to the fact that while most of the discussion in this book has been on exploring the shifting and hegemonic character of secularism, and while activists have framed their discourse within this hegemony, their (re)articulations go well beyond a model of religious governance. It is about a vision of citizenship and alternatives ways of being that challenge the deep-seated 'resilience of patriarchy' (Beaman, 2012: 244) entrenched in many articulations of modern politics, regardless of whether they are religious or secular – a vision that resonates in many ways with the on-going 'spirit of Gezi'.

It is difficult for me to end this journey without briefly reflecting on the fact that over the years of writing this book debates over banning headscarves, bandanas, long skirts, *niqabs*, *burqas* and other types of garments have become almost the norm, especially in western countries, affecting a very diverse range of women from basketball players, to day care owners, to students in universities. The summer of 2013 has proven to be a good example of this current climate. The imagination of French journalists and policy makers was captured by a controversial report of the HCI on religion in universities, in which it proposed a restriction on the wearing of headscarves in that setting. A little later, the province of Quebec was confronted by similar debates over the possible presentation of a 'Charter of Quebec Values' in the fall of that same year, in which the minority government headed by the Party Quebecois would ban public servants from wearing visible religious symbols. The more I think about these obsessions, the more I wonder whether these do not share similarities with the dynamics discussed by Wendy Brown in her study of why modern nation-states are obsessed with the construction of walls to 'protect' their borders (2010). It may be a sign indicating, here as well, the deep crisis of identity that contemporary polities are facing today. In an era where the borders of nation-states are being eroded, and where states are rapidly disinvesting themselves from several of their functions, the focus on this 'other' might be a way for these political formations to symbolically assert their power and create the illusion, or the 'fantasy', to use Rosalyn Deutsche's term, of undisrupted borders (Brown, 2010: 24). In other words, this obsession with 'reforming' Muslim women seems to 'produce' the illusion of an active, invested and stable polity. Thus, not unlike walls, Muslim women's predicaments today participate in producing 'not the future of an illusion, but the illusion of a future aligned with an idealized past' (Brown, 2010: 133). These reflections are important ones. While they are well outside the focus of this book, they merit our attention and are an eager invitation to embark on new and much-needed research journeys.

Notes

1 This distinction between choice and imposition is, as discussed by others (e.g. Brown, 2000), not devoid of its paradoxes. While it is easy to draw a discursive line between those two notions, in practice it is much harder. One wonders, therefore, if despite the attempts by activists to complicate the language of choice and autonomy, they might not be confronted, in practice, by a recurrent dilemma in which the boundaries between choice and imposition are blurrier than they seem discursively.

2 This option of developing communal networks was mentioned in my interviews, as well as in several written testimonies, including in Chouder *et al.* 2008a. However, it remains a limited route. For instance, in 2009, France had only 7 private Muslim schools, with the first one opening its doors in 2003, while there were 250 Jewish schools and 9,000 Catholic ones (Ben Rhouma, 2009).

3 Jean Baubérot is one of the few French philosophers critical of the March 2004 Law. The option of leaving France was also mentioned in interviews, newspapers articles and several testimonies.

4 For instance, the passing of a law limiting the sale and consumption of alcohol at night in 2013 or Erdogan's suggestion to implement a new anti-abortion law could be interpreted as examples pointing to the imposition of an exclusive, religious-conservative inspired ethic.

Bibliography

15 March Committee. (2005) *The Headscarf ban in French schools: truth unveiled*, Bayane Edition. Available online at www.ihrc.org.uk/attachments/6454_The_headscarf_ban_in_French_school_Internet.pdf (accessed 8 October 2013).

Abu-Lughod, L. (1998) 'Feminist Longings and Postcolonial Conditions', in L. Abu-Lughod (ed.) *Remaking Women. Feminism and Modernity in the Middle East*, Princeton: Princeton University Press.

Achi, R. (2005) 'La laïcité à l'épreuve de la situation coloniale. Usages politiques croisés du principe de séparation des Églises et de l'État en Algérie coloniale. Le cas de l'islam (1907–54)', *La Justice en Algérie de 1830–1962,* Paris: La documentation Française.

——. (2006) 'Les apories d'une projection républicaine en situation coloniale: la dépolitisation de la séparation du culte musulman et de l'Etat en Algérie', in P-J Luizard (ed.) *Le choc colonial et l'islam: les politiques religieuses des puissances coloniales en terres d'islam,* Paris: La Découverte.

Ahmed, L. (1992) *Women and Gender in Islam. Historical Roots of a Modern Debate*, New Haven and London: Yale University Press.

Akbulut, N., Yilmaz, H. and Kaplan, H. (2008) 'We Are Not Free Yet!', Declaration.

AKDER. (2004) *There is no limit in the illegality of the headscarf ban*, 1998–2004, Istanbul, Turkey.

——. (2005) *Assessment of the Women Condition in Turkey According to the Statistics and the General Impacts of the Ban on Women*, Istanbul, Turkey.

——. (2007) *Latest Updates From AKDER on Turkish Women and Some Survey About Turkey 2006–2007*, Istanbul, Turkey.

——. (2008) 'Turban Crisis at Table Tennis', Press Release, 25 April.

Akyol, M. (2011) 'Veiled Women Versus Conservative Men', *Hürriyet Daily News,* April 6.

Amani, A. (2013) 'Turkey's growing constitutional conundrum', *Open Democracy,* March 22.

Al-Ali, N. (2000) *Secularism, Gender and the State in the Middle East: The Egyptian Women's Movement*, Cambrige: Cambridge University Press.

Alemagna, L. (2010) 'Le NPA mal fichu sur le foulard', *Libération*, 5 February.

Anthias, F. and Yuval-Davis, N. (1989) *Woman, Nation, State*, Houndsmills, Basingstoke, Hampshire: Macmillan.

Arat, Y. (1997) 'The project of Modernity and Women in Turkey', in S. Bozdoğan and R. Kasaba (eds) *Rethinking modernity and national identity in Turkey*, Seattle and London: University of Washington Press.

——. (2005) *Rethinking Islam and Liberal Democracy: Islamist Women in Turkish Politics*, Albany, NY: State University of New York Press.

Asad, T. (2003) *Formations of the Secular: Christianity, Islam, Modernity*, Stanford, CA: Stanford University Press.

Aydin, A. (2005) 'An innovative Step towards Resolving Turkey's "Headscarf Conflict": Assessing the Application of the Interactive Conflict Resolution at the Civil Society Organization Level', Masters Thesis, Sabanci University, Turkey.

Baubérot, J. (2004) *Laïcité de 1905–2005, Entre Passion et Raison*, Paris: Seuil.

Beaman, L. (2008) *Defining Harm*, Vancouver: UBC Press.

——. (2012) 'The Status of Women: The Report from a Civilized Society', *Canadian Criminal Law Review*, 16 (2): 223–246.

Becket Fund for Religious Liberty. (2007) 'ECHR: Turkey at Fault for Expelling Merve Kavaçki from Parliament for Wearing Muslim Headscarf', Press Release, 11 April.

Benbassa, E. (1997) *Histoire des Juifs de France*, Paris: Editions du Seuil.

——. (2004) *La République face à ses minorités: Les Juifs hier, les Musulmans aujourd'hui*, Paris: Mille et Une Nuits.

Benli, F. (2006) *Legal Evaluation of the Ban Imposed on University Students who Wear the Headscarf Subsequent to the ECtHR'S Ruling in Leyla Sahin v. Turkey*, Istanbul, Turkey.

Ben Rhouma, H. (2009) 'Rentrée 2009: Les écoles musulmanes font le plein', *Saphir News*, 4 September. Available online at www.saphirnews.com/Rentree-2009-les-ecoles-musulmanes-font-le-plein_a10477.html (accessed 17 October 2013).

Berkes, N. (1998) [1964] *The Development of Secularism in Turkey*, London: Hurst.

Birch, N. (2008) 'Turkey: Headscarved Graduate Students Lead Libertarian Movement', *Eurasia Insight*, 11 March. Available online at www.eurasianet.org/departments/insight/articles/eav031208.shtml (accessed 17 October 2013).

Bouissa, H. (2003) 'L'Islam est-il encore une religion?', *Oumma.com*, 17 December. Available online at http://oumma.com/L-islam-est-il-encore-une-religion (accessed 17 October 2013).

Bouzar, D. (2001) *L'Islam des Banlieues. Les prédicateurs musulmans: nouveaux travailleurs sociaux?* Paris: Editions Syros, 2001.

Bouzar, D. and Kada, S. (2003) *L'une voilée, l'autre pas: le témoignage de deux musulmanes françaises*, Paris: Albin Michel.

Bowen, J. (2007a) *Why the French Don't Like Headscarves: Islam, the State and Public Space*, Princeton: Princeton University Press.

——. (2007b) 'A view from France on the Internal Complexity of National Models', *Journal of Ethnic and Migration Studies*, 33 (6): 1003–16.

——. (2010) 'Secularism: Conceptual Genealogy or Political Dilemma?', *Comparative Studies in Society and History*, 52(3): 680–94.

Brèze, L-T. (1996) *Discours d'ouverture 14ème rencontre annuelle des Musulmans de France: L'Islam dans la République*, UOIF, Paris, 27 December.

——. (2007) *Intervention du président de l'UOIF: De l'authenticité et de sa ligne conduite, 24ème rencontre annuelle des musulmans de France*, UOIF, Paris, 14 April.

Brown, W. (2000) 'Suffering Rights as Paradoxes', *Constellations*, 7 (2): 208–29.

——. (2010) *Walled States, Waning Sovereignty*, London: MIT Press.

Bruce, S. (2002) *God is Dead: Secularization in the West*, Oxford: Blackwell Publishers.

Cady, L. and Hurd Shakman, E. (eds) (2010) *Comparative Secularisms in a Global Age*, New York: Palgrave Macmillan.

Caiero, A. (2005) 'Religious Authorities or Political Actors? The Muslim Leaders of the French Representative Body', in J. Cesari and S. McLoughlin (eds) *European Muslims and the Secular State*, Aldershot; Burlington, VT: Ashgate Publishing.

Calhoun, G., Juergensmeyer, M. and VanAntwerpen, J. (eds) (2011) *Rethinking Secularism*, New York: Oxford University Press.
Capital Women's Platform (2005). *Two page report submitted to the CEDAW Committee by hand.*
Çarkoğlu, A. and Toprak, B. (2007) *Religion, Society and Politics in a Changing Turkey*, Istanbul: TESEV Publications. Available online at www.tesev.org.tr/Upload/Publication/b1d06f12–14c13–14e18-a3b3–8c1555d915d7/RSP%20-%20Turkey%2011%202006.pdf (accessed 5 November 2013).
Casanova, J. (1994) *Public Religions in the Modern World*, Chicago: Chicago University Press.
CCIF. (2005) *Bilan d'activités du CCIF: 2003–2005*, Paris, France. Available online at http://islamophobie.net/rapports/bilan-ccif-2003-2005.pdf (accessed 17 October 2013).
——. (2007) 'Communiqué concernant les mamans voilées exclues des activités scolaires', Press Release, 12 June. Available online at www.islamophobie.net/articles/2007/06/12/communique-concernant-les-mamans-voilees-exclues-des-activites-scolaires (accessed 17 October 2013).
——. (2008) 'Conseil d'Etat une décision dangereuse', Press Release, 13 July. Available online at www.saphirnews.com/CCIF-Conseil-d-Etat-une-decision-dangereuse_a9310.html (accessed 17 October 2013).
——. (2009a) R*apport sur l'Islamophobie en France 2008*, Paris, France. Available online at http://islamophobie.net/rapports/rapport-CCIF-2008.pdf (accessed 17 October 2013).
——. (2009b) *Synthèse du rapport sur l'Islamophobie en France 2008*, Paris, France. Available online at http://islamophobie.net/rapports/synthese-rapport-2008.pdf (accessed 17 October 2013).
——. (2010) *Réflexions et révélations sur la mission d'information parlementaire sur la pratique du port du voile intégral sur le territoire national*, Paris, France. Available online at http://islamophobie.net/rapports/contre-rapport-Gerin.pdf (accessed 7 October 2013).
——. (2011) 'Affaire baby-Loup: la laïcité encore une fois galvaudée', Press Release, 13 September. Available online at http://islamophobie.net/cp/CP_CCIF_BabyLoup_13092011.pdf (accessed 7 October 2013).
——. (2012) *Rapport sur l'Islamophobie en France*, Paris, France. Available online at www.islamophobie.net/sites/default/files/file_attach/rapport_2012_CCIF.pdf (accessed 7 October 2013).
——. (2013) 'Non à l'islamophobisation des esprits', Press Release, 13 January. Available online at www.islamophobie.net/articles/2013/01/23/islamophobie-hci-haut-conseil-integration-laicite-femme-voilee-universite (accessed 7 October 2013).
——. [no date] 'Situation 2: L'accès à une salle de sport' Vos droits, Fiches Pratiques. Available online at www.islamophobie.net/sites/default/files/situation2%20_salle_sport.pdf (accessed 21 October 2013).
CCIF and 15 March Committee. (2005) *Le Bilan de la Loi du 15 Mars 2004 et de ses effets pervers*, Paris, France. Available online at http://islamophobie.net/rapports/CCIF-bilan-loi15mars2004.pdf> (accessed 17 October 2013).
CEDAW. (2005) *Concluding comments: Turkey. CEDAW/C/TUR/CC/4–5*, New York: United Nations. Available online at www2.ohchr.org/english/bodies/cedaw/docs/CEDAW-CC-TUR-0523813E.pdf (accessed 17 October 2013).
——. (2009) *List of issues and questions with regards to the consideration of periodic reports. CEDAW/C/Turc/Q/6*, New York: United Nations. Available online at http://

daccess-dds-ny.un.org/doc/UNDOC/GEN/N09/513/04/PDF/N0951304.pdf?OpenElement (accessed 17 October 2013).

——. (2010) *CEDAW: Concluding observations: Turkey CEDAW/TURC/CO/6, 46 session* (New York: United Nations). Available online at www.ohchr.org/Documents/HRBodies/CEDAW/CEDAW_NGO_Participation_en.pdf (accessed 15 October 2013).

——[no date]. *CEDAW: Information note prepared by OHCHR for NGO participation.* Available online at www.ohchr.org/Documents/HRBodies/CEDAW/CEDAW_NGO_Participation_en.pdf (accessed 17 October 2013).

CEDAW Shadow Report. (2010) *A partial preliminary evaluation by non-governmental organizations of Turkey's Sixth Report on its compliance with the Convention of All Forms of Discrimination Against Women*, Istanbul. Available online at www2.ohchr.org/english/bodies/cedaw/docs/ngos/CPRER_Turkey46.pdf (accessed 17 October 2013).

Çelen, N. (2008) 'Thousands rally in Istanbul to protest coup attempts', *Today Zaman*, 23 June. Available online at www.todayszaman.com/newsDetail_getNewsById.action?load=detay&link=145539&bolum=100 (accessed 5 November 2013).

Çemrek, M. (2004) 'How Could the Rights to Education and Representation Challenge National Security? The Headscarf Conflict in Turkey Revisited', *Human Security Perspectives*, 1 (2): 52–58.

Cengiz, A. (2012) 'Unattended Cyprus issue', *Today Zaman*, 20 June.

Cengiz, O. (2012) 'What do Islamist feminists say about abortion?', *Today Zaman*, 7 June.

Césari, J. (1998) *Musulmans et Républicains. Les jeunes, l'Islam et la France*, Paris: Edition Complexe.

CFPE. (2005) 'Pour les droits des femmes, contre les exclusions, pour un monde solidaire', Press Release, May 2005. Available online at http://cfpe.over-blog.org/article-2029810.html (accessed 22 October 2013).

Chalcraft, J. and Noorani, Y. (2007) 'Introduction', in J. Chalcraft and Y. Noorani (eds) *Counterhegemony in the colony and Postcolony*, New York: Palgrave: Macmillan.

Chirac, J. (2003) *Discours prononcé par M. Jacques Chirac Président de la République relatif au respect du principe de la laïcité dans la République*, Palais de l'Elysée: Paris, 17 December. Available online at www.jacqueschirac-asso.fr/fr/les-grands-discours-de-jacques-chirac?post_id=2371 (accessed 17 October 2013).

Chouder, I., Latrèche, M., and Tévanian, P. (2008a) *Les filles voilées parlent*. Paris: La Fabrique.

Chouder, I., Latrèche, M. and Tévanian, P. (2008b) 'Lettre ouverte aux laïques et féministes de bonne volonté', in E. Chouder *et al.* (eds) *Les filles voilées parlent*, Paris: La Fabrique.

Çinar, A. (2005) *Modernity, Islam and Secularism in Turkey: Bodies, Places and Time*, Minnesota: University of Minnesota Press.

Cindoğlu, D. (2011) *Headscarf Ban and Discrimination: Professional Headscarved Women in the Labor Market*, Istanbul: TESEV Publications. Available online at www.tesev.org.tr/Upload/Publication/2011b868–60a8–492a-a170–0e2dca71b84b/headscarf-book.pdf (accessed 5 November 2013).

Connolly, W. (1999) *Why I am not a Secularist*, Minnesota: University of Minnesota Press.

Conseil d'Etat. (1950), Dlle Jamet, 3 May.

——. (1972), Avis no. 309.354 sur la Laïcité et le Corps Enseignant, 21 September.

——. (1989) Avis no. 346.893 sur le Port de signe d'appartenance à une communauté religieuse, 27 November.
——. (1992) M. Kherouraa et autres, 2 November.
——. (2000) Mlle Marteaux, 3 May.
——. (2004a) Union Française pour la Cohésion Nationale v. Ministère de l'Education Nationale, 8 October.
——. (2004b) Mlle X, 8 October.
——. (2004c) *Rapport Public 2004. Jurisprudence et Avis de 2003. Un siècle de laïcité, Etude et document du Conseil d'Etat*. Paris: La Documentation Française.
——. (2008) Mme M, 26 May.
Coutin, S. and Hirsh, S. (1998) 'Naming Resistance: Ethnographers, Dissents, and States', *Anthropological Quarterly*, 71 (1): 1–17.
Cour Administrative de Paris (2005), Singh v. Ministère de l'éducation Nationale, 19 July.
Cozad, L. (2005) 'The United States' Imposition of Religious Freedom: The International Religious Freedom Act and India,' *India Review*, 4 (1): 59–83.
Crisis Group International. (2006) *La France face à ses musulmans: émeutes, jihadisme et dépolitisation*. Available online at www.crisisgroup.org/~/media/files/europe/172_la_france_face_a_ses_musulmans_emeutes – jihadisme_amended.ashx (accessed 1 November 2013).
Daği, I. (2004) 'Rethinking Human Rights, democracy and the West: post-islamist intellectuals in Turkey', *Critique: Critical Middle Eastern Studies*, 13 (2): 135–51.
——. (2005) 'Transformation of Islamic Political Identity in Turkey: Rethinking the West and westernization', *Turkish Studies*, 6 (1): 21–37.
——. (2008) 'Turkey's AKP in Power', *Journal of Democracy*, 19 (3): 25–30.
Dale, J. (2007) 'Transnational legal conflict between peasants and corporations in Burma: human rights and discursive ambivalence under US Alien Tort Claims Act', in M. Goodale and S-E. Merry (eds) *The Practice of Human Rights: Tracking Law Between the Global and the Local,* New York: Cambridge University Press.
Danchin, P. (2011) 'Islam in the secular nomos of the European Court of Human Rights', *Michigan Journal of International Law*, 32, 664–747.
Darif, K. (2004) 'Bricolages identitaires des Musulmans dans l'espace politique français: cas de l'UOIF'. Mémoire de DEA de science politique, option 'Monde arabe et musulman' sous la direction of Vincent Geisser, Institut d'Etudes Politiques d'Aix-en-Provence, France.
Davison, A. (2003) 'Turkey, a "Secular" State?: The Challenge of Description', *South Atlantic Quarterly*, 102 (2/3): 333–50.
Deeb, L. (2006) *An Enchanted Modern: Gender and Public Piety in Shi'i Lebanon*, Princeton: Princeton University Press.
Deringil, S. (1993) 'The invention of tradition as Public Image in the Late Ottoman Empire 1808 to 1908', *Comparative Studies in Society and History*, 35 (1):3–29.
Diène, D. (2004) *UN Special Rapporteur on contemporary forms of racism, racial discrimination, xenophobia and related intolerance. Annual Report 2004. E/CN.4/2004/18*, Geneva: United Nations. Available online at http://daccess-dds-ny.un.org/doc/UNDOC/GEN/G04/104/76/PDF/G0410476.pdf?OpenElement (accessed 24 March 2014).
Djavann, C. (2003) *Bas les voiles!*, Paris: Gallimard.
Douzinas, C. (2007) *Human Rights and Empire: The Political Philosophy of Cosmopolitanism*, Abingdon, UK; New York, NY: Routledge-Cavendish.
Deutsche, R. (1996) *Evictions. Art and Spatial Politics*, Cambridge, Massachusetts: MIT Press.

——. (1999) 'The Question of Public Space', American Photography Institute National Graduate Seminar Proceedings, New York: The Institute. Available online at http://iwalewapublicspace.files.wordpress.com/2012/02/rosalyn-deutsche–the-question-of– public-space_.pdf (accessed 1 November 2013).

ECtHR. (2001) Dalhab v. Switzerland, 15 February.

——. (2004) Leyla Sahin v. Turkey, 24 June.

——. (2005) Leyla Sahin v. Turkey,10 November.

——. (2007) Kavakci v. Turkey, 5 April.

——. (2007) Zengin v. Turkey, 9 October.

——. (2008) Dogru v. France, 4 December.

——. (2008) El Morsli v. France, 4 March.

——. (2008) Kervanci v. France, 4 December.

——. (2009) Aktas v. France, 30 June.

——. (2009) Bayrak v. France, 30 June.

——. (2009) Gamaleddyn v. France, 30 June.

——. (2009) Ghazal v. France, 30 June.

——. (2009) J. Singh v. France, June 30.

——. (2009) R. Singh v. France, June30.

Elle. (2003) 'Elle s'engage contre le voile islamique', *Elle*, 8 December.

Elver, H. (2012) *The Headscarf Controversy. Secularism and Freedom of Religion*, New York: Oxford University Press.

Ensaroğlu, Y. (2004) 'Din özgürlüğü ve "bize özgü" laiklik' [Freedom of Religion and Laicism are Unique to Us] (Mazlumder), Press Release, 19 July. Available online at www.mazlumder.org/yayinlar/detay/makaleler/8/din-ozgurlugu-ve-bize-ozgu-laiklik/934 (accessed 17 October 2013).

Esposito, J. (2000) 'Introduction: Islam and Secularism in the Twenty-First Century', in Azzam Tamimi and John Esposito (eds) *Islam and Secularism in the Middle East* London: C. Hurst & Co.

Fernando, M. (2010) 'Reconfiguring freedom: Muslim piety and the limits of secular law and public discourse in France', *American Ethnologist*, 37 (1):19–35.

Ferrari, S. (2005) 'The Secularity of the State and the Shaping of Muslim Representative Organizations in Western Europe', in J. Césari and S. McLoughlin (eds) *European Muslims and the Secular State,* Aldershot; Burlington, VT: Ashgate.

Fetzer, J. and Soper, C. (2007) 'Religious Institutions, Church-State History and Muslim Mobilisation in Britain, France and Germany', *Journal of Ethnic and Migration Studies*, 33 (6): 933–44.

Fisher Onar, N. (2011) 'Turkey's democracy, Europe's imperative', *Open Democracy*, June 23.

Gaspard, F. and Khosrokhavar, F. (1995) *Le Foulard et la République*, Paris: Découverte.

Geisser, V. and Zemouri, A. (2006) *Marianne & Allah: Les politiques français face à la 'question musulmane'*, Paris: La Découverte.

Gellner, E. (1983) *Muslim Society*, Cambridge: Cambridge University Press.

Gerin, A. (2010) *Rapport d'Information – Au nom de la mission d'information sur les pratiques du voile intégral sur le territoire national*, French National Assembly: Paris. Available online at http://www.assemblee-nationale.fr/13/rap-info/i2262.asp (accessed 17 October 2013).

Gibson, N. (2007) 'Faith in the Courts: Religious Dress and Human Rights', *The Cambridge Law Journal*, 66 (3): 657–97.

Gökariksel, B. (2007) 'Feminist Geography of Veiling: Gender, Class and Religion in the Making of Modern Spaces and Subjects in Istanbul', in K. Morin and J-K. Guelke (eds) *Women, Religion, and Space*, Syracuse, NY: Syracuse University Press.

Gökariksel, B and Mitchell, K. (2005) 'Veiling, secularism, and the neoliberal subject: national narratives and supranational desires in Turkey and France', *Global Networks*, 5 (2):147–65.

Göle, N. (2005) *Interpénétrations: L'Islam et l'Europe*, Paris: Galaade Editions.

——. (2007) 'The Making and Unmaking of Europe in its Encounter with Islam: Negotiating French Republicanism and European Islam', in N. Karagiannis and P. Wagner (eds) *Varieties of World-making beyond globalization,* Liverpool: Liverpool University Press.

——. (2010) 'The Civilizational, Spatial, and Sexual Powers of the Secular', in M. Warner *et al.* (eds) *Varieties of Secularism in a Secular Age.* Harvard University Press.

Goodale, M. and Merry, S-E. (2007) *The Practice of Human Rights: Tracking Law Between the Global and the Local*, New York: Cambridge University Press.

Grigoriadis, I. (2009) 'Islam and democratisation in Turkey: secularism and trust in a divided society', *Democratization*, 16 (6): 1194–1213.

Gümüşcü S. (2010) 'Class, Status, and Party: The Changing Face of Political Islam in Turkey and Egypt', *Comparative Political Studies*, 43 (7): 835–61.

Gurrey, B. (2010) 'Ilhem Moussaid: la jeune femme voilée qui ébranle l'identité du NPA', *Le Monde*, 10 February.

HALDE. (2007a) Délibération no. 2007 – 117, 14 May.

——. (2007b) Délibération no. 2007 – 210, 3 September.

——. (2008) Délibération no. 2008 – 193, 15 September.

Harding, S. (2013) 'Beyond the "Secularism Tic" – An Interview with Feminist Philosopher Sandra Harding', interview with N. Flores in Ms. Blog, July 19. Available online at http://msmagazine.com/blog/2013/07/19/beyond-the-secularism-tick-an-interview-with-feminist-philosopher-sandra-harding/> (accessed 29 October 2013).

Haut Conseil à l'Intégration (HCI). (2007) *Projet de charte de la laïcité dans les services publics – Avis à Monsieur le Premier ministre.* Available online at http://www.hci.gouv.fr/IMG/pdf/AVIS_Charte_Laicite.pdf (accessed 17 October 2013).

——. (2010) *Avis relatif à l'expression des religions dans les espaces publics.* Available online at www.hci.gouv.fr/Avis-relatif-a-l-expression-des.html (accessed 7 October 2013).?

——. (2011a) *Charte de la laïcité dans les services publics.* Available online at www.hci.gouv.fr/IMG/pdf/Charte_laicite_2–4.pdf (accessed 7 October 2013).?

——. (2011b) *Avis de la neutralité religieuse en entreprise.* Available online at www.hci.gouv.fr/IMG/pdf/HCI-Avis-De_la_neutralite_religieuse_en_entreprise–Septembre_2011.pdf (accessed 16 October 2013).

Haynes, J. (2005) 'Religion and International relations after "9/11"', *Democratization*, 12 (3): 398–413.

Houston, C. (1997) 'Islamic Solutions to the Kurdish Problem: Late Rendezvous or Illegitimate Shortcut', *New Perspectives on Turkey*, 16: 1–22.

Human Rights Watch. (2004a) 'Turkey: Headscarf Ban Stifles Academic Freedom', Press Release, 28 June. Available online at www.hrw.org/en/news/2004/06/28/turkey-headscarf-ban-stifles-academic-freedom (accessed 17 October 2013).

——. (2004b) 'France: Headscarf Ban Violates Religious Freedom', Press Release, 26 February. Available online at http://www.hrw.org/en/news/2004/02/26/france-headscarf-ban-violates-religious-freedom (accessed 17 October 2013).

Huntington, S. (1993) 'The Clash of Civilizations' *Foreign Affairs* 72 (3): 22–49.

Inter-Parliamentary Union (IPU). (2002) 'Turkey: Case No TK/66 – Merve Safa Kavakci, Resolution adopted unanimously by the IPU Council at its 171 session', Resolution, 27 September. Available online at http://www.ipu.org/hr-e/171/Tk66.htm (accessed 17 October 2013).

Jahangir, A. (2006a) *UN Special Rapporteur on freedom of religion and belief. Annual Report 2006. E/CN.4/2006/5*, Geneva: United Nations. Available online at http://daccess-dds-ny.un.org/doc/UNDOC/GEN/G06/101/40/PDF/G0610140.pdf?OpenElement (accessed 17 October 2013).

——. (2006b) *UN Special Rapporteur on freedom of religion and belief. Annual Report 2006 – Mission to France September 2005. E/CN.4/2006/5/Add.4*, Geneva: United Nations. Available online at http://daccess-dds-ny.un.org/doc/UNDOC/GEN/G06/117/19/PDF/G0611719.pdf?OpenElement (accessed 17 October 2013).

——. (2009 a) *UN Special Rapporteur on freedom of religion and belief. Annual Report 2008. A/HRC/10/8*, Geneva: United Nations. Available online at http://daccess-dds-ny.un.org/doc/UNDOC/GEN/G09/101/04/PDF/G0910104.pdf?OpenElement (accessed 17 October 2013).

——. (2009b) *UN Special Rapporteur on freedom of religion and belief, Annual Report 2008 – Summary of cases transmitted to Governments and replies received. A/HRC/10/8/ Add.1*. Geneva: United Nations. Available online at http://daccess-dds-ny.un.org/doc/UNDOC/GEN/G09/109/80/PDF/G0910980.pdf?OpenElement (accessed 17 October 2013).

Jakobsen, J. and Pellegrini, A. (eds) (2008) *Secularisms*, Durham: Duke University Press.

Joseph, S. and Slyomovics, S. (2000) 'Introduction', in S. Joseph and S. Slyomovics (eds) *Women and Power in the Middle East*, Philadelphia: University of Pennsylvania Press.

Jospin, L. (1989) Circulaire Jospin, 12 November. Available online at www.islamlaicite.org/article133.html (accessed 17 October 2013).

Kandiyoti D. (1991a) 'Identity and its Discontents: Women and the Nation', *Millenium – Journal of International Studies*, 20 (3):429–43.

——. (1991b) 'End of Empire: Islam, Nationalism and Women in Turkey', in D. Kandiyioti (ed.) *Women, Islam & the State*, Philadelphia: Temple University Press.

——. (1997) 'Gendering the Modern: On Missing Dimensions in the Study of Turkish Modernity', in S. Bozdoğan and R. Kasaba (eds) *Rethinking Modernity and National Identity in Turkey*, Seattle and London: University of Washington Press.

——. (1998) 'Some Awkward Questions on Women and Modernity in Turkey', in L. Abu-Lughod (ed.) *Remaking Women. Feminism and Modernity in the Middle East*, Princeton University Press.

Kant, I. (1979) [1793] *La Religion dans les limites de la simple raison*, Paris: Librairie Philosophique.

Kavakçı, M. (2005) 'ECHR: Turkey at Fault for Expelling Merve Kavaçki from Parliament for Wearing Muslim Headscarf', Press Release, 11 April. Available online at www.freepreach.org/index.php/article/373.html?PHPSESSID=011bf0769d2c48f7c070189a60dd6981 (accessed 21 October 2013).

——. (2010) *Headscarf Politics in Turkey*, New York: Palgrave MacMillan.

Keddie, N. (1997) 'Secularism and the State: Towards Clarity and Global Comparison', *New Left Review*, 226: 21–40.

Keck, M. and Sikkink, K. (1998) *Activists beyond Borders: Advocacy Networks in International Politics*, Ithaca and London: Cornell University Press.

Kepel, G. (1987) *Les banlieues de l'Islam*, Paris: Le Seuil.

Kejanlioğlu, B and Taş, O. (2009) 'Regimes of Un/veiling and Body Control: Turkish Students Wearing Wigs', *Social Anthropology/Anthropologie Sociale*, 17 (4): 424–38.

Kimble, S. (2006). 'Emancipation Through Secularization: French Feminist Views of Muslim Women's Condition in Interwar Algeria', *French Colonial History*, 7:109–28.

Kintzler, C., Taguieff, P-A., Teper, B. and Tribalat, M. (2003) 'Pour une loi interdisant le port des signes religieux à l'école publique', *Libération,* 6 May.

Kirişci, K. (2000) 'Disaggregating Turkish Citizenship and Immigration Practices', *Middle Eastern Studies*, 36 (3):1–22.

Knott, K. (2010) 'Theoretical and methodological resources for breaking open the secular and exploring the boundary between religion and non-religion', *Historia Religionum*, 2: 115–33.

——. (2005) *The Location of Religion: A Spatial Analysis*, London: Equinox Publishing.

Kurban, D. (2003) 'Confronting Equality: The Need for Constitutional Protection of Minorities on Turkey's Path to the European Union', *Columbia Human Rights Law Review,* 35:151–214.

——. (2004/5) 'Unravelling a trade-off: reconciling minority rights and full citizenship in Turkey', *European Yearbook of Minority Issues*, 4: 341–72.

Kuru, A. (2006) 'Reinterpretation of Secularism in Turkey: The Case of the Justice and Development Party', in H. Yavuz (ed.) *Emergence of a New Turkey: Islam, Democracy and the AK Parti*, Salt Lake City: University of Utah Press.

——. (2007) 'Passive and Assertive Secularism: Historical Conditions, Ideological Struggles and State Policies', *World Politics*, 59 (4): 568–94.

——. (2008) 'Secularism, State Policies and Muslims in Europe: Analyzing French Exceptionalism', *Comparative Politics*, 41 (1):1–19.

——. (2009). *Secularism and State Policies Toward Religion: The United States, France, and Turkey*, New York: Cambridge University Press.

Kuru, A. and Stepan, A. (2012) 'Laïcité as an "ideal type" and a continuum. Comparing Turkey, France, and Senegal', in A. Kuru and A. Stepan (eds) *Democracy, Islam and Secularism in Turkey*, New York: Columbia University Press.

Laborde, C. (2005) 'Secular Philosophy and Muslim Headscarves in Schools', *Journal of Political Philosophy*, 13 (3): 305–29.

Lapidus, I. (1996) 'State and Religion in Islamic Societies', *Past & Present*, 151 (1): 3–27.

Laurence, J. and Vaisse, J. (2006) *Integrating Islam: Political and Religious Challenges in Contemporary France*, Washington, DC: The Brookings Institute Press.

Le Bars, S. (2007a) 'Michèle Alliot-Marie veut améliorer la formation des imams en France', *Le Monde,* 7 July.

——. (2007b) 'La formation d'imams à l'Institut catholique provoque des remous chez les musulmans', *Le Monde*, 8 October.

——. (2008) 'Une Marocaine en burqa se voit refuser la nationalité française', *Le Monde*, 11 July.

——. (2010) 'Le communautarisme assumé des "Dérouilleurs"', *Le Monde,* 27 January.

——. (2012) 'Le Sénat vote l'extension de la neutralité religieuse pour les "nounous" à domicile', *Monde Blog,* 18 January. Available online at http://religion.blog.lemonde.fr/2012/01/18/le-senat-vote-l%E2%80%99extension-de-la-neutralite-religieuse-pour-les-nounous-a-domicile (accessed 7 October 2013).

Lentin, R. (1999) 'Constitutionally Excluded: Citizenship and (Some) Irish Women', in N. Yuval-Davis and P. Werbner (eds) *Women, Citizenship and Difference*, London and New York: Zed Books.

Lewis, B. (1993) *Islam and the West*, London: Oxford University Press.
Lewis, T. (2007) 'What not to wear: Religious Rights, the European Court, and the Margin of Appreciation', *International and Comparative Law Quarterly*, 56 (2): 395–414.
Mahmood, S. (2006) 'Secularism, Hermeneutics, and Empire: The Politics of Islamic Reformation', *Public Culture*, 18 (2): 323–47.
——. (2009) 'Religious Reason and Secular Affect: An Incommensurable Divide?' in T. Asad, W. Brown, J. Butler and S Mahmood, *Is Critique Secular? Blasphemy, Injury and Free Speech*, Berkeley, CA: The Townsend Center for the Humanities.
Mamans Toutes Egales (MTE). (2011) 'Pourquoi devriez-vous nous soutenir?' Press Release. Available online at https://sites.google.com/site/mamanstoutesegalestest/ (accessed 7 October 2013).
Mardin, S. (1993) 'Religion and Secularism in Turkey', in A. H. Hourani *et al.* (eds), *The Modern Middle East*, Los Angeles and Berkeley: University of California Press.
——. (1995) 'Laïcité en Turquie et en France: Proposition pour une meilleur comparaison', *Cahier d'Etudes sur la méditerranée et le monde Turco-Iranien*, 19.
Marshall, J. (2006) 'Freedom of Religious Expression and Gender Equality: Sahin v Turkey', *The Modern Law Review*, 69 (3): 452–61.
Maussen, M. (2007) 'Islamic Presence and Mosque Establishment in France. Colonialism, Arrangements for Guestworkers and Citizenship', *Journal of Ethnic and Migration Studies,* 33 (6): 981–1002.
McDougall, G. (2008) *UN Report of the independent expert on minority issues – Annual Report 2007 – Mission to France (19–28 September 2007). A/HRC/17/23/ Add.2*, Geneva: United Nations. Available online at http://daccess-dds-ny.un.org/doc/UNDOC/GEN/G08/114/02/PDF/G0811402.pdf?OpenElement (accessed 17 October 2013).
McGoldrick, D. (2006) *Human Rights and Religion: The Islamic Headscarf Debate in Europe*, Oxford and Portland, Oregon: Hart Publishing.
Ministry of Interior. (2001) *Principes et Fondements Juridiques Régissant les Rapports entre les Pouvoirs Publics et le Culte Musulman en France.*
Ministry of National Education [Ministère de l'éducation nationale]. (2004) *Circulaire Fillon no. 2004–084*, 18 May. Available online at www.education.gouv.fr/bo/2004/21/MENG0401138C.htm (accessed 17 October 2013).
——.(2012) *Orientations et instructions pour la préparation de la rentrée 2012*. Available online at www.education.gouv.fr/pid25535/bulletin_officiel.html?cid_bo=59726 (accessed 7 October 2013).
Moghadam, V. (2003) *Modernizing Women: Gender and Social Change in the Middle East*?, London: Lynne Rienner Publishers.?
Moors, A. (2009) 'The Dutch and the face-veil: The politics of discomfort', *Social Anthropology*, 17 (4): 393–408.
Moors, A. and Salih, R. (2009) '"Muslim women" in Europe: Secular normativities, bodily performances and multiple publics', *Social Anthropology*, 17 (4): 375–78.
Najmabadi, A. (2006) 'Gender and Secularism of Modernity: How Can a Muslim Woman Be French?', *Feminist Studies*, 32 (2): 239–55.
Öktem, K. (2011) 'Turkey's Passive Revolution and Democracy', *Open Democracy*, June 9.
Osanloo, A. (2009) *The Politics of Women's Rights in Iran*, Princeton: Princeton University Press.
Özdalga, E. (1998) *The Veiling Issue, Official Secularism and Popular Islam in Modern Turkey*, Taylor & Francis.

Özdemir, Ş. (2008) 'Turkey's headscarf issue to be appealed to UN for first time', *Today Zaman*, 15 May.

Pateman, C. (1988) *The Sexual Contract*, Stanford: Stanford University Press.

——. (1989) *The Disorder of Women: Democracy, Feminism and Political Theory*, Stanford: Stanford University Press.

Philippe, B. (1997) *Être juif dans la société française. Du Moyen Âge à nos jours*, Editions Complexe.

Ramadan, T. (2004) 'Manifester, Pourquoi?', *Libération*, 14 January. Available online at http://oumma.com/Manifester-pourquoi (accessed 17 October 2013).

Richard, A. (2011) *Rapport sur la Proposition de loi Mme Francoise Laborde*. Available online at www.senat.fr/rap/l11–144/l11–144.html (accessed 7 October2013).

Rossinot, A. (2006) *La laïcité dans les services publics: Rapport du Groupe de Travail – Présidé par M. André Rossinot*. Available online at http://www.islamlaicite.org/IMG/pdf/Rapport_Rossinot.pdf (accessed 17 October 2013).

Saïd, E. (1979) *Orientalism*, New York: Vintage Books.

Salih, R. (2003) *Gender in Transnationalism: Home, Longing and Belonging Among Moroccan Migrant Women*, London: Routledge.

——. (2009) 'Muslim women, fragmented secularism and the construction of interconnected "publics" in Italy', *Social Anthropology*, 17 (4): 409–23.

Salton, H. (2007) 'Veiled threats? Islam, Headscarves and Religious Freedom in America and France', PhD Thesis, New-Zealand: Auckland University.

Sandel, M. (1998) 'Religious Liberty: freedom of choice or freedom of conscience' in R. Bhargava (ed.) *Secularism and its Critics*, Oxford: Oxford University Press, New Delhi.

Sarkozy, N. (2004) *La République, les Religions et l'Espérance*, Paris: Editions du Cerf.

Schreier, J. (2007) 'Napoléon's Long Shadow: Morality, Civilization, and Jews in France and Algeria, 1808 –1870', *French Historical Studies*, 30 (1): 77–103.

Scott, J. (1996) *Only Paradoxes to Offer: French Feminists and the Rights of Man*, Cambridge, Mass: Harvard University Press.

——. (2007) *The Politics of the Veil*, Princeton: Princeton University Press.

Shakman Hurd, E. (2008). *The Politics of Secularism in International Relations*, Princeton: Princeton University Press.

——. (2012) 'International politics after secularism', *Review of International Studies*, 38: 943–61.

——. (2013) 'Rescued by law? Gender and the global politics of secularism', in L. Cady and T. Fessenden (eds) *Religion, the Secular, and the Politics of Sexual Difference* New York: Columbia University Press.

Shively, Kim. (2005) 'Religious Bodies and the Secular State: The Merve Kavakçi Affair', *Journal of Middle East Women's Studies*, 1 (3): 46–72.

Silvestri, S. (2007) 'Asserting Islam in the EU: actors, strategies, and priorities', in F. Foret (ed.) *L'espace public européen à l'épreuve du religieux*, Bruxelles: Institut d'Etudes Européenes.

Smith, A-M. (1998) *Laclau and Mouffe: The Radical Democratic Imaginary*, London and New York: Routledge.

Smith, T. (2005) 'Civic Nationalism and Ethnocultural Justice in Turkey', *Human Rights Quarterly*, 27 (2): 436–70.

Soysal, Y. (1994) *Limits of Citizenship: Migrant and Postnational Membership in Europe*, Chicago: University of Chicago Press.

Stasi, B. (2003) *Rapport de la Commission de Réflexion sur l'Application du Principe de Laïcité dans la République Remis au Président de la République le 11 Décembre 2003*, Paris: La Documentation Française. Available online at http://lesrapports.ladocumentationfrancaise.fr/BRP/034000725/0000.pdf (accessed 17 October 2013).

Ssenyonjo, M. (2007) 'The Islamic veil and freedom of religion, the rights to education and work: A survey of recent international and national cases', *Chinese Journal of International Law*, 6(3): 653–710.

Tavernise, S. (2008a) 'Rebellion in Turkey: Putting on a headscarf', *The New York Times*, 9 February. Available online at www.nytimes.com/2008/02/09/world/europe/09benli.html?pagewanted=all&_r = 0 (accessed 5 November 2013).

——. (2008b) 'Youthful Voice Stirs Challenge to Secular Turk', *The New York Times*, 13 October. Available online at www.nytimes.com/2008/10/14/world/europe/14turkey.html?pagewanted=all (accessed 5 November 2013).

Taylor, C. (1998) 'Modes of Secularism' in R. Bhargava (ed.) *Secularism and its Critics*, Oxford: Oxford University Press.

——. (2003) *Modern Social Imaginaries*, Durham: Duke University Press.

——. (2007) *A Secular Age*, Cambridge, MA: Belknap Press of Harvard University Press.

Ternisien, X. (2002) *La France des Mosquées*, Paris: Editions Albin Michel.

Today Zaman. (2008) 'Summary of the Indictment Against the Ruling AK Party'. Available online at www.todayszaman.com/newsDetail_getNewsById.action?load=detay& link = 138111 (accessed 17 October 2013).

The Executive Committee for NGO Forum on CEDAW-Turkey. (2004) *Shadow Report on the 4th and 5th Combined Periodic Country Report for Turkey*. Available online at http://www.iwraw-ap.org/resources/turkey_Flying_Broom_(Eng).pdf (accessed 17 October 2013).

Troper, M. (2000) 'French Secularism, or Laïcité', *Cardozo Law Review*, 21: 1267–84.

Turam, B. (2006) *Between Islam and the State: The Politics of Engagement*, Stanford: Stanford University Press.

Union des Familles Laïques. (2003) 'Non au voile islamique à l'école publique! Oui à la construction de mosquée dans la société civile', Petition, 4 April.

United Nations Beijing Declaration (1995). Available online at http://www.un.org/womenwatch/daw/beijing/platform/declar.htm (accessed 5 November 2013).

United Nations Committee on the Rights of the Child (2004). *Second Periodic Report on France. CRC/C/15/Add.240*. Geneva: United Nations. Available online at http://daccess-dds-ny.un.org/doc/UNDOC/GEN/G04/424/28/PDF/G0442428.pdf?OpenElement (accessed 17 October 2013).

United Nations Human Rights Committee. (2008) *Consideration of reports submitted by states parties under article 40 of the Covenant, Concluding observations of the Human Rights Committee – France. CCPR/C/FRA/C04*. Geneva: United Nations. Available online at http://tbinternet.ohchr.org/_layouts/treatybodyexternal/Download.aspx?symbolno=CCPR%2fC%2fFRA%2fCO%2f4&Lang=en (accessed 17 October 2013).

——. [no date] General Comments. Available online at http://tbinternet.ohchr.org/_layouts/treatybodyexternal/TBSearch.aspx?Lang=en&TreatyID=8&DocTypeID=11 (accessed 17 October 2013).

Vakulenko, A. (2007) 'Islamic Dress in Human Rights Jurisprudence: a Critique of Current Trends', *Oxford Human Rights Law Review*, 7 (4): 717–39.

Vigerie, A. and Zelensky, A. (2003) '"Laïcardes" puisque féministes', *Le Monde*, 29 May. Available online at http://mapage.noos.fr/anne.zelensky/laicarde.pdf (accessed 17 October 2013)

White, J. (2002) *Islamist Mobilization in Turkey: A Study in Vernacular Politics*, Seattle: University of Washington Press.

Williams, R. (1977) *Marxism and Literature*, Oxford: Oxford University Press.

Wilson, E. (2012) *After Secularism. Rethinking Religion in Global Politics*, New York: Palgrave Macmillan.

Wilson, R. (1997) 'Human Rights, Culture and Context: An Introduction', in R. Wilson (ed.) *Human rights, culture and context: an anthropological perspectives,* London: Pluto Press.

——. (2007) 'Conclusion: Tyrannosaurus lex: the anthropology of human rights law and transnational law', in M. Goodale and S-E. Merry (eds) *The Practice of Human Rights: Tracking Law Between the Global and the Local*, New York: Cambridge University Press.

Yavuz, H. (2003) *Islamic Political Identity in Turkey*, Oxford: Oxford University Press.

Yildiz, E. (2013) 'Alignments of Dissent and Politics of Naming: Assembling Resistance in Turkey', *Jadaliyya*, June 4. Available online at www.jadaliyya.com/pages/index/12001/alignments-of-dissent-and-politics-of-naming_assem (accessed 15 October 2013).

Yuval-Davis, N. (1997a) *Gender and Nation*, London: Sage Publications.

——. (1997b) 'Women, Citizenship and Difference', *Feminist Review*, 57: 4–27.

——. (2001) 'The "Multi-Layered Citizen"', *International Feminist Journal of Politics*, 1(1): 119–36.

——. (2009) 'Women, Globalization and Contemporary Politics of Belonging Gender', *Technology and Development,* January/April 13: 1–19

Yuval-Davis, N., Anthias, F. and Kofman, E. (2005) 'Secure borders and safe haven and the gendered politics of belonging: Beyond social cohesion', *Ethnic and Racial Studies*, 28(3): 513–35.

Yuval-Davis, N. and Werbner, P. (1999) 'Introduction: Women and the New Discourse of Citizenship', in N. Yuval-Davis and P. Werbner (eds) *Women, Citizenship and Difference,* London and New York: Zed Books.

Zappi, S. (2010) 'Le NPA confronté à de vives critiques pour présenter une candidate voilée', *Le Monde*, 8 February.

Zıbak Dişli, F. (2011) 'Why Is the AKP Reluctant to Address the Headscarf Ban?', *Today's Zaman*, October 14.

Zürcher, E. and van der Linden, H. (2004) 'Searching for the Fault-Line', in WRR, Netherland Scientific Council for Government Policy (ed.) *The European Union, Turkey and Islam*, Amsterdam: Amsterdam University Press. Available online at www.uni-marburg.de/isu/inhaltinfos/seminarbeschreibungen2011/pflichtlektuere2011/zuercher.pdf (accessed 5 November 2013).

Index

Abdülhamid II, Sultan 23
abortion: and Turkish religious activists 111–12
AK Party 49, 52–53, 97–98, 111, 140; formation of 97; and headscarf bans 98; and women wearing headscarves in Parliament 57–58
Akbulut, Neslihan 109
AKDER (Women Rights Organization Against Discrimination) 49, 98–99, 125–26
Aktas vs France 133
Alevis 28–29, 107
Algeria, colonial 26–27, 32, 36, 77
Algerian Jews 26
Algerian Muslims: in France 26–27
Anthias, F. 7
anti-colonial resistance: and women 8
Arat, Y. 35, 36
Asad, T. 3
assertive secularism 5, 141
Aubry, Martine 1
autonomy 11, 78–79, 145, 147; dichotomy between submission and 33; neutrality and personal 78; and religious freedom 79–80
Avis Marteaux (2000) 46–47

Bas les voiles ('Taking off the veils') 92*n*
Baubérot, J. 25
Beaman, L. 140
Becket Fund for Religious Liberty 124
Beijing Declaration (1995) 105
Benbassa, E. 26
beur movement 73
Bouteyre, Abbé 46
Bowen, J. 22
Brown, Wendy 104, 121, 151
burqa 51, 54
businesses: extending neutrality requirement to French 59–60; and women wearing headscarves in Turkish 61–62

Capital Women's Platform 98, 99, 125
Catholic Institute (Paris) 142
CCIF (Collective Against Islamophobia in France) 75, 76, 83, 84, 120–21
CEDAW (UN Convention on the Elimination of All Forms of Discrimination against Women) 105, 116*n*, 124–26, 145; Shadow Report (2010) 101, 105, 115*n*
CEPT (School For All Collective) 75, 76, 87
Césari, J. 73
CFCM (French Council of the Muslim Cult) 27, 84, 91*n*
CFPE (Collective Feminists For Equality) 40*n* 75, 76, 85, 87
challenges
childcare: extending neutrality requirement to French 60; *see also* day care
Chirac, President 50, 71
CHP (Republican People's Party) 53
Christianity 5, 21, 133–34
Cindoğlu, D. 60–61
Circulaire Jospin 46
citizenship 32, 44, 141, 147, 150; and France 25, 26, 27, 28, 31, 33; and French Muslim activists 86, 87, 88–90; gendered character of 19*n* 32; and Turkey 28, 34, 121, 125
class 40*n* 44
Collective Against Islamophobia in France *see* CCIF

Collective Feminists For Equality *see* CFPE
Collective School For All *see* CEPT
colonialism 7–8
Concordat 22
Conseil Constitutionel 92*n*
Conseil d'Etat 46, 71, 119, 128, 143; jurisprudence of 80–82
Council of Higher Education (YÖK) (Turkey) 51, 53
Council of State (Turkey) 49

Daği, I. 97
Dale, J. 122
Danchin, P. 133
Davison, A. 24
day care 45, 60, 76, 82, 149, 150
Demirel, Süleyman 56
Deutsche, Rosalyn 151
Diène 128–29
Directorate of Religious Affairs (Turkey) 24, 28, 107–8; *see also Diyanet*
Diyanet 108
Dogru case 131, 132

Ecevit, Bülent 56
ECtHR (European Court of Human Rights) 119, 126, 145, 146; approach to secularism 131, 133; judgements on secularism and religious freedom 130–35; and Merve Kavakçı case 123–24; and neutrality 134–35
EMF (Muslim Students of France) 75, 91*n*
Engaged French and Muslim Women (FFME) 73
Erbakan, Necmettin 96, 97
Erdoğan, Tayyip 97, 111
Ergenekon trial 57
European Convention on Human Rights (ECHR) 101
European Court of Human Rights *see* ECtHR
Evren, President 52

family relations: regulation of 37
Felicity Party 97
Fernando, M. 148
FFME (Engaged French and Muslim Women) 73
15 March Committee 75, 120, 137*n*
France: Algerian Muslims in 26–27; attempts to regulate Islam in 27; banning of wearing headscarves/religious symbols in public schools 1–2, 6, 33, 43, 50, 70–71, 127, 131–32; and charter of *laïcité* 54–55; and citizenship 25, 26, 27, 31, 33; coalition between French Right and Left 71; establishment of the *Consistoire* (1808) 26; exclusion of pious women from society 43–45; extending neutrality requirement to citizens in the 'private' realm 58–60; extending neutrality requirement to users beyond schools and universities 53–55; extending neutrality requirement to users of public services 49–51, 71; formation of Muslim associations 73; gender equality 25, 32–33; historical exclusion of women in 30–33; Jews in 25–26; Law (1905) 27, 35, 36, 37–38, 76–80, 142, 143; Law (2004) 49–50, 54, 58, 69, 70, 76–88, 127, 128, 129, 135, 143; Law (2010) 58–59; Muslims living in 71–73, 87; neutrality of public servants 46–48; number of girls wearing headscarves 72; protests against headscarf ban 2, 75; relationship between religion and the state 2, 22, 23, 37–38, 77, 142; and religious minorities 25–28; training programme for Imams 142
Free Thought and Education Rights Association (Özgür-der) 99
French Council of the Muslim Cult *see* CFCM
French Muslim activists 69–93, 112, 143–44; and 15 March Committee 75; and 2004 Law 76–88; Collective Against Islamophobia in France (CCIF) 75, 76, 83, 84, 120–21; Collective Feminists For Equality (CFPE) 40*n*, 75, 76, 85, 87; description of 74–76; and distinction between private expressions of faith and public behaviour 89; fighting against 'special treatment' 83–86; and jurisprudence of the *Conseil d'Etat* and other courts 80–82, 88; Mothers All Equal Collective (MTE); and neutrality 80–81, 86, 88, 143; organisations created 75–76; overview and paradigm shift of 71–74; protecting of 'universal' values as citizens 96–98; and School For All

Collective (CEPT) 75; seeking equality of treatment as French citizens 83–88; specialising in litigation at national level to protect religious freedom 119–21, 135–36; use of international rights mechanisms 121, 136; vision of *laïcité* 87–89
French Revolution 25, 31

gender/gender equality 11, 25; France 25, 32–33; and headscarves 104–6; and nationalism 7; and neutrality 45; and religion 24–25; and secularism 8, 75, 135, 141; Turkey 25, 34
Gerin report (2010) 47, 54
Gibson, N. 134
Gökariksel, B. 8–9
Göle, N. 33
Gramscian idea of hegemony 22
Grigoriadis, I. 98

HALDE (High Authority for the Fight Against Discrimination and for Equality) 47, 81, 83
HCI (High Council of Integration) 51, 58, 59, 84, 150
headscarf bans 6–7, 10, 12, 14, 17, 142–43; beyond schools and universities 53–58; challenging 17–18, 148–49; and ECtHR judgements 131; in France 1–2, 6, 33, 50, 70–71, 127, 131–32; and French Muslim activists *see* French Muslim activists; infringement on individual rights 2, 100, 101, 144, 145; and international human rights bodies 119; in Turkey 2, 49; and Turkish religious activists; *see* Turkish religious activists
headscarves: and gender equality 104–6; and Merve Kavakçı affair 49, 55–57, 122–24; as part of a culture of non-discrimination 107–10; and public servants 46–49; and right to religious freedom 101–3, 107, 144; and students 49–52; types of interpretation as a sign/symbol 130; wearing of by politicians in Turkey 55–58; and women working in Turkish firms 61
hegemony 10; *see also* secularism, hegemonic character of
High Authority for the Fight Against Discrimination and Equality *see* HALDE
High Council of Integration *see* HCI
homosexuality: and Turkish religious activists 108–9
human rights discourse: and Turkish religious activists 94–95, 98, 99–100; *see also* international human rights bodies
Human Rights Watch 124

ICCPR (UN International Covenant on Civil and Political Rights) 101
immigrant women 8
INGOs: and Merve Kavakçı case 123–24
Inter-Parliamentary Union (IPU) 123–24
international forums 145
international human rights bodies 122–35; decisions of as illustration of the hegemony of secularism 126–35; and French activists 121, 136; reasons for bringing complaints to 122; and Turkish religious activists 123–26; *see also* CEDAW; ECtHR
interview process 14–16
Iran 106, 145
Iraq war 110
Islam 21; attempts to regulate in France 27; 'control versus separation' thesis 5, 21; distinction between social and political 97

Jahangir, A. 127, 128, 129
Jews 66*n*; in France 25
JMF (Young Muslims of France) 75, 91*n*

Kada, Saida 73–74
Kandiyoti, D. 7, 53
Kant, Immanuel 39*n*
Kaplan, Hilal 109, 111
Kavakçı, Merve 49, 55–57, 122, 123–24
Kejanlioğlu, B. 34
Kemal, Mustapha 4, 23
Kervanci case 131
Kherouaa Affair (1992) 46
Kirişci, K. 30
Kurban, D. 29
Kurds 29
Kuru, A. 5, 71, 98
Kutan, Recai 56, 97

Laborde, C. 23
Laurence, J. 71, 72
Lausanne Treaty (1923) 29, 108
Le Bars, S. 148–49

Le Bel, Philippe 22
Le Pen, Marine 43
League of Education 71

McGoldrick, D. 52, 119
Mahmood, S. 130
MAZLUMDER (Organization of Human Rights and Solidarity of the Oppressed People) 98, 99, 100
micro-approach 3, 9, 140–41
migration 8
Mothers All Equal Collective (MTE) 69, 76, 77, 85, 86, 89, 136
Moussaid, Ilhem 1, 2, 55
Muslims' Collective of France (CMF) 75, 91
Muslim Spirituality and Participation (PSM) 75
Muslim Students of France *see* EMF

Najmabadi, A. 33
Napoleon Bonaparte 22, 25
National Security Council (Turkey) 51
National View movement 96
nationalism: and gender 7
Navaro-Yashin 35
neutrality 11, 22, 24–25, 45, 77–78, 80, 142, 143; and ECtHR 134–35; extending of to citizens in the 'private' realm 58–62; extending of to users beyond schools and universities 53–58; extending of to users of public services 49–53; and French Muslim activists 80–81, 86, 88, 143; and gender equality 45; of public servants 46–48; and Turkish politicians 55–58; and UN experts 129, 135
New Anti-Capitalist Party (NPA) 1
niqab 51, 54, 83

Organization of Human Rights and Solidarity of the Oppressed People *see* MAZLUMDER
Ottoman Empire 96; centralization reforms 23, 33–34; relationship between state and religion 23
overlapping consensus model 113–14
Özal, Prime Minister 52
Özdalga, E. 48

Pateman, C. 32
politicians: and wearing of headscarves in Turkey 55–58
politics: and religion 21–22

Quebec 85, 150–51

Ramadan, Tariq 75, 87, 89
regulation 17
religion: and gender 24–25; and politics 21–22; and secularism 4, 9; separation from state *see* separation; transcending division between secularism and 140–51
religious duty 147
religious freedom 63; and autonomy 79–80; ECtHR judgements on 130–35; and headscarves 101–3, 107, 144; paradoxes of 103–4; specialising in litigation by French activists to protect 119–21; UN experts' positions on 127–30
religious minorities: in France 25–28; in Turkey 28–30, 107–8
Republican People's Party (CHP) 53
rights-based discourse 118–39; *see also* human rights discourse
Rossinot report (2006) 47, 54

Sahin, Leyla 131, 132, 134
Salton, H. 46
Sandel, M. 104
Saudi Arabia 106, 145
Schreier, J. 26
Scott, Joan 6, 31–32
secularism(s): comparative tradition of 5–6; conceptualising 10–11; excavating power of 3–5; ECtHR judgements on 130–35; and French Muslim activists 87–88; and gender/gender equality 8, 75, 135, 141; hegemonic character of 3–4, 10–11, 38, 88, 126–34, 136, 141; languages of 11, 21–40; paradigmatic status of 4, 5; and religion 4, 9; researching 12–16; transcending division between religion and 140–51; UN experts' position on 127–30, 134, 135; and women 43–44
separation (between religion and the state) 2, 3, 5, 11, 17, 21–24, 33; and France 35, 36, 37–38, 77, 78, 142, 143; and Turkey 38, 124
Shakman Hurd, Elizabeth 3, 4, 5, 22, 39, 114, 118, 135
Sharia law 34
Shively, Kim 56
Special Rapporteur 127, 128, 129
Stasi report (2003) 47, 50, 51

state: separation between church and *see* separation (between religion and the state)
students: extension of neutrality requirement to in France 49–50

Taş, O. 34
Taylor, Charles 113–14
teachers: and neutrality in France 46–47
türban 51–52, 64*n*
Turkey 149–50; Alevis in 28–29, 107; challenges to headscarf bans 2, 18; and citizenship 25, 26, 27, 28, 31, 33; coalition against the Iraq war 110; Constitution (1982) 116*n*; discrimination against non-Muslim minorities in 28, 29–30; economic liberalization and democratization 95, 109, 150; EU integration issue 29, 96, 97–98, 115*n*; exclusion of pious women from society 43–45; extending of neutrality requirement to users of public services 51–53; extension of neutrality requirement to private realm 60–62; gender equality 25, 34; Gezi Park protests 140; growth of Islamic elites and political parties 95–96; headscarf ban 2, 49, 51, 131; Kurds in 29, 108; neutrality of public servants 48–49; politicians as subject to the neutrality requirement 55–57; regulation on dress code for civil servants 48–49; relationship between religion and the state 23–24, 38, 124; religious minorities in 28–30, 107–8; rise of Islamic parties in 35; soft coup (1997) 2, 49, 96–98, 99; Turkish-Islamic synthesis programme 52; women in 30–31, 33–36, 57–58, 106–7
Turkish religious activists 70, 94–117, 144, 150; and 1997 coup 99; and abortion 111–12; coalitions with other organizations 110, 113; emphasis on headscarves being part of a wider culture of prohibition 107–10; headscarf ban seen as a direct discrimination against women 104–6; and headscarf bans 100–101, 100–103, 111, 144; headscarf petition (2008) 109; and human rights discourse 94–95, 98, 99–100; issues involved with 99; linking demands to wider civic projects 109–10; making parallels between headscarves and hair length 102; 'no headscarf, no vote' campaign 57, 111; organisations involved with 98–99; position towards homosexuality 108–9; questioning of legitimacy of Directorate of Religious Affairs 107; and rights of religious minorities 107–8; use of international human rights bodies 123–26
Turkish-Islamic Synthesis programme 95

UN Convention on the Elimination of All Forms of Discrimination against Women *see* CEDAW
UN Declaration on the Elimination of All Forms of Intolerance and Discrimination Based on Religion and Belief (1981) 101
UN experts 134, 145, 146; and neutrality 129, 135; position on secularism 127–30, 134, 135, 145
UN Human Rights Committee 127
UN International Covenant on Civil and Political Rights (ICCPR) 101
Union Francaise Pour la Cohésion Nationale v Ministere de l'Education (2004) 92*n*
Union of the Islamic Organizations of France *see* UOIF
universities: headscarf bans in French 150; and neutrality in France 51; prohibition of headscarves in Turkish 51–52
University of Marseille 142
UOIF (Union of the Islamic Organizations of France) 75, 90*n*

Vaisse, J. 71, 72
veil 8; *see also* headscarves

Welfare Party (Turkey) 35, 36, 40*n*, 95–97
White, J. 36
Williams, R. 10, 11
Wilson, E. 118
women 6–9, 24–25, 37; and anti-colonial protests 8; battle over place and role of 7–8; as 'border-guards' 8, 25, 33, 35–36; exclusion of pious women from French and Turkish

societies 43–66; historical exclusion of in France 30–33; and the nation-state 30–36; and secularism 43–44; in Turkey 33–36, 57–58
Women Rights Organization Against Discrimination *see* AKDER

Yavuz, H. 95
Yildiz, E. 140
Yilmaz, Havva 109
YÖK (Council of Higher Education) 51, 53
Young Muslims of France *see* JMF
Yuval-Davis, N. 7, 8

For Product Safety Concerns and Information please contact our EU
representative GPSR@taylorandfrancis.com
Taylor & Francis Verlag GmbH, Kaufingerstraße 24, 80331 München, Germany

www.ingramcontent.com/pod-product-compliance
Ingram Content Group UK Ltd.
Pitfield, Milton Keynes, MK11 3LW, UK
UKHW022124190926
475702UK00013B/1637

* 9 7 8 0 4 1 5 7 9 0 8 6 4 *